Teens
at Risk

OPPOSING
VIEWPOINTS®

Other Books of Related Interest

Opposing Viewpoints Series

America's Children
Child Abuse
Child Welfare
Crime and Criminals
Gangs
Juvenile Crime
Media Violence
Suicide
Teenage Pregnancy
Teenage Sexuality
Tobacco and Smoking
Violence

Contemporary Issues Companion Series

Eating Disorders

Current Controversies Series

Crime
Family Violence
Smoking
Teen Addiction
Violence in the Media
Youth Violence

At Issue Series

Date Rape
Rape on Campus
Sex Education
Single-Parent Families
Smoking

Teens
at Risk

OPPOSING
VIEWPOINTS®

David L. Bender, Publisher
Bruno Leone, Executive Editor
Bonnie Szumski, Editorial Director
Brenda Stalcup, Managing Editor
Scott Barbour, Senior Editor
Laura K. Egendorf, Book Editor
Jennifer A. Hurley, Book Editor

OPPOSING
VIEWPOINTS®
SERIES

Greenhaven Press, Inc., San Diego, California

Library of Congress Cataloging-in-Publication Data

Teens at risk : opposing viewpoints / Laura K. Egendorf, book editor,
Jennifer A. Hurley, book editor.
        p.   cm. — (Opposing viewpoints series)
    Includes bibliographical references and index.
    ISBN 1-56510-949-X (lib. bdg. : alk. paper). —
    ISBN 1-56510-948-1 (pbk. : alk. paper)
    1. Socially handicapped teenagers—United States. 2. Problem
youth—United States. 3. Juvenile delinquency—United States.
4. Teenage pregnancy—United States. 5. Teenagers—Substance
use—United States. I. Egendorf, Laura K., 1973– . II. Hurley,
Jennifer A., 1973– . III. Series.
HV1431.T44 1999
362.74—dc21   98-23191
                                                             CIP

Greenhaven Press, Inc., P.O. Box 289009
San Diego, CA 92198-9009

"CONGRESS SHALL MAKE NO LAW...ABRIDGING THE FREEDOM OF SPEECH, OR OF THE PRESS."

First Amendment to the U.S. Constitution

The basic foundation of our democracy is the First Amendment guarantee of freedom of expression. The Opposing Viewpoints Series is dedicated to the concept of this basic freedom and the idea that it is more important to practice it than to enshrine it.

CONTENTS

Chapter 3: How Can Teen Pregnancy Be Prevented?

Chapter 4: What Role Do the Media and Government Play in the Problem of Teen Substance Abuse?

WHY CONSIDER OPPOSING VIEWPOINTS?

"The only way in which a human being can make some approach to knowing the whole of a subject is by hearing what can be said about it by persons of every variety of opinion and studying all modes in which it can be looked at by every character of mind. No wise man ever acquired his wisdom in any mode but this."

John Stuart Mill

In our media-intensive culture it is not difficult to find differing opinions. Thousands of newspapers and magazines and dozens of radio and television talk shows resound with differing points of view. The difficulty lies in deciding which opinion to agree with and which "experts" seem the most credible. The more inundated we become with differing opinions and claims, the more essential it is to hone critical reading and thinking skills to evaluate these ideas. Opposing Viewpoints books address this problem directly by presenting stimulating debates that can be used to enhance and teach these skills. The varied opinions contained in each book examine many different aspects of a single issue. While examining these conveniently edited opposing views, readers can develop critical thinking skills such as the ability to compare and contrast authors' credibility, facts, argumentation styles, use of persuasive techniques, and other stylistic tools. In short, the Opposing Viewpoints Series is an ideal way to attain the higher-level thinking and reading skills so essential in a culture of diverse and contradictory opinions.

In addition to providing a tool for critical thinking, Opposing Viewpoints books challenge readers to question their own strongly held opinions and assumptions. Most people form their opinions on the basis of upbringing, peer pressure, and personal, cultural, or professional bias. By reading carefully balanced opposing views, readers must directly confront new ideas as well as the opinions of those with whom they disagree. This is not to simplistically argue that everyone who reads opposing views will—or should—change his or her opinion. Instead, the series enhances readers' understanding of their own views by encouraging confrontation with opposing ideas. Careful examination of others' views can lead to the readers' understanding of the logical inconsistencies in their own opinions, perspective on why they hold an opinion, and the consideration of the possibility that their opinion requires further evaluation.

EVALUATING OTHER OPINIONS

To ensure that this type of examination occurs, Opposing Viewpoints books present all types of opinions. Prominent spokespeople on different sides of each issue as well as well-known professionals from many disciplines challenge the reader. An additional goal of the series is to provide a forum for other, less known, or even unpopular viewpoints. The opinion of an ordinary person who has had to make the decision to cut off life support from a terminally ill relative, for example, may be just as valuable and provide just as much insight as a medical ethicist's professional opinion. The editors have two additional purposes in including these less known views. One, the editors encourage readers to respect others' opinions—even when not enhanced by professional credibility. It is only by reading or listening to and objectively evaluating others' ideas that one can determine whether they are worthy of consideration. Two, the inclusion of such viewpoints encourages the important critical thinking skill of objectively evaluating an author's credentials and bias. This evaluation will illuminate an author's reasons for taking a particular stance on an issue and will aid in readers' evaluation of the author's ideas.

As series editors of the Opposing Viewpoints Series, it is our hope that these books will give readers a deeper understanding of the issues debated and an appreciation of the complexity of even seemingly simple issues when good and honest people disagree. This awareness is particularly important in a democratic society such as ours in which people enter into public debate to determine the common good. Those with whom one disagrees should not be regarded as enemies but rather as people whose views deserve careful examination and may shed light on one's own.

Thomas Jefferson once said that "difference of opinion leads to inquiry, and inquiry to truth." Jefferson, a broadly educated man, argued that "if a nation expects to be ignorant and free . . . it expects what never was and never will be." As individuals and as a nation, it is imperative that we consider the opinions of others and examine them with skill and discernment. The Opposing Viewpoints Series is intended to help readers achieve this goal.

David L. Bender & Bruno Leone,
Series Editors

Greenhaven Press anthologies primarily consist of previously published material taken from a variety of sources, including periodicals, books, scholarly journals, newspapers, government documents, and position papers from private and public organizations. These original sources are often edited for length and to ensure their accessibility for a young adult audience. The anthology editors also change the original titles of these works in order to clearly present the main thesis of each viewpoint and to explicitly indicate the opinion presented in the viewpoint. These alterations are made in consideration of both the reading and comprehension levels of a young adult audience. Every effort is made to ensure that Greenhaven Press accurately reflects the original intent of the authors included in this anthology.

INTRODUCTION

"Suicide is the nation's second leading cause of death among teenagers."

—Chintan Turakhia

"For both sexes and all races, teenagers experience the lowest suicide rates of any age group except pre-teens."

—Mike Males

According to a 1997 nationwide survey conducted by the Public Agenda Foundation and the Advertising Council, a vast majority of adults—nine out of ten—are pessimistic about the future of today's youth. As analysts of the survey conclude, "Americans are convinced that today's adolescents face a crisis." Many social critics contend that the stresses of modern-day society—including violence in the schools, deteriorating family security, and an overdose of disturbing media images—put teens at risk of never reaching their full potential. Teens who have trouble coping with such enormous pressures, some maintain, resort to drug and alcohol use, violence, sexual relationships that often result in pregnancy or sexually transmitted diseases, and sometimes suicide.

However, other commentators criticize the tendency to view teenagers as "troubled" and insist that today's teenagers face no more hardships than those of past generations. Furthermore, these critics argue that many of the problems teens encounter—in particular, academic competition, financial worries, and relationship issues—are nothing new. As writer Andrea Young Ward contends, "Gangs and drug abuse are not unique to the '90s." In fact, some say that the elimination of social taboos, which previously prevented people from speaking openly about sex, drugs, and other sensitive issues, has made it easier for teenagers to cope with problems.

In judging the condition of today's youth, researchers often look to suicide rates as an indicator of how teens are doing. Some assert that teen suicide rates are rising, reflecting an overall downward trend for today's youth. The American Association of Suicidology reports that between 1980 and 1994, suicide rates increased 30 percent for teens aged fifteen to nineteen. The increase in teenage suicide rates, observers claim, is glaring evidence that teens are distressed, desperate, and without hope for the future.

These commentators allege that among certain groups of teenagers, the incidence of suicide is rising at a horrifying rate. For example, according to one statistic, the suicide rate for fifteen- to nineteen-year-old black males has increased 164 percent between 1980 and 1992—and continues to rise. Moreover, many researchers believe that a significant number of suicides committed by young African-American males go unreported. As columnist Fern Shen notes, the suicide of adolescent black males "often is masked by labels such as 'drug overdose' or by situations in which the victim purposely provokes a police officer or other person to kill him." Journalist and political commentator Clarence Page refers to the tendency of young black males to place themselves in highly dangerous situations as "suicide by other means."

Another group at a high risk of suicide, some maintain, is gay teens. According to a 1989 report by the Department of Health and Human Services, 30 percent of five hundred gay and lesbian youths interviewed in San Francisco had attempted suicide at least once. Social critics say that the isolation gay teens experience, due to fears of rejection or attempts to conceal their sexual identity, puts them at a serious risk of suicide. Furthermore, notes one government study, gay teens are more likely to engage in the types of behaviors that increase their chances of committing suicide, including drug use and sexual activity.

With surveys documenting that 60 percent of teens personally know a teenager who has tried to commit suicide, it seems as though suicide is pandemic among today's youth. However, the notion that teen suicide rates are skyrocketing does not go undisputed. A number of critics maintain that flawed statistics create a deceptive picture about teens. Mike Males, author of *The Scapegoat Generation: America's War on Adolescents*, offers a different explanation for the increasing numbers of teen suicides. In the past, he maintains, many teen suicides committed with a firearm were labeled "accidents" due to the social stigma surrounding teenage suicide; today, the correct labeling of firearm deaths as suicides gives the false impression that teen suicide has increased, when actually it has remained nearly the same.

Moreover, some argue that teen suicide rates do not provide a clear picture of the condition of teens in general. For example, according to Males, teen suicide rates in the state of California have decreased by 30 percent since 1970, despite the concurrent rise in homelessness, AIDS, and gang violence—not to mention a greater availability of guns and deadly drugs. The fact that teen suicide is declining while risky behavior is increasing, claim observers, suggests that teen suicide might not be an accurate way to assess the overall situation of teens.

Furthermore, says Males and others, teenage suicide, while horrible from any standpoint, can be put into perspective when the rate of teen suicide is compared to that of other age groups. Excluding young children, teenagers are the least likely group to commit suicide—far less likely than adults. In fact, the group most likely to commit suicide is the elderly, who have a suicide rate 2.5 times that of teenagers.

Numerous researchers also dispute the notion that gay teenagers are at a high risk of committing suicide. While a variety of media sources have reported that gay and lesbian teenagers are two to three times more likely than heterosexual teens to commit suicide, other commentators contend that these claims are unsubstantiated. They allege that the statistic about gay teen suicides originated from a single essay written by a San Francisco social worker who based his figures on methodologically flawed studies. In fact, a 1994 panel composed of social analysts and mental health advocates found that "there is no population-based evidence that sexual orientation and suicidology are linked in some direct or indirect manner."

Some of those who feel teen suicide is not as common as it is portrayed to be argue that it is dangerous to overstate the problem of teen suicide: If teens feel "everybody is doing it," they may begin to view suicide as an acceptable way of coping with their struggles. Others declare that "copycat suicides" are a myth. As Mary Kluesner, President of Suicide Awareness/Voices of Education notes, "There are no documented scientific studies, only rumor and assumed belief, that contagion is a reality. Suicide contagion is very, very rare."

The suicide rate is just one barometer of the quality of teens' lives. Other signals include the rates of teen pregnancy, drug use, and crime. These and other issues are addressed in *Teens at Risk: Opposing Viewpoints*, which contains the following chapters: What Factors Put Teens at Risk? How Can Society Deal with Teenage Crime and Violence? How Can Teen Pregnancy Be Prevented? What Role Do the Media and Government Play in the Problem of Teen Substance Abuse? Throughout these chapters, the authors assess the risks that today's teens face and present potential solutions to these problems.

CHAPTER 1

WHAT FACTORS PUT TEENS AT RISK?

Chapter Preface

Former vice president Dan Quayle brought the issue of single parenthood into the limelight in the early 1990s, when he criticized the television show *Murphy Brown* for its positive portrayal of single parenthood. Quayle and a number of other commentators argue that teenagers from single-parent families are more inclined to engage in risky behavior than those from traditional two-parent families. David Popenoe, a critic of single parenthood, maintains that "the decline of fatherhood is a major force behind . . . crime and delinquency; premature sexuality and out-of-wedlock births to teenagers; deteriorating educational achievement; [and] depression, substance abuse, and alienation among adolescents."

Those who allege that single parenthood puts teenagers at risk cite two reasons for their views. First, they claim, children in single-parent families receive half of the attention, supervision, and financial resources as those from two-parent families. Second, critics of single-parent families maintain, children without fathers miss out on critical lessons about competition, initiative, risk-taking, and independence.

However, others dismiss the notion that a traditional family structure is essential to raising a child successfully. They contend that other familial factors, not single parenthood, influence teen behavior. For example, the National Longitudinal Study on Adolescent Health found that the most important deterrent to risky adolescent behavior was "a feeling of connectedness and love from parents"—a conclusion that held true for both single- and two-parent families. David Demo, a professor at the University of Carolina, argues that because of idyllic television families such as the Cunninghams of the program *Happy Days* and the Cleavers of *Leave It to Beaver*, "a lot of people just assume that [the two-parent family] is the healthiest, ideal family structure." When it comes to the well-being of teenagers, however, Demo maintains that "family structure is not the most important influence."

Those who believe single-parent families place teenagers at risk feel that the only solution is a return to the traditional family structure. Those who view single parenthood as a viable alternative to two-parent families say that society should focus on helping single parents succeed, rather than criticizing them. The question of whether single parenthood puts teens at risk, along with related issues, is debated in the following chapter.

> "Up to 15% of 16- to 19-year-olds are at risk of never reaching their potential and simply becoming lost in society."

A VARIETY OF FACTORS PUT TEENS AT RISK

Gene Stephens

Gene Stephens contends in the following viewpoint that a variety of factors are responsible for the risks teens face. He maintains that today's teens are at risk due to a combination of social problems—including teenage pregnancy, the growing number of single-parent families, poverty, and child abuse—as well as individual problems such as truancy, substance abuse, and feelings of hopelessness. In order to help teens at risk, Stephens advocates the implementation of community-based youth programs. Stephens is a professor of criminal justice at the University of South Carolina.

As you read, consider the following questions:

1. How does Stephens define "at risk" teens?
2. In the author's opinion, how does teen pregnancy place youths at risk?
3. What are the eight characteristics of Stephens's plan to help teens at risk?

Reprinted from Gene Stephens, "Youth at Risk: Saving the World's Most Precious Resource." This article originally appeared in the March/April 1997 issue of The Futurist. Used with permission from the World Future Society, 7910 Woodmont Ave., Suite 450, Bethesda, MD 20814.

Child-care advocates claim that up to 15% of 16- to 19-year-olds are at risk of never reaching their potential and simply becoming lost in society. Others would add to this category children of any age if they are at risk of not becoming self-supporting adults, headed for a life in institutions for delinquency, crime, mental illness, addiction, and dependency. We could also describe as "at risk" those teens and preteens who take on child rearing themselves and drop out of school.

The task of saving these children has become increasingly formidable. Compounding the problem are the expanding gap between the rich and poor, the increasing number of single-parent households, the rise of homes where both parents work, the growing gun culture, and the recent increase in negative attitudes about children, such as courts that treat younger and younger children as adult criminals.

As a result, children lose hope for the future. They turn to peers for attention; they turn to guns for protection, security and status; and they turn to sex and drugs for comfort and relief of boredom. The gang too often becomes their "family"—the only place where they receive attention and approval.

Criminologist James Fox of Northeastern University predicts that the murders committed by teenagers (4,000 in the United States in 1995) will skyrocket as the 39 million children now under age 10 swell the ranks of teenagers by 20% in the first decade of the twenty-first century. The result could be a juvenile crime wave such as the United States has never seen.

SIGNS OF HOPE

Yet, such a catastrophe is not inevitable. There are some signs of hope: a slightly decreased birth rate among teenagers in the mid-1990s, a rising bipartisan concern about "saving the children," burgeoning community-based experiments for meeting the needs of youth, and a movement to regard poor prenatal care, poor parenting skills, child abuse, and child neglect as public-health problems.

Beyond this, a striking change in the rearing of children in many families has been observed. Countering the trend toward ignoring or even abusing children is a trend toward cherishing and nurturing them. Thousands or even millions of young parents are taking turns working while the other stays at home and makes child care almost a full-time vocation. There is an unrecognized renaissance in parenting progressing quietly in neighborhoods across the nation and possibly the world.

Of course, having youth at risk is not a problem unique to

the United States. Wars, social upheaval, rapidly changing economic systems, political instability, and cultural animosity have placed millions of children at risk around the world. Children die of starvation while others wander aimlessly in search of home and family.

JUVENILE ARRESTS, 1980 TO 1994

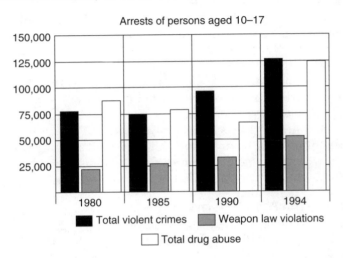

Arrests of persons aged 10–17

■ Total violent crimes ■ Weapon law violations

□ Total drug abuse

U.S. Federal Bureau of Investigation, *Statistical Abstract of the United States* 1996.

Singling out specific problems is difficult, for most are interrelated. For example, children left alone without adult attention are more likely to experiment with sex and drugs. Teenagers who try drugs are more likely to be involved in delinquent behavior. Children who experiment with sex increase their likelihood of becoming unmarried teenage parents. Youngsters who are physically and sexually abused are more likely to adopt abusive behavior toward others. Clearly, however, the following are major factors in the dilemma.

TEENAGE PREGNANCY

Many child advocates see teenage pregnancy as the main problem. Children having children puts both generations at risk and often leads to poverty, poor health care, truancy, and underemployment. The dimensions of the issue—as reported by the National Commission on Children, the United States Census Bureau, and others—are staggering:

- Every year, one in 10 teenage females becomes pregnant—

more than 3,000 a day.
- One of four teenage mothers will have a second child within one year of her first child's birth.
- Most teenage mothers are single and receive no support from the father.
- Eight of 10 teenage mothers do not finish high school.

THE ROLE OF SINGLE PARENTHOOD

About one-fourth of the families in America are headed by a single parent—usually the mother. In the Hispanic community, it is one-third; among black families, it is one-half. Most of the children in these families were born to teenagers.

According to the Centers for Disease Control (CDC), 85% of all children exhibiting behavioral disorders come from father-less homes. Other statistical findings indicate that children from fatherless homes are: 32 times more likely to run away; nine times more likely to drop out of high school; 14 times more likely to commit rape; 10 times more likely to be substance abusers; and 20 times more likely to end up in prison.

POVERTY AND POOR HEALTH CARE

Whereas 75% of single-female-headed households are in poverty at least some of the time, and 33% are chronically poor, poverty is also endemic to a majority of young households. Already, one in three children under 6 lives below the poverty line.

About half of the homeless are families with children. A million divorces each year create new female-headed households below the poverty line.

CDC and other agencies have found that at least 25 million children in the United States have no health care. This means that they are taken to the hospital emergency room or to non-professionals for health problems. Without change in health provider arrangements, half of the nation's children could be without health care by the year 2000. Already, most unwed mothers receive no prenatal care.

Lack of health care too often equals stunted ability to learn, life-altering health problems, lowered ability to cope in a free-market system, and, as a result, greater likelihood of drug abuse, delinquency, and crime.

CHILD ABUSE

There is substantial evidence of child abuse or neglect in the background of every known serial killer. In most cases, the abuse was physically or sexually severe.

Beyond blatant abuse, neglect itself—ignoring the child's physical and emotional needs—is a form of abuse that scars the child as much or more than beatings.

Child abuse and neglect are often called the "silent epidemic" in the United States. Alleged abuse more than quadrupled between the mid-1970s and the mid-1990s to more than 3 million cases a year reported (and 1 million substantiated). A Gallup Poll reported that physical abuse cases were 16 times greater than reported rates, and sexual abuse was 10 times greater.

The U.S. Department of Justice reports that abused or neglected children are 40% more likely to be arrested as juvenile delinquents and adult criminals; three times as likely to use drugs and alcohol, get into fights, and deliberately damage property; and four times as likely to steal and be arrested. It is also reported that one in eight neglected children was later arrested for a violent offense.

CHRONIC TRUANCY AND SCHOOL DROPOUT

On the average school day, as many as 15% of junior and senior high school students are not in school. For too many, this is a pattern that leads to dropout.

Truants represent a large portion of those arrested for daytime break-ins and thefts, and dropouts are over-represented in jails and prisons.

The Census Bureau reports that earnings of students without a high school diploma average far below the poverty line.

ALCOHOL AND DRUG ABUSE

Polls of youth indicate that nine out of 10 teenagers drink alcohol to some extent by the time they finish high school, and a majority have used illegal drugs. A study of 1,200 school dropouts in California found their weekly alcohol-use rates were twice as high as in-school counterparts, and their use of hard drugs was two to five times as high. Dropout drug users were much more likely to be involved in violent and criminal activities. One-third said they had sold drugs in the past year, and twice as many dropouts as in-school students said they belonged to a gang.

The Gallup Poll reported that 70% of 16- to 24-year-olds believe that the world was a better place when their parents were their age, and 56% said it will be worse for their own children. A joint *Washington Post*, Kaiser, and Harvard survey reported that the belief that "most people can be trusted" fell from 54% to 35%, and trust in government dropped from 76% to 25% over a three-decade period ending in 1995. At-risk youth, in particular, say they "live for today" and see no hope for their future.

CRIME AND HOMICIDE

In 1996, the Justice Department reported that the juvenile homicide rate had almost doubled in over a decade, and blacks and males were by far the most likely to be killed.

The major correlating factor was an increase in the use of firearms. Guns were also found to be the single factor that could account for tripling the number of juvenile homicide offenders over the decade. Justice predicts another doubling of crime by juveniles by 2010 if current trends continue.

Tragically, most victims of juvenile violence are other juveniles, often children who are not even involved in the dispute. . . .

A PLAN TO HELP TEENS AT RISK

The plan that follows represents a consensus from groups to whom I've given the same assignment over the past decade: "Develop a program to turn your community's youth into productive, happy, law-abiding adults." These groups have included students from high school to graduate school, practitioners from police to social service workers, and community leaders, all participating in brainstorming and planning sessions to alleviate the youth-at-risk problem.

Here is a comprehensive plan based on my 10-plus years' experience with these exercises.

1. *Commit to positive reinforcement* through community and school-based parenting classes (mandatory in schools), ongoing media campaigns, positive attention, and recognition in all schools (preschool through high school) and community-based programs.

2. *Promote nonviolent conflict resolution* among peers through mandatory educational programs for students, parents, teachers, counselors, administrators, media, and community campaigns.

3. *Encourage mentoring* for all children. Civic, business, and community campaigns should recruit and train mentors, matching them by needs and temperament. Programs such as Big Brothers and Big Sisters should be expanded.

4. *Establish community-school partnerships* to offer before- and after-school tutoring. Enlist youth to perform services to the community to enhance their stake in society.

5. *Develop community-oriented proactive policing programs* that begin with a philosophy of prevention. Examples of prevention programs include midnight basketball leagues, police-youth athletic leagues, neighborhood housing project substations, and foot pa-

trols. These all involve partnerships of police, parents, church, business, civic, and community organizations.

6. *Initiate ethical and cultural awareness programs* that build on partnerships among family, church, school, media, civic, business, and other community groups. These programs would emphasize finding common ground on basic values, such as respect, responsibility, and restraint.

7. *Design youth opportunity programs* to provide all children the chance to reach their potential, regardless of circumstances. Such programs could be run through school, business, and community partnerships that provide in-school jobs and child care, career counseling and training, opportunity scholarships, and recognition for achievement.

8. *Set up peer counseling hotlines* to help youth help each other through the trying times of adolescence.

To this basic plan we may also consider in the future adding more dramatic (though often controversial) measures, such as birth-control implants, health monitoring and treatment implants, behavioral control implants in extreme cases, computer-assisted brain implants, and educational implants. But these measures should only be considered after reaching consensus concerning ethical issues.

In addition, we must focus on justice where delinquency and crime occur. Youth offenders must recognize the consequences of their actions on the victim, the victim's family, and the community. The harm must be ameliorated and restored through mediation and arbitration, restitution, service to the victim and community, reclamation, and reconciliation.

CHILDREN WANT ATTENTION

Every community can develop programs guided by this model. But all plans must adopt certain guiding principles that permeate the approach.

Children want attention above everything. Thus, giving attention reinforces behavior and denying attention extinguishes behavior. Both praise and punishment are attention, and both will reinforce behavior that gets that attention.

It is important to instill optimism and faith in the future in all children, as they are the key to success. The very nature of adolescence is to challenge authority, but most children drift through this troubled period and become law-abiding adults unless they become labeled as delinquents, criminals, or losers.

Surely we can see the need to reach out and lend a hand to the world's most precious resource.

> "U.S. teenagers today are, by nearly
> every important measure, healthier,
> better educated, and more responsible
> than teens of the past."

TEENS ARE NOT AT RISK

Kirk A. Astroth

In the following viewpoint, Kirk A. Astroth refutes the notion that today's teens are at risk; in fact, Astroth claims, statistics show that older generations are generally worse off than teenagers. He maintains that the portrayal of teens as troubled and "out of control" is solely a product of ephebiphobia—adults' fear and hatred of adolescents. Astroth is an extension specialist in the State 4-H Office at Montana State University, Bozeman.

As you read, consider the following questions:

1. According to Astroth, what is responsible for the rise in teen admissions to psychiatric hospitals?
2. In the author's view, why are the statistics on teen suicide misleading?
3. What groups are more likely to commit suicide than teens, in Astroth's opinion?

Reprinted from Kirk A. Astroth, "Beyond Ephebiphobia: Problem Adults or Problem Youths?" *Phi Delta Kappan*, January 1994, by permission of the author and Phi Delta Kappa International.

It is common today to hear that almost half of all young people between the ages of 10 and 17 are at risk of school failure, substance abuse, delinquency, and teenage pregnancy. Indeed, it would appear that troubled youths are no longer the exception but have become the dysfunctional rule. Young people today are typically portrayed as an aberrant pariah class that suffers its own distinct "epidemics" bearing no relationship to adult patterns of behavior. Are today's young people really so different?

Given the barrage of adolescent problems uncovered by so-called researchers, it should come as a shocking surprise to learn that U.S. teenagers today are, by nearly every important measure, healthier, better educated, and more responsible than teens of the past. Moreover, the Iowa Youth Poll for 1991, published by the Iowa State University Extension Service, revealed that most young people feel satisfied with their lives and generally positive about themselves.

Today's Teens Lead Healthy Lives

Not only are today's teens healthier than teens of the past, but they are typically healthier than the adults who seem so ready to label them as "at risk." Even in such cities as Los Angeles, it is estimated that 90% to 95% of all young people are not involved in gangs. Yet we are bombarded with alarms about rising gang activity in our big cities.

Like previous generations of adults, we appear to be suffering from ephebiphobia—a fear and loathing of adolescence. Nearly every generation of young people has been chastised for being "out of control" or aberrant in some way. Adult claims of degeneration among the young can be found in nearly every previous decade. For example, the cover of the 6 September 1954 issue of *Newsweek* blared: "Let's Face It: Our Teen-Agers Are Out of Control." The article inside lamented a "national teen-age problem—a problem that is apparently getting worse." And why? "Too much divorce, too few normal homes," claimed one sociologist. Others denounced "salacious, sadistic comic books." Today, we might blame MTV.

Adults Are Biased Against Teens

Unfortunately, the notion of "youth at risk" has become a lens through which we view all young people, so that today adolescence is seen as some incurable social disease. For example, a study of teenage drinking in the 1950s describes patterns that are the same as those of teens today. In reality, today's teens behave in ways very similar to those of teens of the past and very much like those of today's adults.

The recent sharp increase in teen psychiatric admissions is one manifestation of our pathological treatment of today's youth. Since 1980 adolescent psychiatric admissions have increased 250% to 400%, but "it's not because teens are suddenly so much crazier than they were a decade ago," according to Lynette Lamb. The Children's Defense Fund suggests that at least 40% of these juvenile admissions are inappropriate, may violate the civil rights of the "patients," and are a result of parents' inability to deal with adolescent behavior.

TEENS ARE MUCH LESS LIKELY THAN ADULTS TO COMMIT SUICIDE					
U.S. suicides per 100,000 persons of each age group, sex, and race, 1991					
Age group	Total	Male	Female	White	Nonwhite
10–14	1.5	2.3	0.7	1.6	1.0
15–19	11.0	17.6	3.7	11.8	7.8
All 10–19	6.2	10.0	2.2	6.7	4.4
20–24	14.9	25.4	3.9	13.6	11.3
25–34	15.2	25.0	5.4	16.0	11.3
35–44	14.7	24.0	6.5	15.9	8.1
All 20–44	14.9	24.7	5.5	15.5	9.9
45–64	15.5	24.4	7.1	16.6	7.9
Over 65	19.7	40.2	6.0	21.0	8.4
All ages >10	14.4	23.9	5.6	15.5	8.4

National Center for Health Statistics, *Vital Statistics of the United States 1991*, 1995.

Though commonplace, such a pathological perspective on adolescence exaggerates the negative. Stanton Peele, a Princeton University psychologist, has observed that today's views often define adolescence itself as a diseased state. He points out that research is usually skewed toward the maladjusted young, which has created a myth of the prevalence of adolescent maladjustment.

As astonishing as it may sound, today's teens lead healthier lives than most young and middle-aged adults. Teens have lower rates of suicide, violent death, unwed pregnancy, drug abuse, smoking, and drunken driving. When youth problems do occur, adult influence is apparent. For example, in Montana "nearly 60% of 'teen' pregnancies are [caused] by men over the age of 21," according to Mike Males. Only 29% of all "teen" pregnancies actually involve two teenagers. The most important thing adults can do about the "epidemic of teen pregnancy" in Montana and other states is to stop impregnating teenagers.

AN "EPIDEMIC" OF TEEN SUICIDE?

To illustrate the point that we've become too negative about the current generation of young people, let's look at one other area: teen suicide. The oft-quoted statistics cited to dramatize this epidemic are that nearly 6,000 teens kill themselves annually and that suicides have tripled since the 1950s. But let's look at the data.

First, we have to ask ourselves what seems like a simple question: Who is a teenager? Federal data for 1990 show 13.6 suicides per 100,000 population for people between the ages of 15 and 24. The "teen" suicide rate of 6,000 comes from this same age group—a group that includes more than just teens. What we also fail to ask is how this rate compares to the rate for other age groups. If we are going to be accurate when we discuss "teen" suicide, we should be looking at the suicide rate for 13- to 19-year-olds, not 15- to 24-year-olds. Census data show that the suicide rate for 10- to 19-year-olds is about 10 per 100,000, one of the lowest rates for any age group. More teens die each year from cancer (13 per 100,000) than from suicide.

While I don't wish to minimize the tragedy of any pointless deaths, especially teen suicides, I want us to put the issue in perspective and stop needlessly alarming communities about a "teen suicide epidemic." If we are truly concerned about high suicide rates, we should be devoting more attention to older citizens. Senior citizens over the age of 85 have a suicide rate of 22.5 per 100,000—2.5 times the rate for 10- to 19-year-olds. Those between 75 and 84 years of age have a suicide rate of 26.1 per 100,000; those between 65 and 74 years of age have a suicide rate of 18.1 per 100,000. And rates for Americans 65 and older rose 21% from 1980 to 1986. So who's at risk?

In 1956, 10,000 teens died from violent causes, including 1,100 from firearms (a toll that almost surely includes many hidden suicides) and 5,200 from traffic deaths. This total death rate has changed little over the years. What has changed, though, is our honesty about how teens die. During the 1950s, many deaths from firearms were classified as "accidental"; we now accurately list them as suicides.

ADULTS COMMIT SUICIDE MORE THAN TEENS

The reality is that teens as a whole are less likely to commit suicide than any other age group except preteens. In fact, Montana's teen suicide rate is not rising, and youth suicide levels and trends appear to be linked to those of adult suicide. Occupational surveys consistently show that parents and teachers are twice as likely, counselors and psychologists are four times as likely, and school administrators are six times as likely to commit suicide as are high school students. Today's teens are more justified in worrying that a parent, adult relative, teacher, or counselor will commit suicide than the other way around. Yet we do not question the health of all grown-ups as a result.

Today's mythology that most or all youths are "at risk" scatters valuable resources and dilutes efforts to help the minority of youths who are genuinely troubled. While the problems faced by our young people are serious, I want to caution against framing the issue as an "epidemic." Certainly, some of our young people are troubled. Precisely because such problems as suicide, drug addiction, and delinquency are enormous tragedies, we must be clear about the nature and extent of the problems as we study and seek to prevent them. Blanket approaches that inflate the numbers of youths "at risk" are not only ineffective but also undermine the effectiveness of what should be carefully targeted preventive measures.

| "If I were a Hollywood producer who put before the eyes of impressionable kids images that glorify violence . . . , I would find it awfully hard to sleep at night."

MEDIA VIOLENCE PUTS TEENS AT RISK

Mona Charen

In the following viewpoint, Mona Charen maintains that violent media images inspire teens to commit violent crimes. Because children are saturated in violent media from such an early age, the author claims, they become numb to violence and are therefore prone to aggressive behavior. Charen is a syndicated columnist.

As you read, consider the following questions:

1. On what basis does Charen state that the nation suffers from a "moral meltdown"?
2. What inspired fourteen-year-old Michael Carneal to open fire on a group of friends, according to Charen?
3. In the author's opinion, how is the entertainment media able to influence actions?

Reprinted from Mona Charen, "Do Movies Make Kids Kill?" *Conservative Chronicle*, December 24, 1997, by permission of Mona Charen and Creators Syndicate.

It is sad evidence of our internal carnage that we seem to have become an expert nation of mourners. The latest version, from Paducah, Ky., was so well stage-managed and professional—complete with live coverage by CNN—that it seemed almost planned.

The 14-year-old accused killer, Michael Carneal, entered his high school during the pre-school hours carrying five guns. He found the room where a group of his friends were holding a prayer meeting and began shooting to kill. Three girls were shot dead. Another six were wounded. One is permanently paralyzed from the waist down.

The young man in custody is described by one and all as the product of a good family. His father is a prominent Paducah attorney. The family attends church regularly. The accused killer's sister will be valedictorian this year at the high school now stained with blood. The boy himself, while small and unprepossessing, was at no time considered to be unbalanced or mentally disturbed.

He was, by all accounts, a fairly normal boy who seethed at being the butt of teasing by his contemporaries, leaving the troubling question: How could a normal child commit such a despicable crime? How could he shoot down his friends in cold blood?

A Moral Meltdown

The overall crime rate in the United States is dropping. And while this is reassuring news, it does not quiet the concern that this nation is in the grip of a serious moral meltdown. For while the absolute number of crimes is down, the nature of crimes committed, particularly by the very young, continues to shock and dismay us.

Normal teenaged girls have given birth in toilet bowls and then left their offspring in trash bins. Other normal kids have lured strangers to their homes—in New Jersey it was a pizza delivery man—for the pure pleasure of killing. In New York in 1997, two middle-class teenagers killed a wino they had met in Central Park and then attempted to mutilate his body so that police would be unable to identify him.

The streets of inner cities are pockmarked by the sites of casual murders; murders for sneakers, murders for clothes, murders over basketball games and murders because someone "dissed" someone else.

Michael Carneal says he was inspired by the movie *The Basketball Diaries*, which features a dream sequence in which a kid who is teased gets revenge by killing his classmates with a shotgun. The scenes are vivid and gory. At first blush, they would seem to repel anyone.

Horsey. Reprinted by special permission of North America Syndicate.

But our kids are marinated in violence from an early age. The images they see and hear—from Nine Inch Nails to Marilyn Manson—are so grotesque that they dull the senses.

Now it is fashionable to say that Hollywood never made anyone pick up a gun, that the people who do kill would have done so anyway and copycat crimes merely reflect the lack of creativity on the part of criminals.

HOW THE MEDIA ENCOURAGES VIOLENCE

Nonsense. The entertainment media convey a sense of what is within the realm of the possible. If everyone on prime-time television is sleeping around, there is no question that this influences the viewers' sense of what is proper and acceptable. A few years ago, the movie *The Money Train* portrayed a criminal firebombing the ticket booth of a New York subway. Within a few weeks of the movie's release, three copycat crimes had taken place. Harry Kaufman, who worked inside one of those booths, was condemned to days of torture from third-degree burns and ultimately death.

The veneer of civilization is very thin. Almost all of us have the capacity under the right circumstances to behave savagely. Some of us need only a little encouragement.

Clearly, the causes of violence are complex. But there have always been tormented teenagers. Only recently have they thought it reasonable to blow their classmates away with shotguns. If I were a Hollywood producer who put before the eyes of impressionable kids images that glorify violence and revel in pornography (the sexual and the violent kind), I would find it awfully hard to sleep at night.

| "Claims that TV causes violence bear little relation to real behavior."

MEDIA VIOLENCE DOES NOT PUT TEENS AT RISK

Mike Males

Mike Males, author of *The Scapegoat Generation: America's War on Adolescents*, argues in the following viewpoint that real violence, not media violence, is responsible for juvenile crime. He maintains that teens who engage in risky behavior are often mimicking the behavior of their parents or other adults, not the violence they see depicted in television programs, films, and other media.

As you read, consider the following questions:

1. What proof does Males offer that media violence does not cause teen violence?
2. According to Males, what is America's "biggest explosion in felony violence"?
3. In the author's opinion, what influence do cigarette ads have on teens?

Reprinted from Mike Males, "Stop Blaming Kids and TV," *The Progressive*, October 1997, by permission of *The Progressive*, 409 E. Main St., Madison, WI 53703.

"**C**hildren have never been very good at listening to their elders," James Baldwin wrote in *Nobody Knows My Name*. "But they have never failed to imitate them." This basic truth has all but disappeared as the public increasingly treats teenagers as a robot-like population under sway of an exploitative media. White House officials lecture film, music, Internet, fashion, and pop-culture moguls and accuse them of programming kids to smoke, drink, shoot up, have sex, and kill.

So do conservatives, led by William Bennett and Dan Quayle. Professional organizations are also into media-bashing. In its famous report on youth risks, the Carnegie Corporation devoted a full chapter to media influences.

Progressives are no exception. *Mother Jones* claims it has "proof that TV makes kids violent." And the Institute for Alternative Media emphasizes, "the average American child will witness . . . 200,000 acts of [TV] violence" by the time that child graduates from high school.

THE PREVALENCE OF REAL VIOLENCE

None of these varied interests note that during the eighteen years between a child's birth and graduation from high school, there will be fifteen million cases of real violence in American homes grave enough to require hospital emergency treatment. These assaults will cause ten million serious injuries and 40,000 deaths to children. In October 1996, the Department of Health and Human Services reported 565,000 serious injuries that abusive parents inflicted on children and youths in 1993. The number is up four-fold since 1986.

The Department of Health report disappeared from the news in one day. It elicited virtually no comment from the White House, Republicans, or law-enforcement officials. Nor from Carnegie scholars, whose 150-page study, "Great Transitions: Preparing Adolescents for a New Century," devotes two sentences to household violence. The left press took no particular interest in the story, either.

All sides seem to agree that fictional violence, sex on the screen, Joe Camel, beer-drinking frogs, or naked bodies on the Internet pose a bigger threat to children than do actual beatings, rape, or parental addictions. This, in turn, upholds the Clinton doctrine that youth behavior is the problem, and curbing young people's rights the answer.

Claims that TV causes violence bear little relation to real behavior. Japanese and European kids behold media as graphically brutal as that which appears on American screens, but seventeen-year-olds in those countries commit murder at rates lower than those of American seventy-year-olds.

Likewise, youths in different parts of the United States are exposed to the same media but display drastically different violence levels. TV violence does not account for the fact that the murder rate among black teens in Washington, D.C., is twenty-five times higher than that of white teens living a few Metro stops away. It doesn't explain why, nationally, murder doubled among nonwhite and Latino youth over the last decade, but declined among white Anglo teens. Furthermore, contrary to the TV brainwashing theory, Anglo sixteen-year-olds have lower violent-crime rates than black sixty-year-olds, and Anglo thirty-year-olds. Men, women, whites, Latinos, blacks, Asians, teens, young adults, middle-agers, and senior citizens in Fresno County—California's poorest urban area—display murder and violent-crime rates double those of their counterparts in Ventura County, the state's richest.

Confounding every theory, America's biggest explosion in felony violent crime is not street crime among minorities or teens of any color, but domestic violence among aging, mostly white baby boomers. Should we arm Junior with a V-chip to protect him from Mom and Dad? . . .

CHILDREN IMITATE ADULTS

I worked for a dozen years in youth programs in Montana and California. When problems arose, they usually crossed generations. I saw violent kids with dads or uncles in jail for assault. I saw middle-schoolers molested in childhood by mom's boyfriend. I saw budding teen alcoholics hoisting forty-ouncers alongside forty-year-old sots. I also saw again and again how kids start to smoke. In countless trailers and small apartments dense with blue haze, children roamed the rugs as grownups puffed. Mom and seventh-grade daughter swapped Dorals while bemoaning the evils of men. A junior-high basketball center slept outside before a big game because a dozen elders—from her non-inhaling sixteen-year-old brother to her grandma— were all chain smokers. Two years later, she'd given up and joined the party.

As a rule, teen smoking mimicked adult smoking by gender, race, locale, era, and household. I could discern no pop-culture puppetry. My survey of 400 Los Angeles middle schoolers for a 1994 *Journal of School Health* article found children of smoking parents three times more likely to smoke by age fifteen than children of non-smokers. Parents were the most influential but not the only adults kids emulated. Nor did youngsters copy elders slavishly. Youths often picked slightly different habits (like chewing tobacco, or their own brands).

In 1989, the Centers for Disease Control lamented, "75 percent of all teenage smokers come from homes where parents smoke." You don't hear such candor from today's put-politics-first health agencies. Centers for Disease Control tobacco chieftain Michael Eriksen informed me that his agency doesn't make an issue of parental smoking. Nor do anti-smoking groups. Asked Kathy Mulvey, research director of INFACT: "Why make enemies of fifty million adult smokers" when advertising creates the real "appeal of tobacco to youth?"

MEDIA VIOLENCE DOES NOT MAKE TEENS KILL

Thirty-one suburban and rural California counties, with a population of 2.5 million, including 250,000 teenagers, had no teenage murders in 1993. Yet in a state with 4,000 murders that year, these kids saw the same movies, heard the same music, possessed as many guns as those central Los Angeles census tracts with the same youth population, but with more than 200 youth murders. One difference: The youth poverty level of those thirty-one suburban and rural counties is tiny in comparison with central L.A.

Alexander Cockburn, *Nation*, June 3, 1996.

Do ads hook kids on cigarettes? Studies of the effects of the Joe Camel logo show only that a larger fraction of teen smokers than veteran adult smokers choose the Camel brand. When asked, some researchers admit they cannot demonstrate that advertising causes kids to smoke who would not otherwise. And that's the real issue. In fact, surveys found smoking declining among teens (especially the youngest) during Joe's advent from 1985 to 1990.

The University of California's Stanton Glantz, whose exposure of 10,000 tobacco documents enraged the industry, found corporate perfidy far shrewder than camels and cowboys.

"As the tobacco industry knows well," Glantz reported, "kids want to be like adults." An industry marketing document advises: "To reach young smokers, present the cigarette as one of the initiations into adult life . . . the basic symbols of growing up."

The biggest predictor of whether a teen will become a smoker, a drunk, or a druggie is whether or not the child grows up amid adult addicts. Three-fourths of murdered kids are killed by adults. Suicide and murder rates among white teenagers resemble those of white adults, and suicide and murder rates among black teens track those of black adults. And as far as teen pregnancy goes, for minor mothers, four-fifths of the fathers are adults over eighteen, and half are adults over twenty.

The inescapable conclusion is this: If you want to change juvenile behavior, change adult behavior. But instead of focusing on adults, almost everyone points a finger at kids—and at the TV culture that supposedly addicts them.

Groups like Mothers Against Drunk Driving charge, for instance, that Budweiser's frogs entice teens to drink. Yet the 1995 National Household Survey found teen alcohol use declining. "Youths aren't buying the cute and flashy beer images," an in-depth USA Today survey found. Most teens found the ads amusing, but they did not consume Bud as a result.

By squabbling over frogs, political interests can sidestep the impolitic tragedy that adults over the age of twenty-one cause 90 percent of America's 16,000 alcohol-related traffic deaths every year. Clinton and drug-policy chief Barry McCaffrey ignore federal reports that show a skyrocketing toll of booze and drug-related casualties among adults in their thirties and forties—the age group that is parenting most American teens. But both officials get favorable press attention by blaming alcohol ads and heroin chic for corrupting our kids.

Progressive reformers who insist kids are so malleable that beer frogs and Joe Camel and Ace Ventura push them to evil are not so different from those on the Christian right who claim that Our Bodies, Ourselves promotes teen sex and that the group Rage Against the Machine persuades pubescents to roll down Rodeo Drive with a shotgun.

America's increasingly marginalized young deserve better than grownup escapism. Millions of children and teenagers face real destitution, drug abuse, and violence in their homes. Yet these profound menaces continue to lurk in the background, even as the frogs, V-chips, and Mighty Morphins take center stage.

> "Children living in homes where fathers are absent are far more likely to be expelled from or drop out of school, develop emotional or behavioral problems, commit suicide, and fall victim to child abuse or neglect."

THE ABSENCE OF FATHERS PUTS TEENS AT RISK

Wade F. Horn

The number of single-parent families rose from 8 million in 1960 to 24 million in 1995. Wade F. Horn maintains in the following viewpoint that this increase in fatherless families has caused widespread violence, pregnancy, and drug abuse among teenagers. Fathers are an essential part of a child's successful upbringing, the author contends. Horn is a clinical child psychologist, a faculty member at Georgetown University's Public Policy Institute, and president of the National Fatherhood Initiative.

As you read, consider the following questions:

1. According to Horn, what are the two mechanisms by which parents socialize children?
2. In the author's view, why are fathers important?
3. What does Horn cite as the consequences of fatherlessness?

Reprinted from Wade F. Horn, "Why There Is No Substitute for Parents," *Imprimis*, June 1997, by permission of *Imprimis*, the monthly journal of Hillsdale College.

In 1960, the total number of children living in fatherless families was fewer than eight million. Today, that total has risen to nearly twenty-four million. Nearly four out of ten children in America are being raised in homes without their fathers and soon it may be six out of ten. How did this happen? Why are so many of our nation's children growing up without a full-time father? It is because our culture has accepted the idea that fathers are superfluous—in other words, they are not necessary in the "modern" family. Supposedly, their contributions to the well-being of children can easily be performed by the state, which disburses welfare checks, subsidizes midnight basketball leagues, and establishes child-care facilities.

Ideas, of course, have consequences. And the consequences of this idea have been as profound as they have been disastrous. Almost 75 percent of American children living in fatherless households will experience poverty before the age of eleven, compared to only 20 percent of those raised by two parents. Children living in homes where fathers are absent are far more likely to be expelled from or drop out of school, develop emotional or behavioral problems, commit suicide, and fall victim to child abuse or neglect. The males are also far more likely to become violent criminals. As a matter of fact, men who grew up without dads currently represent 70 percent of the prison population serving long-term sentences.

Undeniably, fathers are important for the well-being of children. So, too, are traditional families. They ensure the continuity of civilization by propagating the species and socializing children. Everyone seems to understand the obvious benefits of propagation, but the important role that parents play in socializing children is widely misunderstood and undervalued.

WHY SOCIALIZATION IS IMPORTANT

Socialization can be defined as the process whereby individuals acquire the behavior, attitudes, and values that are not only regarded as desirable and appropriate by society but that have also stood the test of time and proved to be the most humane. Proper socialization requires delaying or inhibiting "impulse gratification" in order to abide by the rule of law and the rule of custom. Well-socialized children have learned, for example, not to strike out at others to get what they want; poorly socialized children have not. Well-socialized children have learned to obey the directions of legitimate authority figures like parents and teachers; poorly socialized children have not. Well-socialized children have learned to cooperate and share with others; poorly socialized children have not.

Much of what is described as "good character" or "virtue" reflects the ability to delay or inhibit impulse gratification. When a child tells the truth, even though he knows that it will result in negative consequences, he is inhibiting the impulse to lie to avoid unpleasantness. When he shows charity to others, he is inhibiting the impulse to behave selfishly. A civil society is dependent upon virtuous citizens who have developed this capacity to delay or inhibit impulse gratification; that is, persons who can control their behavior voluntarily. Without a majority of such citizens, storekeepers would have to post armed guards in front of every display counter, women would live in constant fear of being raped by roaming bands of marauding men, and children would be left to the mercy of those who would exploit them. Fortunately, well-socialized children generally become well-socialized adults. Unfortunately, poorly socialized children generally do not. There are few statements one can make with complete certitude, but here is one: When families fail in their task to socialize children, a civil society is not possible. Herein lies the awesome responsibility of parenting.

TWO MECHANISMS OF SOCIALIZATION

Parents socialize children through two mechanisms. The first is teaching through direct instruction reinforced by a combination of rewards and punishments for acceptable and unacceptable behavior. The second is teaching by example. Of the two, the latter is the more important mechanism since most complex human behavior is acquired through observational learning. Children are much more likely to do as a parent *does* than as a parent *says*. This is why parents who lie and cheat tend to raise children who lie and cheat, despite any direct instruction to the contrary. As Benjamin Franklin once observed, the best sermon is indeed a good example.

Please note that I have not asserted that the state—or as it is euphemistically referred to these days, the "village"—is necessary for the proper socialization of children. Rather, it is parents who are necessary, and this means a mother *and* a father. There are, of course, thousands of single mothers who are doing a heroic job of parenting and beating the odds. I do not mean to denigrate their efforts. Yet there is a great deal of hard evidence to suggest that when fathers are absent, boys tend to develop poor conduct. They "act out" their aggressive impulses, sometimes quite violently, toward others. Girls also tend to act out when fathers are absent, but in a different way; they become rebellious and promiscuous.

MOTHERS AND FATHERS PARENT DIFFERENTLY

No matter what the advocates of "gender-free parenting" may say, mothers and fathers do parent differently. Mothers tend to be more verbal, whereas fathers are more physical. Mothers also tend to encourage personal safety and caution, whereas fathers are more challenging when it comes to achievement, independence, and risk-taking. And mothers tend to be stronger comforting figures than fathers who are more intent upon establishing and enforcing rules governing the behavior of their children.

The fact that mothers and fathers parent differently is not to say that one group does it "right" or "better" than the other. What children need to develop good character is the combination of what mothers and fathers bring to the parenting equation. Take the fact that mothers tend to be nurturers and fathers tend to be disciplinarians. Parenting experts used to believe that families socialize children best when both parents adopt a nurturing but permissive role, demonstrating high levels of love and low levels of control. Decades of research have shown, however, that when children are reared this way they act out through chronic bad behavior. Permissiveness as a "parenting style" simply doesn't work. Boys and girls need a high level of nurturing balanced by a high level of control. Those who are reared in families that exhibit this combination are friendlier, more energetic, and better behaved. Those who are reared by single mothers, therefore, are warm and affectionate but have difficulty learning self-discipline. Conversely, those who are reared by single fathers are obedient but often plagued by anxiety and insecurity.

WHY ARE FATHERS IMPORTANT?

It has also been fashionable for those pushing for gender-free parenting to assert that the physical play of fathers has no beneficial impact on child-rearing. Many self-proclaimed child experts exhort fathers to stop playing with the kids and do more housework. Some even claim that the rough-and-tumble play of fathers teaches aggression and should be avoided. But new clinical studies reveal that the physical play of fathers actually gives children much-needed practice in regulating their emotions and behavior and helps them develop the capacity to recognize the emotional cues of others.

The point is not to force a choice between the parenting role of mothers or fathers but to suggest that they work best when they work together. This view contrasts sharply with the "two pair of hands" argument, which holds that when it comes to parenting, two people are better than one and it makes no difference whether they are mothers or fathers. In reality it matters greatly to whom the "two pairs of hands" are attached. Kids don't need impersonal "caregivers"; they need loving moms and dads.

Reprinted by permission of Chuck Asay and Creators Syndicate.

Fathers are also critical to the proper socialization of children because they teach by example how to keep negative impulses in check. It is through boys' observation of the way their fathers deal with frustration, anger, and sadness that they learn how men should cope with such emotions. It is also through the observation of how fathers treat mothers that boys learn how men should treat women. If fathers treat mothers with dignity and respect, then it is likely that their sons will grow up to treat women with dignity and respect. If fathers treat mothers with contempt and cruelty, then it is likely that their sons will, too. Fathers are also critical for the healthy emotional development of girls. If girls experience the love, attention, and protection of fathers, then they are likely to resist the temptations of seeking such things elsewhere—often through casual sexual relations at a very young age. Finally, fathers are important in helping children make the difficult transition to the adult world. Boys require an affirmation that they are "man enough." Girls require an affirmation that they are "worthy enough."

Given this understanding, what should we expect when fatherlessness becomes the norm? We don't need a crystal ball to find the answer. As I indicated earlier, nearly four out of every ten children are being raised absent their fathers right now. The result is that juveniles are the fastest growing segment of the criminal population in the United States. Between 1982 and 1991, the rate at which children were arrested for murder increased 93 percent; for aggravated assault, 72 percent; for rape, 24 percent; and for automobile theft, 97 percent. Although homicide rates have increased for all ages, those for teenagers have increased more rapidly than for adults.

The teen population is expected to grow by 20 percent over the next decade, and this is precisely the generation most likely to be reared without fathers. The prospect has led many sociologists, criminologists, and law enforcement agencies to conclude that shortly after the turn of the twenty-first century we will see an adolescent crime wave the likes of which has never been seen before in this country. If that were not enough, we know that each and every day:

- 7,700 children become sexually active;
- 1,100 children have abortions;
- 2,500 children are born out of wedlock;
- 600 children contract syphilis or gonorrhea; and
- six children commit suicide.

Fatherlessness is not solely responsible for these tragedies, but it certainly is a major cause. Indeed, all the available evidence suggests that improving the well-being of our children—and ultimately our nation—depends upon finding ways to bring fathers back into the home.

> "Most children of single parents do not drop out of school, get arrested, abuse drugs, or suffer long-term emotional distress."

THE ABSENCE OF FATHERS DOES NOT PUT TEENS AT SIGNIFICANT RISK

Stephanie Coontz

Stephanie Coontz maintains in the following viewpoint that broad generalizations about the risks associated with single parenthood perpetuate the myth that two-parent families are always better than single-parent families. In fact, she contends, there are potential advantages and disadvantages to both single-parent and two-parent families. Moreover, the author argues that two-parent families that are abusive or conflict-ridden can be more harmful to children than families in which no father is present. Stephanie Coontz, a family historian at the Evergreen State College in Olympia, Washington, wrote *The Way We Never Were: American Families and the Nostalgia Trap* (1992) and *The Way We Really Are: Coming to Terms with America's Changing Families* (1997).

As you read, consider the following questions:

1. According to the author, what are the potential disadvantages of two-parent families?
2. What does Coontz cite as the potential advantages of single-parent families?
3. What are the greatest periods of stress for two-parent families and for single-parent families, in the author's view?

Excerpted from Stephanie Coontz, "The American Family and the Nostalgia Trap," *Phi Delta Kappan*, March 1995, by permission of the author and Phi Delta Kappa International.

There is no denying that children need more than one caring adult in their lives, or that family breakup is a potent cause of childhood distress. Why, then, complain "profamily" advocates, can't we simply revive the "cultural consensus" that, "on the average, an intact, two-parent family is best"?

The problem is that such seemingly innocuous generalizations encourage preconceived notions that a particular "intact" family does have a responsible, involved mother and father and that a particular single-parent or reconstituted family does not have its own strengths. People end up in single-parent homes for a variety of reasons, some of which even the most radical right-wingers would acknowledge as valid. And there is much wider variation among children from single-parent families, including never-married ones, than there is between the averages for each category.

GENERALIZATIONS ABOUT DIVORCED FAMILIES

Broad generalizations about family types ignore critical variations and usually reflect serious methodological errors. For example, in 1989 Judith Wallerstein published a long-term study of middle-class children of divorced families, claiming that almost half of the children of divorced parents experience long-term pain, worry, and insecurity that adversely affect their love and work relationships. It was Wallerstein's work that laid the foundation for Barbara Whitehead's claim in the April 1993 Atlantic Monthly that "the evidence is in." But this supposedly definitive study was based on a self-selected sample of only 60 couples. It did not compare the children of divorced couples with those of nondivorced ones to determine whether some of their worries and adjustment problems might have stemmed from other factors, such as work pressures, general social insecurities, or community fragmentation. Moreover, the sample was drawn from families already experiencing difficulty and referred to a divorce clinic for therapy. According to Andrew Cherlin and Frank Furstenberg, "Only a third of the sample was deemed to possess 'adequate psychological functioning' prior to the divorce."

More careful research yields much lower estimates of the risks associated with single parenthood. In February 1993 Paul Amato published a review of nearly every single quantitative study that had been done on divorce. Although he found some clear associations with lower levels of children's well-being, these were, on average, "not large." A meta-analysis of such studies, published in the Psychological Bulletin, also found "modest" differences overall, noting that the more carefully controlled the studies, the smaller the differences they reported. The "large majority" of children of divorce, wrote 11 family researchers in response to Whitehead's misuse of their data, do not experience long-term problems. Most children of single parents do not drop out of school, get arrested, abuse drugs, or suffer long-term emotional distress. Only a minority of such children do experience severe problems. Meanwhile, children from high-conflict marriages or even ones in which the father has simply withdrawn often do worse in the long run than do children of divorced or never-married parents. A RAND Corporation study reports that marital conflict has a stronger relation with youthful delinquency and aggression than does parental absence per se. . . .

STIGMATIZATION HARMS SINGLE-PARENT FAMILIES

Certainly, one-parent families face serious challenges. After all, it's hard enough for two parents to raise children in a society in which rampant consumerism is constantly rubbing against rampant inequality. But most families can meet the challenges, so long as these are not multiplied by intense economic stress, deteriorating social support systems, and the very same social stigma that the family-values crusaders believe to be part of the cure for our family problems. Indeed, one review of the literature on single-parent families found that the only situations in which children of one-parent families suffered losses of self-esteem were those in which single-parent families were stigmatized.

Such stigmatization remains widespread, even among people who should know something about the effects of self-fulfilling prophecies. Teachers shown a videotape of a child engaging in a variety of actions consistently rate the child much more negatively on a wide range of dimensions when they are told that he or she comes from a single-parent family than when they believe the child comes from an intact family. And even though serious antisocial behavior is overwhelmingly related to economic circumstances rather than to family form, children from one-parent families are far more likely to be arrested and prosecuted for the same offenses for which children from two-parent families are released to their parents.

In other words, the main policy recommendation of the new family-values crusaders would exacerbate the problems they hope to solve. Multiplying the stigmas against single parents may deter some couples from divorce or prevent some women from having babies out of wedlock, but it's unlikely to reverse the larger trend toward the declining centrality of lifelong marriage. Nor will it help the millions of children who, for better or worse, are already in one-parent families. In the real world, only 50.8% of all youths live with both biological parents; 24% live in one-parent families; 21.1% live in stepfamilies.

THERE IS NO PERFECT FAMILY STRUCTURE

I am in favor of educating parents about the potential problems associated with divorce and rearing children alone. But we need to reject the false notion that there is one perfect family form that automatically protects children, while others automatically put them at risk. We should choose more sensitive and delicate tools than the blunt instruments that the family-values crusade employs in its effort to hammer all families into one mold. In addition to grasping the historical variability of family life, we must analyze the individual strengths, weaknesses, resources, and vulnerabilities of today's diverse families in light of their particular circumstances. Different family structures tend to produce different stress points, but ultimately it is the processes families develop within their different structures that count most in determining the outcomes for family members.

SINGLE MOTHERS CAN RAISE SUCCESSFUL CHILDREN

Critical as it may be to encourage fathers to nurture their families, there needs to be an acknowledgment that the alternative is not necessarily damnation. Understanding what permits many single mothers to raise successful children may be every bit as important as understanding the power of paternal love.

Ellis Cose, *Newsweek*, October 31, 1994.

Take the male breadwinner/female homemaker model. In an economy in which work, home, and school are in different locations, this form potentially provides children with more time, more supervision, and more help with homework; the mother has more chances to meet with teachers, help out in the schools, and chauffeur children to extracurricular activities. This family structure seems to be especially beneficial to the health and happiness of men, so long as they can live up to their provider role. Yet these families often isolate the mother and lower her self-esteem. Homemakers with young children, for example, tend to be more depressed than other groups of women. Furthermore, such families may have a tough time adjusting to rapid economic change. Parents with strong values about male breadwinning are more likely than other parents to experience conflict and severe distress if the father faces economic setbacks or the mother has to seek a job.

Two-earner families have less family time together, and they are more likely to quarrel over housework, sometimes to the point of rupture. Yet Arlie Hochschild's study of two-earner couples found that both men and women were happiest in marriages that had worked out egalitarian relations. Furthermore, families with a working mother are more likely to raise children who respect women—no small advantage in a world in which women are rapidly becoming the majority of the workforce and old-fashioned notions of women's place are a potent cause of workplace hostilities.

THE ILLUSION OF HEALTHY TWO-PARENT FAMILIES

Both types of two-parent families have the potential advantage that more than one adult is available to the child. Parents can back each other up with regard to discipline, compensate for each other's weaknesses, spell each other in tasks and time, and model healthy conflict resolution or negotiation. On the other hand, this potential is not always fulfilled. Many two-parent families have the illusion that a father's presence provides them with some magic psychological shield. This attitude may lead the mother to avoid confronting damaging paternal behavior rather than risk a split. Other traditional families have fathers who are effectively absent, and therapist Deborah Luepnitz has remarked that such an unacknowledged or ambiguous loss may in the long run be more difficult to grieve than a sharp break.

Children stuck in high-conflict marriages or ones in which a father is angry and withdrawn often have worse long-term problems than children in single-parent families. One recent study of adolescent self-esteem found no differences by family structure. However, the lowest self-esteem of all groups was found in teens of two-parent families whose fathers had low levels of interest in them. Such youngsters, lacking even the excuse of the father's absence to explain his disengagement, were more likely to blame themselves for their father's lack of interest. It is also more possible for two-parent families to hide problems of abuse, incest, and alcoholism from the outside world than it is for one-parent families.

Even harmonious couples need to beware of certain pitfalls. Thinking themselves complete and self-sufficient, they may not give their children enough exposure to experiences and values that differ from their own. Such families occasionally foster an inward orientation that hinders a child from striking out in new directions or learning to appreciate difference in others. I was raised in neighborhoods in which all adults felt free to act parentally toward everyone's children, and I have noticed that, when I continue this tradition by commenting on something dangerous or hurtful that local children may be doing, some youths from two-parent families are the most hostile in their response: "You can't tell me that; you're not my mom."

POTENTIAL ADVANTAGES OF SINGLE-PARENT FAMILIES

Single-parent families have only one parent in the home to provide financial and emotional resources. When one adult is sad or angry, the whole household is upset; it takes single-parent families longer to recover from economic reverses. These are serious handicaps. Yet in many communities, female-headed families were historically an adaptive way of compensating for high male unemployment and persistent poverty. For example, an African American colleague of mine has described how his single mother's very lack of a stable marriage gave her the flexibility to link him up with a huge network of matrilineal kin and fictive cousins. She moved him in with whatever friends or relatives were employed or had contacts with successful men in the black community. He thus gained access to mentoring that his own irregularly employed (though never entirely absent) father could not provide. Today, my friend argues, the cutbacks in social programs, the growth of unemployment, and the increasing isolation of poor inner-city blacks from job networks make single motherhood less likely to be such an adaptive coping mechanism. Yet the community collapse that makes single motherhood more difficult also increases its likelihood, and heaping more guilt on the mothers does not help.

Adults in single-parent families spend less time supervising homework or interacting with teachers than adults in two-parent families, an obvious drawback. But they also spend more time talking with their children, a behavior that can lead to accelerated cognitive development and emotional empathy, so long as the parent takes care not to confide too much anger or distress. (Ironically, children of mothers who have made a conscious choice to be single and do not go through the intense grief and bitterness of a failed relationship have a potential advantage here.) In addition, adolescents in single-parent families face fewer pressures to conform to traditional gender roles. They tend to have greater maturity and feelings of efficacy than teens in two-parent families. Depending on the dynamics of the family, these characteristics can lead to more risk-taking or to more breadth and depth of thinking—or to both. In terms of academics, the absence of a father tends to be associated with lower mathematics achievement for boys but higher verbal skills. Yet the average math deficit is just as great for boys in two-parent families with low paternal involvement—a point that again directs our attention to family processes rather than family structures.

Single parents are less likely to pressure their children into social conformity and more likely to praise good grades than are parents in two-parent households—both of these, behaviors that tend to produce higher academic performance. Here single-parent families have a potential advantage over many two-parent families. But single parents are more likely to get upset and angry when their children receive bad grades, a reaction that encourages defiance and a further decline in grades.

All these variables are further complicated by the fact that they play out differently according to the race, class, and ethnicity of the family; they also have different impacts on children depending on their age, sex, individual temperament, and interaction with siblings. The negative impacts of single parenthood, interestingly, tend to be greatest among groups whose cultural values most emphasize two-parent families and paternal authority and least among those who have a history of tolerance and support for single mothers. Sara McLanahan and Gary Sandefur found that family disruption is most likely to produce harmful effects among Hispanics and least likely to do so among blacks, with whites falling in between.

Are Children in Stepfamilies at Risk?

The contradictory data on stepfamilies also illustrate the problem with overgeneralization. While remarriage tends to reduce the stresses associated with poverty and economic insecurity, some studies suggest that, taken as a whole, children in stepfamilies face the same added risks of emotional problems as do children in one-parent families; they are actually more likely to repeat a grade than are children of never-married mothers. Yet in a recent long-term, ongoing government study, 80% of children in stepfamilies were judged to be doing well psychologically, compared to 90% in intact biological families.

Numerous researchers have suggested that girls have more problems in stepfamilies than boys, yet one recent study found not more problems for girls but merely more articulated worries. Researchers Andrew Cherlin and Frank Furstenberg point out that "stepfamilies are even less alike as a group than are nuclear families." They also cite "tremendous variation in the way parents manage the transition" to a blended family. The lack of norms and support systems for such transitions, rather than the family form itself, probably accounts for most of the problems observed in stepfamilies.

Different family forms experience different stress points over time as well. The period of greatest stress for two-parent families is generally the first few years after the birth of a child—sometimes because the husband resents his wife's transfer of time, energy, and services to the infant; sometimes because the wife resents the father's lack of such transfer. Interestingly, considerable anecdotal evidence indicates that unwed mothers with flexible jobs and financial security experience less stress during the early months, because the mother does not have to balance two relationships and two sets of needs.

The greatest period of stress for single-parent families occurs in the early teen years, when youngsters begin to demand more freedom from parental control. It's easier to wear a parent down when she or he has no ally to help resist a child's insistence that "everybody else's parents" say it's okay. Thus single parents are apt to relinquish parental decision-making prerogatives too early, a behavior that encourages negative forms of deviance in children. However, this problem can be almost entirely eliminated when another adult joins the household on a stable basis, whether that adult is a relative, a lover, or a friend. . . .

THE NEED FOR ADJUSTMENT

Children today are a precious and threatened resource. They make up only 26% of the population, and they are the poorest of any age group in the nation. Yet it is these children—not just our own children, but all children—who will grow up to appreciate the work we leave behind, to provide for the elderly (us!), to contribute to the Social Security fund on which we all depend. Either that or they will not do any of these things. It is up to all of us, not just to parents, to decide which it will be, because we are all affected by the way these children turn out.

We cannot return to "traditional" family forms and expectations that were at least partly mythical in the first place.

To help our children move successfully into the 21st century we need to stop organizing our institutions and values around the notion that every family can—or should—have one adult totally available at work and another totally available at home. We have to adjust our economic programs, schools, work policies, expectations of family life, and moral reasoning to the realities of family diversity and the challenges of global transformation. The new family-values crusade, no matter how sincere the motives of its participants, points us backward rather than forward.

| "Adult society keeps many young people in emotional and mental turmoil by sending them mixed signals about important moral, ethical and legal issues."

INCONSISTENT MESSAGES ABOUT MORALITY PUT TEENS AT RISK

Edward Grimsley

In the following viewpoint, Edward Grimsley contends that adults put teens at risk by subjecting them to mixed messages about moral issues such as using illegal drugs and having sex. Grimsley asserts that adults are shirking their duty to be constructive role models for children, thereby causing confusion among teens about what is acceptable behavior. Grimsley is a nationally syndicated columnist.

As you read, consider the following questions:

1. How are adults hypocritical on the issue of illegal drugs, according to Grimsley?
2. In the author's opinion, what mixed signals do adults send about sex?
3. According to the author, how do the media promote society's hypocrisy about sexual values?

Reprinted from Edward Grimsley, "Mixed Signals to an Embattled Generation," The Washington Times, July 28, 1996, by permission of Edward Grimsley and Creators Syndicate.

Upstanding adult citizens everywhere rail against the young who commit crimes against society, but society is committing one of the most heinous crimes of all against the young.

This nation's grown men and women who are supposed to serve as constructive role models for the young are, instead, engaging in child abuse by subjecting them to acute moral, social and psychological pain and suffering.

One man who is concerned about what the adult society of America is doing to the young is Dr. George R. Holmes, a noted child psychiatrist. A recent *Washington Times* article quoted him as saying modern teen-agers and even pre-adolescents "are experiencing a wide variety of negative influences that no previous generation has had to confront." The results include "higher rates of delinquency, psychiatric illness and deaths among teenagers."

ADULTS SEND MIXED MESSAGES TO YOUTH

Contemporary news stories seemed to confirm Dr. Holmes' theory. They made it distressingly clear that adult society keeps many young people in emotional and mental turmoil by sending them mixed signals about important moral, ethical and legal issues.

One such issue is the use of illegal drugs. Over and over, adults warn children that they flirt with disaster by such acts as smoking joints and snorting cocaine. Drug users, say the adults, will disgrace themselves and their families, incur the wrath of the law and imperil their livelihoods.

Every day, the law does indeed punish many ordinary young people from ordinary neighborhoods for using illegal drugs. Many have gone to jail merely for possessing a single marijuana joint.

But the young can learn from news stories that some people who use illegal drugs and admit it get cushy jobs in the White House. One even became president of the United States. It's true that President Bill Clinton insists he never inhaled, but American anti-drug laws do not stipulate that a user must inhale to commit an illegal act. Mr. Clinton violated the law simply by holding a joint.

Also from news stories the young learn that some people who are charged with the most serious drug offenses go not to prison but back to their football teams to continue to earn bundles of money. Oh, these privileged individuals may have to vacuum a few hospital room floors and perform other community services over a period of time, but most young people who are behind bars on drug charges would much prefer that kind of "punishment" to time in prison.

CONFLICTING SIGNALS ABOUT SEX CONFUSE TEENS

Conflicting signals like these make it difficult for the young to know whether using drugs will bring them punishment, disgrace and ruin, or rewards, prestige and success.

Possibly even more confusing are the signals adult society sends about sex. It admonishes the young to abstain from sex outside marriage, and in some instances even threatens to put them in jail if they don't.

That's happening in Gem County, Idaho. To discourage unwed teen-agers from getting pregnant, County Prosecutor Douglas Varie has begun to charge those who do and their boyfriends with violating the state's law against fornication.

That Mr. Varie's objective is laudable is undebatable. But is he in fairness also enforcing the anti-fornication law against unmarried adults? Young people who read the news stories about his actions will find no indication he is raiding the motels and hotels of his area in search of trysting grown-ups.

THE LOSS OF MORAL STANDARDS

One reason why so many young people are having sex is the loss of objective moral standards. Their models are adults who abandon integrity about as quickly as they abandon their spouses. In one generation, we have passed from the free distribution of *Gideon Bibles* to the free distribution of condoms.

Cal Thomas, *Conservative Chronicle*, October 15, 1997.

But young readers could learn from another story that while Gem County's adult prosecutor is punishing teen-agers for fornication, the adults who run the Army are doing nothing to prevent it. At least 70 American soldiers in Bosnia have become pregnant since the peacekeeping mission began in December 1995, yet the Army has punished not a single woman or her boyfriend for engaging in illicit sex.

While it restricts the consumption of alcoholic beverages and cigarettes, the Army has no ban on sexual relations between unmarried couples—unless one is an officer and the other is an enlisted man or woman. Then the Army might punish them for violating its prohibition on fraternization between social unequals.

This suggests that teen-agers in Idaho who wish to engage in illicit sex should join the Army first.

THE HYPOCRISY OF ADULTS

In addition to these particular conflicting stories about sex, there are stories about famous adults who engage in sex with people to whom they are not married: princes, princesses, movie stars, television performers, politicians and other VIPs. Instead of jailing these violators of the laws against illicit sex, society seems to condone their conduct.

It is too bad the young cannot sue America's adult society for damages for sending such hypocritical signals about right and wrong. Hitting grown-ups in their wallet might induce them to be more honest in making and enforcing the rules of life.

"A heightened anger toward homosexuals, plain conservative values on the parts of parents, and a general malaise for homosexuals . . . either forces or drives these youths to the street."

GAY TEENS ARE AT RISK

Rosemarie Buchanan

Rosemarie Buchanan asserts in the following viewpoint that gay teens are at risk of becoming homeless because they are sometimes rejected or cast out by family members. Furthermore, the author maintains, gay teens are more likely to abuse drugs or alcohol in response to feelings of alienation. Buchanan is a writer based in Chicago.

As you read, consider the following questions:

1. What percentage of youths at the Outside In homeless shelter classify themselves as gay, according to Buchanan?
2. Why is it difficult to estimate how many homeless teens are gay, in Buchanan's view?
3. In the author's opinion, why do some gay teens seek the streets?

Excerpted from Rosemarie Buchanan, "Young, Homeless, and Gay," *Human Rights*, Winter 1995, ©1995 American Bar Association. Reprinted with permission.

The teenager had nowhere to go, except to join the growing numbers like him who have taken to living on the streets. He was lucky, however, and found Terry Person, program director for Community United Against Violence, a service agency for homeless youth in San Francisco. Speaking about the boy, Person says, "He's an unusual case because he came to San Francisco with parental permission. He came from Kansas and stayed with friends, then found himself on the street."

Person is talking about a gay teen whose parents kicked him out of his family because of his sexuality.

While statistics are scant, it is now believed that a disproportionate number of gay and lesbian teens can be found among the country's homeless population.

Some shelters, like Person's, are struggling to help, either by offering counseling or providing critical job training. Their programs can be seen as models for other agencies or shelters facing this issue.

Outcast by Their Families

These teens are homeless not by choice, but because they are no longer welcome within their families.

A case study performed on a social service agency for young people in Oregon illustrates what social workers see day to day in their dealings with young street people: Many of them are gay, are unsure of their sexuality or are confused about their identity.

Some say a heightened anger toward homosexuals, plain conservative values on the parts of parents, and a general malaise for homosexuals in our society either forces or drives these youths to the street.

How Many Homeless Youth Are Gay?

David Allen, a lawyer in Portland, Oregon, analyzed data collected by Outside In, a medical and counseling agency serving homeless young people. Allen is one of the shelter's former board members.

According to the agency's findings, about 20 percent of Outside In's clients classified themselves as gay, lesbian or bisexual as of 1993. During the following year, that number increased to 30 percent.

A nationwide sex survey published by the University of Chicago estimated that 3 percent of men surveyed designated themselves as homosexual and about 1.5 percent of female respondents said they were lesbian. In these terms, the number of homosexual youth at Outside In is at least 10 times the average.

In addition, the Outside In study found that 9 percent at the Portland shelter classify themselves as "unsure" of their sexual identity.

"And even that figure may be low," Allen contends. "Seventy-one percent of respondents characterize themselves as heterosexual, but there is undeniably a greater incentive to adopt the latter rather than the former label. An unknown number of 'straight' respondents are probably more accurately characterized as 'unsure' at best.". . .

AN EXPLOSIVE ISSUE FOR FAMILIES

At Community United Against Violence, Person believes that many gay and lesbian youths end up in shelters because of their identity problems.

"They come out to their parents and get kicked out, or are in the coming-out process and start exhibiting," she says. "They don't know why they feel uncomfortable, but it leads to family conflict."

Allen agrees. "Homosexuality is an explosive issue for many families, an issue which can be resolved in the short term by expulsion of the 'disruptive' child from the family circle. Young people with acute sexual-identity crisis are likely to abuse drugs or alcohol out of frustration and/or alienation; chronic substance abuse in turn precipitates family breakup."

To help gay and lesbian homeless teens, Community United Against Violence chiefly provides job search assistance, believing that these youths are in a transition time. While they are discovering their sexuality, what they really need is to move back into society through employment.

Another shelter, the Larkin Street Youth Center in San Francisco, deals with more dire problems, offering intensive counseling to deal with immediate problems of prostitution and drug abuse.

"I think the proportion of gay and lesbian youth is very high [out of] the ones we see here," says Leslie Laughlin, who works at Larkin. "A lot of it has to do with their coming out. Once they get to be about 13, they're thrown out. It's 'Hit the road; go to San Francisco.'"

Allen contends that teens who express uncertainty about their sexuality are both pushed and pulled toward the street.

"Sexual minority youth from small towns and cities or conservative regions frequently find adolescence a living hell," he believes. "They become the victims of a cycle of diminished expectations. They may not only be pushed from the home; they may be 'pulled' to the street as the road toward the realization of self."

"SURVIVAL SEX"

Laughlin adds that many homeless under the age of 15 engage in "survival sex" because they can't get a minimum wage job, which doesn't automatically classify them as gay or lesbian.

"They may be doing what it takes to get the money to live, and not be gay or lesbian, but just very practical and desperate," says Patricia Hanrahan, director of the American Bar Association's (ABA) Commission on Homelessness and Poverty.

"There are men who have sex with men because it's simply something they do," says Mark Agrast, senior legislative assistant for Congressman Jerry Studds. "That kind of thing is an empirical problem with kids who may be gay," adds Agrast, who is also a former chair of the Rights of Lesbians and Gay Men committee of the ABA's Section of Individual Rights & Responsibilities.

COMING OUT TO FAMILIES CAN BE DANGEROUS

[Gay, lesbian, and bisexual youth] get kicked out of homes, abused, and disowned; parents refuse to speak to their child or force them to seek "reparative" therapy. While coming out can indeed be liberating—and for some people is a necessity to maintain their sanity—for young people still emotionally and financially dependent on their parents, it can all too often be a dangerous thing.

Laura Lorenzen, In the Family, January 1998.

Because few studies have been done on the issue of gay homeless teens, quantitative information is hard to come by on the subject. The Hedric-Martin Institute, which is the largest social service agency for gay and lesbian youth, estimates that at least 40 to 50 percent of the homeless population in New York City is composed of gay or lesbian teens.

Andy Humm, policy coordinator for the New York–based institute, said statistically, this population is difficult to define. Many youth may cast themselves as heterosexual while performing homosexual acts.

Based on the center's experience, Humm suggested that about 26 percent of gay and lesbian youths leave home, and many of those end up on the streets. They are then frequently exposed to sexually transmitted diseases, from both sexual partners and drug abuse.

Why Do Some Gay Teens Seek the Streets?

At Outside In, roughly 67 percent of the clients admit to using alcohol and/or drugs, possibly as a result of feeling out of place in society and within their families. It's possible that teens seek the streets to support a drug habit.

But Allen believes the streets offer even a more substantial pull: validation of the kids' identity.

"The streets may be the first place a young gay or lesbian experiences validation," Allen notes. On the streets, gay males not only publicly identify as gay—a critical prerequisite to other developmental tasks of adolescence—but also get paid for it through prostitution. As harmful as that may be in the long run, in the short run they are receiving rewards and approvals, and joining a community," Allen adds.

All is not bleak for these teens, however. Person's organization helps move teens from the shelter to society through job training programs. Although a disproportionate number of homosexual or uncertain teens make their way to the streets, it doesn't mean they will stay there.

PERIODICAL BIBLIOGRAPHY

The following articles have been selected to supplement the diverse views presented in this chapter. Addresses are provided for periodicals not indexed in the *Readers' Guide to Periodical Literature*, the *Alternative Press Index*, the *Social Sciences Index*, or the *Index to Legal Periodicals and Books*.

Nell Bernstein	"Learning to Love," *Mother Jones*, January/February 1995.
Mona Charen	"How to Raise a Killer," *Conservative Chronicle*, June 18, 1997. Available from PO Box 37077, Boone, IA 50037-0077.
Alexander Cockburn	"The War on Kids," *Nation*, June 3, 1996.
Greg Donaldson	"Throwaway Youth," *New York Times*, July 3, 1994.
Bettyann H. Kevles and Daniel J. Kevles	"Scapegoat Biology," *Discover*, October 1997.
Mike Males	"Poverty, Rape, Adult/Teen Sex: Why 'Pregnancy Prevention' Programs Don't Work," *Phi Delta Kappan*, January 1994.
Bronwyn Mayden	"Child Sexual Abuse: Teen Pregnancy's Silent Partner," *Children's Voice*, Winter 1996. Available from Child Welfare League of America, 440 First St. NW, 3rd Fl., Washington, DC 20001-2085.
David Popenoe	"A World Without Fathers," *Wilson Quarterly*, Spring 1996.
Karen S. Schneider	"Mission Impossible," *People Weekly*, June 3, 1996.
Joseph P. Shapiro and Missy Daniel	"Teenage Wasteland?" *U.S. News & World Report*, October 23, 1995.
Arlene Skolnick and Stacey Rosencrantz	"The New Crusade for the Old Family," *American Prospect*, Summer 1994.
Norman Solmon	"'Teen People' and the Souls of Young Folks," *Liberal Opinion Week*, January 26, 1998. Available from PO Box 880, Vinton, IA 52349-0880.
Charlene Marmer Solomon	"Latchkey Kids," *Parents*, March 1994.
Ruby Takanishi and Jane Sims Podesta	"Years of Wonder—and Risk," *People Weekly*, November 13, 1995.
M. Witwer	"Early Sexual Activity, but Not Childhood Sexual Abuse, Increases the Odds of Teenage Pregnancy," *Family Planning Perspectives*, July 1, 1997. Available from the Alan Guttmacher Institute, 120 Wall St., New York, NY 10005.

CHAPTER 2

HOW CAN SOCIETY DEAL WITH TEENAGE CRIME AND VIOLENCE?

CHAPTER PREFACE

In March 1998, the U.S. Department of Education released a report showing that 47 percent of public schools reported at least one serious or nonviolent crime during the 1996–97 school year. Another 10 percent reported at least one serious violent crime. The problem of school violence persists, as indicated by a string of fatal shootings that took place during the 1997–98 school year. In all, over a dozen people were shot to death and more than forty people were wounded. Of the suspects in the shootings, almost all were teenagers, while one was an eleven-year-old.

The deadly attacks have prompted many people to wonder if and how schools can be made safer. Some observers assert that the answer is in limiting the access these teenagers and preteens have to guns. In an editorial in *USA Today* following the Arkansas tragedy, in which four students and a teacher were killed and ten others wounded, Jonathan Kellerman criticized a culture that teaches children how to hunt and use guns. "Handing a frightfully immature, troubled human being a firearm and encouraging him to stalk and kill animals is beyond absurd," he wrote. Laws that restrict juvenile access to guns have gained support in recent years. As of this writing, fifteen states hold adults criminally liable if they do not keep loaded guns inaccessible to children or if they do not use a gun lock. Similar federal legislation has been proposed in Congress.

Other people contend that access to guns is not at fault, asserting that poor parenting is the cause of these crimes. An editorial by Zach Myles in the University of Virginia's student newspaper concluded, "Blaming juvenile violence on lax gun control laws and television violence is a copout. Americans regularly express that sentiment, however, giving would-be parents an excuse for raising dishonorable children. In fact, the real blame should rest on those who hold responsibility to mold the child—his parents."

Whether the cause is inadequate parenting, too many guns, or other factors, incidents of teen violence have led to various proposed solutions to this problem. Ways to reduce teenage crime and violence, in the schools and elsewhere, are considered by the authors in the following chapter.

| "Detaining a rapist or murderer in a juvenile facility until the age of 18 or 21 isn't even a slap on the hand."

VIOLENT JUVENILE CRIMINALS SHOULD BE TREATED AS ADULTS

Linda J. Collier

Violent crimes by youths, such as the 1998 school shooting in Jonesboro, Arkansas, in which four students and one teacher were killed, point to a need to treat some juvenile criminals as adults, argues Linda J. Collier in the following viewpoint. She asserts that the juvenile justice system is outdated because it was designed to deal with the vandals and petty thieves of an earlier era, not today's juvenile murderers and rapists. Collier, a Pennsylvania lawyer who has worked in Philadelphia's juvenile court, maintains that the states should set a uniform minimum age for trying violent youths as adults.

As you read, consider the following questions:

1. How much has crime by juveniles increased since 1984, according to statistics cited by Collier?
2. According to the author, what is the operating principle of juvenile adjudications?
3. In Collier's view, what is one reason for the lack of consistency in waiver laws?

Reprinted from Linda J. Collier, "Doing Adult Time for an Adult Crime," *The Washington Post National Weekly Edition*, April 6, 1998, by permission of the author.

When prosecutor Brent Davis said he wasn't sure if he could charge 11-year-old Andrew Golden and 13-year-old Mitchell Johnson as adults after the slaughter on March 24, 1998, in Jonesboro, Arkansas, I cringed. But not for the reasons you might think. I knew he was formulating a judgment based on laws that have not had a major overhaul for more than 100 years. I knew his hands were tied by the long-standing creed that juvenile offenders, generally defined as those under the age of 18, are to be treated rather than punished. I knew he would have to do legal cartwheels to get the case out of the juvenile system. But most of all, I cringed because today's juvenile suspects—even those who are accused of committing the most violent crimes—are still regarded by the law as children first and criminals second.

JUVENILE CRIME HAS INCREASED

As astonishing as the Jonesboro events were, this is hardly the first time that children with access to guns and other weapons have brought tragedy to a school. Only weeks before the Jonesboro shootings, three girls in Paducah, Kentucky, were killed in their school lobby when a 14-year-old classmate allegedly opened fire on them. Authorities said he had several guns with him, and the alleged murder weapon was one of seven stolen from a neighbor's garage. And the day after the Jonesboro shootings, a 14-year-old in Daly City, California, was charged as a juvenile after he allegedly fired at his middle-school principal with a semiautomatic handgun.

It's not a new or unusual phenomenon for children to commit violent crimes at younger and younger ages, but it often takes a shocking incident to draw our attention to a trend already in progress. According to the U.S. Department of Justice, crimes committed by juveniles have increased by 60 percent since 1984. Where juvenile delinquency was once limited to truancy or vandalism, juveniles now are more likely to be the perpetrators of serious and deadly crimes such as arson, aggravated assault, rape and murder. And these violent offenders increasingly include those as young as the Jonesboro suspects. Since 1965, the number of 12-year-olds arrested for violent crimes has doubled and the number of 13- and 14-year-olds has tripled, according to government statistics.

Those statistics are a major reason why we need to revamp our antiquated juvenile justice system. Nearly every state, including Arkansas, has laws that send most youthful violent offenders to the juvenile courts, where they can only be found "delinquent" and confined in a juvenile facility (typically not past age 21). In recent years, many states have enacted changes in their juvenile crime laws, and some have lowered the age at which a juvenile can be tried as an adult for certain violent crimes. Virginia, for example, has reduced its minimum age to 14, and suspects accused of murder and aggravated malicious wounding are automatically waived to adult court. Illinois is now sending some 13-year-olds to adult court after a hearing in juvenile court. In Kansas, a 1996 law allows juveniles as young as 10 to be prosecuted as adults in some cases. These are steps in the right direction, but too many states still treat violent offenders under 16 as juveniles who belong in the juvenile system.

PERSONAL EXPERIENCES

My views are not those of a frustrated prosecutor. I have represented children as a court-appointed guardian ad litem, or temporary guardian, in the Philadelphia juvenile justice system. Loosely defined, a guardian ad litem is responsible for looking after the best interest of a neglected or rebellious child who has come into the juvenile courts. It is often a humbling experience as I try to help children whose lives have gone awry, sometimes because of circumstances beyond their control.

My experience has made me believe that the system is doing a poor job at treatment as well as punishment. One of my "girls," a chronic truant, was a foster child who longed to be adopted. She often talked of how she wanted a pink room, a frilly bunk bed and sisters with whom she could share her dreams. She languished in foster care from age 2 to 13 because her drug-ravaged mother would not relinquish her parental rights. Initially, the girl refused to tolerate the half-life that the state had maintained was in her best interest. But as it became clear that we would never persuade her mother to give up her rights, the girl became a frequent runaway. Eventually she ended up pregnant, wandering from place to place and committing adult crimes to survive. No longer a child, not quite a woman, she is the kind of teenage offender for whom the juvenile system has little or nothing to offer.

A brief history: Proceedings in juvenile justice began in 1890 in Chicago, where the original mandate was to save wayward children and protect them from the ravages of society. The system called for children to be processed through an appendage of the family court. By design, juveniles were to be kept away from the court's criminal side, the district attorney and adult correctional institutions.

ATTITUDES TOWARD VIOLENT JUVENILES

By race, ethnicity, community, and whether respondent is a crime victim, United States, 1994[a]

Question: "In your view, should juveniles who commit violent crimes be treated the same as adults, or should they be given more lenient treatment in a juvenile court?"

	Treated the same as adults	Given more lenient treatment	Treated tougher[b]	Depends[b]	Don't know
National	68%	13%	[c]	16%	3%
Race, ethnicity					
White	69	12	[c]	16	3
Black	71	17	[c]	11	1
Hispanic	64	15	[c]	19	2
Community					
City	70	7	1	17	5
Suburb	68	15	[c]	16	1
Small town	66	17	[c]	16	1
Rural area	69	14	[c]	15	2
Victim of crime	71	8	1	15	5

[a] Percents may not add to 100 because of rounding.

[b] Response volunteered.

[c] Less than 0.5 percent.

Source: Bureau of Justice Statistics, *Sourcebook of Criminal Justice Statistics 1994.*

Typically, initial procedures are informal, non-threatening and not open to public scrutiny. A juvenile suspect is interviewed by an "intake" officer who determines the child's fate. The intake officer may issue a warning, lecture and release; he may detain the suspect; or, he may decide to file a petition, subjecting the child to juvenile "adjudication" proceedings. If the law allows, the intake officer may make a recommendation that the juvenile be transferred to adult criminal court.

AN OUTDATED SYSTEM

An adjudication is similar to a hearing, rather than a trial, although the juvenile may be represented by counsel and a juvenile prosecutor will represent the interests of the community. It is important to note that throughout the proceedings, no matter which side of the fence the parties are on, the operating principle is that everyone is working in the best interests of the child. Juvenile court judges do not issue findings of guilt, but decide whether a child is delinquent. If delinquency is found, the judge must decide the child's fate. Should the child be sent back to the family—assuming there is one? Declare him or her "in need of supervision," which brings in the intense help of social services? Remove the child from the family and place him or her in foster care? Confine the child to a state institution for juvenile offenders?

This system was developed with truants, vandals and petty thieves in mind. But this model is not appropriate for the violent juvenile offender of today. Detaining a rapist or murderer in a juvenile facility until the age of 18 or 21 isn't even a slap on the hand. If a juvenile is accused of murdering, raping or assaulting someone with a deadly weapon, the suspect should automatically be sent to adult criminal court. What's to ponder?

With violent crime becoming more prevalent among the junior set, it's a mystery why there hasn't been a major overhaul of juvenile justice laws long before now. Will the Jonesboro shootings be the incident that makes us take a hard look at the current system? When it became evident that the early release of Jesse Timmendequas—whose murder of 7-year-old Megan Kanka in New Jersey sparked national outrage—had caused unwarranted tragedy, legislative action was swift. Now New Jersey has Megan's Law, which requires the advance notification of a sexual predator's release into a neighborhood. Other states have followed suit.

It is unequivocally clear that the same type of mandate is needed to establish a uniform minimum age for trying juveniles as adults. As it stands now, there is no consistency in state laws governing waivers to adult court. One reason for this lack of uniformity is the absence of direction from the federal government or Congress. The Bureau of Justice Statistics reports that adjacent states such as New York and Pennsylvania respond differently to 16-year-old criminals, with New York tending to treat offenders of that age as adults and Pennsylvania handling them in the juvenile justice system.

THE LONG-TERM SOLUTION

Federal prosecution of juveniles is not totally unheard of, but it is uncommon. The Bureau of Justice Statistics estimates that during 1994, at least 65 juveniles were referred to the attorney general for transfer to adult status. In such cases, the U.S. attorney's office must certify a substantial federal interest in the case and show that one of the following is true: The state does not have jurisdiction; the state refuses to assume jurisdiction or the state does not have adequate services for juvenile offenders; the offense is a violent felony, drug trafficking or firearm offense as defined by the U.S. Code.

Exacting hurdles, but not insurmountable. In the Jonesboro case, prosecutor Davis has been exploring ways to enlist the federal court's jurisdiction. Whatever happens, federal prosecutions of young offenders are clearly not the long-term answer. The states must act. As far as I can see, the next step is clear: Children who knowingly engage in adult conduct and adult crimes should automatically be subject to adult rules and adult prison time.

| "We seem almost always to respond to teenagers with an authoritarianism in the name of clarity and standards."

JUVENILE CRIMINALS SHOULD NOT BE TREATED AS ADULTS

William Ayers

Trying youths as adults is a faulty approach to juvenile crime, contends William Ayers in the following viewpoint. Ayers argues that juveniles placed in adult prisons are more likely to be sexually assaulted, to commit suicide, and to return to crime after they are released. He asserts that a more appropriate approach to juvenile crime is to provide young people with better educational and employment opportunities. Ayers is a professor of education and a university scholar at the University of Illinois at Chicago. He is also the author of *A Kind and Just Parent: The Children of Juvenile Court.*

As you read, consider the following questions:

1. According to Ayers, what is the "schizophrenic view of children"?
2. Why has youth murder increased, in the author's opinion?
3. Why do "zero tolerance" policies cause neglect, according to Ayers?

Reprinted from William Ayers, "The Criminalization of Youth," *Rethinking Schools*, Winter 1997/1998, by permission of the author.

Our culture embraces a schizophrenic view of children: We romance childhood as a time of innocence and beauty, and we simultaneously construct an image of original sin and elemental evil lurking in those little bodies. Children are angels and devils—pure and wicked, clean and corrupt, lambs and devils. When children are left to themselves, however, our culture assumes the demon child has the upper hand. The Exorcist and Village of the Damned are popular manifestations, The Lord of the Flies its most enduring expression. Young people today find themselves in a peculiarly precarious landscape—reified as consumers, demonized as a threat, they inhabit a cultural fault-line that is bumpy for all and fatal for some.

A HOPELESS VIEW OF YOUTH

While these contradictions have been a part of our culture for over a century (before the Victorian age, children were miniature adults and the goal was to grow up as quickly as possible), a more hopeless view of children and adolescence is now taking hold. What is more, this view is backed by legislative proposals such as trying more children and teens as adults, building more youth prisons, and codifying the "three strikes and you're out" approach even for children.

An ominous new language of bestiality and disease has gained popularity to describe particular young people as unlike any we have ever known. "Violent juvenile crime is a national epidemic," declares Rep. Bill McCollum (R-FL), and "today's superpredators are feral, presocial beings with no sense of right and wrong." Over time the rhetoric takes hold. As Michael Doring wrote in the spring of 1997 in The Chicago Tribune, "The political consensus developing in favor of fundamental national changes in juvenile justice comes down to this: A child stops being a child when he picks up a gun."

Rep. McCollum declares that "the really bad news" is that "America will experience a 31% increase in teenagers" in coming years. The kids themselves are the trouble. Among them, he says, are "the highly crime-prone males—teen-agers from fatherless homes growing up in neighborhoods where gangs, drugs and violence are commonplace and consequences for misbehavior are almost nonexistent." McCollum insists that the threat is palpable: "A juvenile who commits cold-blooded murder can be walking in your neighborhood in less than a year."

Rep. McCollum is backing up his rhetoric with legislative clout. He has proposed the Juvenile Crime Control Act of 1997 (originally called the Superpredator Incapacitation Act) which calls for $1.5 billion in incentive grants to states to encourage automatic transfers to adult courts for juveniles charged with certain crimes, escalating predetermined punishment for repeat juvenile offenders, as well as sanctions for their parents, and the public release of previously sealed juvenile criminal records. With its aggregation of certain youth into a convenient and manageable mob and its one-size-fits-all simplicity, it passed the House 286-132 and moves, with the Clinton administration's support for key provisions, inexorably toward the Senate. Rep. McCollum's bill represents a decisive withdrawal from a century of difficult, uneven progress in relation to juvenile justice, undermining the fundamental thesis that a child in crisis, a child in trouble, is still a child. [As of March 1998, no action had been taken on the Senate floor.]

Rep. McCollum relies on an entirely inaccurate popular impression that youth crime is a runaway train, reckless, out of control, unpredictably dangerous, picking up speed as it careens down the track toward our town or neighborhood. We read about teenagers being "wild in the streets" and of a "ticking demographic time bomb," the 3-year-olds of today morphing overnight into tiny monsters in sneakers.

The truth is more complicated. The overwhelming majority of kids are not criminals—less than one-half of 1% of youth 10–17 are charged with violent crimes. In fact, youth crime is relatively flat over decades and juvenile arrests for violent offenses have declined dramatically since 1994. Youth murder is up, it's true, but why? Access to guns. What would have been a terrible incident twenty years ago—a brutal fight, a kid hit by another kid with a baseball bat—is now too often fatal. Today the immature, impulsive kid can get a gun.

THE TRUTH ABOUT ADOLESCENT CRIME

While each instance of youth-on-youth violence is alarming, the hidden, terrible truth is that most murder victims under 18 are killed by adults; 70% of the murderers of children in 1994 were adults, and it is six times more likely that a parent will kill his or her teenage child than the other way around.

Under Rep. McCollum's bill, we would return to the practices of the 19th century, erasing the distinctions between children and adults, thrusting youngsters into adult courts and prisons, ensuring that they are preyed upon sexually and physically, hardened and destroyed. Six in 10 juveniles tried as adults are non-violent offenders, and headline-grabbing youth crimes account for less than 1% of all juvenile delinquency. But once in adult prisons, youth are twice as likely to be beaten or to commit suicide and five times as likely to be sexually assaulted. Those who survive have higher recidivism rates than kids charged with similar offenses but kept under the supervision of juvenile courts. Ironically, McCollum-type proposals—tough-sounding but ineffective—contribute to rising crime rates.

Dan Wasserman ©1997 Boston Globe. Distributed by the Los Angeles Times Syndicate. Reprinted by permission.

Transferring children as young as 13 years old automatically to adult courts without a juvenile hearing is already creating a peculiarly American gulag for the poor in states that have vigorously pursued this approach. In Rep. McCollum's own Florida, one of the severest get-tough states, youth sentenced to adult courts return to criminal activity and commit consistently more serious crimes than their counterparts who remain under the jurisdiction of juvenile courts. Florida's approach—which denies judges the opportunity to examine the specific circumstances of each case, uncovering the particular problems and possibilities in each situation, and then opens confidential records just as disaffected young people are struggling to reintegrate into society—is an economic death sentence for many. It guarantees a growing population that is hurt, hopeless, and angry.

We seem almost always to respond to teenagers with an authoritarianism in the name of clarity and standards. For example, "zero tolerance" seems to be becoming a favorite phrase, promoted as clarifying what might have been perceived as murky, ambiguous. It's odd though: I don't have any murkiness at all on drug abuse, for example. I think cigarettes are toxic, alcohol poisonous—heavier drugs are even worse—and so I don't use them, and I strongly disapprove of their use. What does saying I have "zero tolerance" for them add? It sounds tougher, perhaps, but what would I do, for example, what action would I take if I saw someone abusing alcohol? Kill them? Jail them? Punch them out? Expel them? Sounding tough is quite a different thing from prescribing what that toughness entails. And since contexts and circumstances are always specific and often complex, wise prescriptions will likely be various.

Furthermore, saying I have "zero tolerance" for alcohol gives it an oddly privileged position. How much tolerance do I have for sexual abuse? For bigotry? Intolerance or disrespect? Meanness or thoughtlessness? Well, it's clear that these are complicated. "Zero tolerance" simplifies, closes the door to conversation. Move into more complicated issues and the need for conversation only intensifies. Young people, in particular, need steady grown-ups to talk to, to think with, to bounce back off of. Closing the door is a form of abandonment, of neglect.

SETTING LIMITS

We should refine our standard and ask, what if this were my child? The question cannot be about some abstract child, every child, the mob of children. That turns other people's children into things, objectifies them. To ask, is it good enough for my child?—not, is it a perfect arrangement for my child?—is to begin to set limits of acceptability. Personalizing our approach to juveniles does not mean that there are no serious consequences to action or behavior, but it does remind us that a child who breaks the law will return to society someday, and that among our central goals must be recovery. It reminds us that our efforts on behalf of our children and other people's children must include cleaning up their environment—removing adult-controlled toxic elements like guns and drugs—and a sustained struggle to provide productive work, decent schools, and community centers to support and challenge them, to engage their hopes and dreams and capacities. We must fight for the obvious: a child in crisis, a child in trouble, is still a child.

"Injunctions represent a breakthrough
strategy in the effort to undermine
youth street gangs."

GANG INJUNCTIONS CAN PREVENT
TEENAGE VIOLENCE

Roger L. Conner

In the following viewpoint, Roger L. Conner argues that gang
injunctions, court orders that prohibit gang members from performing certain activities such as congregating in specific public
areas, help reduce violence. Such injunctions should be upheld
by the courts, Conner maintains, despite the protests of the
American Civil Liberties Union (ACLU), which claims that the
orders are unconstitutional. He asserts that injunctions are an effective form of intervention that make it harder for gangs to engage in criminal activity and recruit new members. Conner is
executive director of the Center for the Community Interest, a
nonpartisan organization that helps citizens regain control over
public spaces and defends public policies that balance community responsibility and individual liberties.

As you read, consider the following questions:

1. What approaches are needed in the antigang effort, according
   to Conner?
2. Why are some otherwise legal acts enjoined, according to the
   author?
3. According to the Supreme Court, as cited by the author, what
   is the only type of association that is constitutionally
   protected?

Reprinted from Roger L. Conner, "A Gangsta's Rights," The Responsive Community, Winter
1995/1996, by permission of The Responsive Community.

A hallmark of the U.S. Constitution is that fundamental rights extend even to those people whom many would consider the least deserving—perhaps especially to such people. But in California, a court has interpreted this principle so broadly as to prevent communities from reigning in those who make their neighborhoods unlivable.

THE BATTLE OVER GANG INJUNCTIONS

The case in question grew out of an innovative tactic, pioneered by Los Angeles District Attorney Gil Garcetti and pro bono lawyers from the law firm of Latham & Watkins. The strategy is to obtain injunctions that prohibit gang members from engaging in certain activities. The efforts have been so effective that they have been duplicated throughout the state. In San Jose, for example, residents of the Rocksprings neighborhood were constantly in fear of two violent street gangs. Gang members staked out their turf with graffiti, loud music, and urine. Gunshots and drug deals were commonplace, and car windows were frequently smashed. So in 1993, the city attorney brought a civil action to have six key gang members declared public nuisances. California District Court Judge Robert Foley sided with the district attorney and issued an injunction prohibiting the gang leaders from activities that harassed and intimidated the entire community. According to San Jose City Attorney Joan Gallo, arrests in the targeted area dropped by 72 percent in two years, and many gang-related problems were largely eliminated. As one enjoined gang member remarked, "There's nothing for me to do anymore."

But then the American Civil Liberties Union (ACLU) brought suit—and won. In *The State of California v. Carlos Acuna, et al.*, the California Court of Appeals vacated the injunction and adopted the ACLU's contention that gang members have a right to the tools and tricks of their trade. The three-judge panel held that activities such as carrying crowbars and chains, possessing "slim jims" and spray paint, engaging motorists in traffic, and climbing trees to maintain lookouts, are all constitutionally protected. The court also maintained that gang members have a right to gather together for such purposes in public places. Apparently uncompelling was the trial court's determination that, as a group, gang members used these actions as a direct means of intimidation, assault, theft, vandalism, drug dealing, and other crimes.

The California Supreme Court has agreed to review the ruling and many California jurisdictions are deeply worried about the outcome. [On January 30, 1997, the court upheld the injunction in a 4-3 ruling.] Injunctions represent a breakthrough strategy in the effort to undermine youth street gangs. The *Los Angeles Times* reported that a civil order in Burbank dissolved a gang-run drug ring entirely. In Panorama City, gang activity was reduced by 70 percent. The Los Angeles County Sheriff noted that in the six months after an injunction took effect, Norwalk police, who had been summoned to a gang-plagued neighborhood an average of eight times a day, were called only *once a month* on gang-related incidents.

The injunctions, by preventing gangsters from flaunting their gang affiliation and congregating in specified public areas, directly attack the sense of collective impunity that drives gang activity. They thus give the community the leverage it needs to face down threats of violence and rebuild a culture of respect. And while supporters admit that civil orders must be only one part of a wider anti-gang effort—an effort that would include education, youth diversion, community policing, and traditional law enforcement—they are powerful preventive tools.

THE ACLU'S REASONING

The ACLU's lawyers insist that it is impermissible for a court to issue a civil order to prohibit gang members from any act that is not expressly illegal. "The issuance of injunctions makes some activities criminal that would not otherwise be criminal," said Amitai Schwartz, the ACLU lawyer challenging the San Jose order. "It's a shortcut for law enforcement [and] an end run around constitutional protections." The Court of Appeals agreed: an individual may be forbidden from illegal acts like dealing drugs, but not from anything that is ordinarily legal. In other words, gang members cannot be prohibited from brandishing heavy chains or crowbars, even when such weapons constitute an implicit threat to anyone who fails to show proper compliance.

The city attorney had countered that any activity that constitutes a public nuisance is a crime. The California Penal Code defines a public nuisance as "anything which is injurious to health, or is indecent, or is offensive to the senses, or an obstruction to the free use of property, so as to interfere with the comfortable enjoyment of life or property by an entire community, or by any considerable number of persons." The appellate court opinion in *Acuna* cited this definition but, adopting the ACLU's reasoning, narrowed the meaning of the word "anything" in the statute to apply only to "criminal activity" as defined by other statutes. Thus, the court held, any activity that could "have legitimate non-criminal purposes . . . may not be judicially enjoined."

It is this holding that most perplexes critics of the ruling. For, in fact, the law is filled with many examples of otherwise lawful acts that are enjoined because, in context, they amount to unreasonable behavior. Abusive spouses are ordered to stay a certain distance from their victims, though walking is itself hardly criminal. Playing music, yelling, and applauding are enjoined when an establishment's noise level consistently disturbs its neighbors, though at a stadium rock concert these activities are legal and encouraged. Other examples abound.

NOT ALL ASSOCIATIONS ARE EQUAL

The ACLU has also used the *Acuna* case to get the courts to broaden the range of association protected by the First Amendment. It is the position of the ACLU that the First Amendment's protection of expression includes all personal association. The San Jose injunction infringes on this right, lawyers argue, by prohibiting gang members from congregating on the four square blocks they call their turf—where, incidentally, not one of them lives. Adopting this view, the California appeals panel stated that "non-criminal associational conduct cannot be enjoined solely on the basis of [gang] membership."

THE COURT'S EXPLANATION

No appeal to freedoms of speech or association warrants authorities turning a blind eye toward the depredations of rampaging youths such as those in Rocksprings. The Supreme Court of California's words are striking: "Often the public interest in tranquillity, security and protection is invoked only to be blithely dismissed, subordinated to the paramount right of the individual. In this case, however, the true nature of the tradeoff becomes painfully obvious. Liberty unrestrained is an invitation to anarchy. Freedom and responsibility are joined at the hip. 'Wise accommodation between liberty and order always has been and ever will be indispensable for a democratic society.'"

Catherine Coles and George Kelling, *Insight*, June 2, 1997.

The U.S. Supreme Court has repeatedly rejected such an interpretation, however, maintaining that the Constitution does not create a right to associate for social purposes. Only association that is directly linked to expressive purposes, such as petitioning the government, is constitutionally protected. In *The City of Dallas v. Stanglin,* for instance, the high court ruled against a dance hall owner who claimed that restricting 14- to 18-year-olds from his club late at night violated their associational rights. Furthermore, in *Bailey v. City of National City*, the court upheld a police department policy that caused an officer to be fired for his "continuous associations" with a known felon. The ruling was based on the grounds that, absent some significant expressive component, laws regulating social relationships are not subject to First Amendment scrutiny. In other words, for constitutional purposes, gang membership is not the equivalent of joining the National Association for the Advancement of Colored People (NAACP) or the Republican Party.

This is not to deny the fact that these injunctions can walk fine constitutional lines at times. Some judges have prohibited wearing gang insignia and displaying gang signs. While the First Amendment extends to all, "fighting words" have never been protected. The California high court should thus permit civil orders in this area when a trial court judge finds that, as a matter of fact, colors and signs are used to intimidate others in the community.

In an era of mandatory minimum sentences and high incarceration rates, civil injunctions provide a viable alternative to criminal convictions—a way for the community to intervene in wayward kids' lives before the trouble gets too serious. Moreover, by making it difficult for gangs to operate, injunctions make it harder for gangs to recruit impressionable youngsters in the first place. The ruling in *Acuna* has left Rocksprings residents afraid that they will be forced once again to keep their children indoors at all times, to return home themselves before dark, and to face violent retaliation for cooperating with police. It is the right of these citizens to the peaceful enjoyment of their homes and streets that deserves protection, and not some ersatz right to operate an intimidating gang.

> "Rather than having oppressive
> ordinances, it would be more
> productive to discuss the factors that
> result in young people joining gangs."

GANG-LOITERING ORDINANCES ARE AN OBJECTIONABLE APPROACH TO REDUCING TEENAGE VIOLENCE

George Brooks

Ordinances that prohibit young people from gathering in public places are reprehensible, argues George Brooks in the following viewpoint. Brooks maintains that these laws are unjust and discriminatory because they target minorities and allow them to be arrested without any evidence of wrongdoing. Instead of condemning gang members, he contends, society needs to understand why youths join gangs and how to intervene in ways that will reduce youth violence. Brooks is the director of advocacy at Kolbe House, the jail ministry of the Archdiocese of Chicago, and a chaplain at Chicago's Cook County Jail.

As you read, consider the following questions:

1. What moral problems are created by gang-loitering ordinances, in the author's view?
2. According to Brooks, what is the responsibility of Christians toward young people who lack family support?
3. How do the U.S. Catholic bishops criticize the criminal-justice system, according to the author?

Reprinted from George Brooks, "Let's Not Gang Up on Our Kids," *U.S. Catholic*, March 1997, by permission of *U.S. Catholic*, published by Claretian Publications, 205 W. Monroe St., Chicago, IL 60606.

L aws based on stereotyping and guilt by association are being passed in the name of crime prevention. Laws that seemed impossible after the McCarthy era now encourage discriminatory and arbitrary law enforcement. Many of these laws are being found unconstitutional. All these laws are morally reprehensible.

OFFENSIVE ORDINANCES

In 1992, a Chicago ordinance provided that "whenever a police officer observes a person whom he reasonably believes to be a criminal street-gang member loitering in any public place with one or more other persons, he shall order such persons to disperse from the area." Failure of the suspect to not promptly obey would authorize his or her arrest. When the Illinois Appellate Court declared the law unconstitutional in 1995, many who saw the ordinance as a valid way to curb gang activity protested loudly. The court's decision was based on the ordinance's failure to include some type of illegal conduct besides loitering. In 1989 an ordinance was upheld in Milwaukee that prohibits "loitering in a place, at a time, or in a manner not used for law-abiding individuals." And in Tacoma, Washington, in 1992, an ordinance was upheld that prohibits loitering "in a manner and under circumstances manifesting the purpose to engage in drug-related activities."

Having my own law firm for 25 years, I find these ordinances legally objectionable. Yet these laws offend and outrage me even more because of my experiences over the past six years as a chaplain at Cook County Jail in Chicago. There I see young people confined for committing no crime other than being in a group. Many are guilty only by association or guilty because they adorned gang colors or gang insignias. Often the gang-loitering ordinance permits young people to be arrested for not doing anything illegal.

There are significant moral problems raised by gang-loitering ordinances. It is troubling when anyone can be singled out because of who they are with or the colors or symbols they are wearing rather than for what they are doing. If the ordinance were applied equally in all communities, regardless of race, ethnicity or social status, the country on the whole would be outraged. Rather than having oppressive ordinances, it would be more productive to discuss the factors that result in young people joining gangs and those conditions that can prevent them from becoming lawbreakers.

As a chaplain, I visit 72 inmates in 12 cellblocks every week as they wait for trial anywhere from a year to three years. The majority of the detainees are gang members, and most are black or Latino. Almost all of them live in poor neighborhoods.

This experience has made me more aware that the criminal-justice system works differently for them. My white, middle-class background did not prepare me for the systemic abuses that are routine for certain members of our society. The abuses start at the time of arrest, continue through bail setting, include plea bargaining, and end up in the sentencing. I hear story after story of young blacks and Latinos being stopped by the police, hassled, verbally abused, and searched.

They are stopped because of their race or ethnicity—not because of doing anything illegal. The presumption of innocence is virtually nonexistent. The poor are unable to post bond, so they remain incarcerated until their overworked public defender can get to their case. This only increases their antagonism for the police and reinforces the belief that it is "us" against the system. The arrest of innocent people can lead to their erroneous convictions. Since 1996, six minorities in Illinois alone have been released from death row in two separate cases because of evidence that absolved them from committing any crime.

Frequently I hear, "Well, if they're not doing anything wrong, why should they care if they get stopped and searched?" That's a nice sound bite, but I don't think many middle-class parents would tolerate their kids being stopped, insulted, and searched on a regular basis.

Recently three Latino young men came out to my home in the suburbs to pick up a couch and some clothes. Their van broke down on the expressway. Rather than getting assistance from the police, the young men and all the contents of the van were searched. They had to walk a mile to call for help. While I was angry about what happened, they were not upset. They expected blatant discriminatory practices; they didn't look at the police as those who would help them but as those who would hassle them.

THE REASONS FOR GANG MEMBERSHIP

In February 1995, the Chicago Crime Commission issued a report saying there were 100,000 gang members in the city. These figures indicate that 10 percent of Chicagoans between the ages of 9 and 40 are gang members. Although I question the methodology for arriving at these figures, the real question is: Are we just going to condemn gang members and lock them up as soon as possible or do we want to do something about the conditions that foster gang membership?

We must understand that young people join gangs for the family they don't have. They join for acceptance and security. They join because they don't have an education or job skills—gangs are how they can survive. Society can urge abrogating gang members' constitutional rights and demand they need family values, but isn't our Christian responsibility to help these kids? Our responsibility when good parents and a good family do not exist is to provide early and continuing intervention in young people's lives.

A Superficial Solution

Injunctions ignore the reality that gang activity is widespread as a result of critical, broad problems that permeate our society. Without addressing deficits in education, job opportunity, recreational resources and—most important—the breakdown of the family, superficial remedies like injunctions will be as effective as treating a heart attack with rubbing alcohol.

Allan Parachini, *Los Angeles Times*, February 23, 1997.

In 1996 Chicago went through a tragic trial of a juvenile. An 11-year-old male, with 28 prior arrests, was suspected of killing an innocent, talented 14-year-old girl. His gang then ordered his murder, which was carried out by 14- and 16-year-olds. Having been sexually abused as a youth and born to a teenage mother and a father who is now in prison, the 11-year-old was a felon at age 9. Early and continuing intervention may have made a difference.

Improving the Conditions

We need to be serious about youth crime. But we can't be serious when each kid does not have a decent and competitive education, a decent place to live, and decent health care. Each Christian has to be involved in changing detrimental conditions. Basic education, job training, conflict resolution, child-care skills, emotional support, substance abuse counseling, and meaningful jobs are all necessary. We can't ignore and lock up a child when those things do not exist.

Why not just immediately lock up the 100,000 gang members? Maybe because from a practical standpoint there aren't enough jail facilities. Or could it be that confining our youth is a violent solution?

In a 1995 letter "Confronting the Culture of Violence," the U.S. Catholic bishops wrote: "We are tragically turning to violence in search of the quick and easy answers to complex human problems. . . . How do we teach the young to curb their violence when we embrace it as the solution to social problems?" The bishops added that our criminal-justice system "does not offer security to society, just penalties and rehabilitation to offenders, or respect and restitution to victims." And they are right.

I first met Keith when he was 20 years old, a ten-year gang member. He dropped out of school when he was in fifth grade. He was arrested on a regular basis, frequently for just hanging out. He saw the police and courts as the enemy. He was usually released within a day or so with nothing being done to change his behavior or improve his life. But in jail, he responded to the influence of chaplains and quit the gang.

In court, Keith was found not guilty by a jury, not on any technicality, but because he hadn't committed any crime. (Keith and two other former gang members were arrested without any evidence of their involvement in a crime.) Today Keith has a job as a mentor for a social service agency and is going to school.

Keith is an example of why we need to build fewer prisons and rebuild more lives. We need to confine fewer young people and do more freeing of spirits and souls. We need to commit fewer people to institutions and commit to all people. It will only be when each member of our faith community takes responsibility to live the gospel that our society will refocus its priorities for the dignity and respect of each person.

| "When boot camps are used as an alternative to confinement, savings can be achieved."

JUVENILE BOOT CAMPS CAN BE EFFECTIVE IN ADDRESSING TEENAGE CRIME

Eric Peterson

In the following viewpoint, Eric Peterson contends that boot camps for juvenile criminals, which provide military-style discipline and physical training, can have positive results. He asserts that participants' academic skills improve and that many of these youths find jobs after leaving the camp. In addition, he claims, boot camps are less costly than traditional confinement. While Peterson concedes that these programs are not as successful as more traditional programs at reducing recidivism, he argues that boot camps can achieve their goals if they follow certain guidelines. Peterson is a program manager in the Office of Juvenile Justice and Delinquency Prevention's (OJJDP) Research and Program Development Division.

As you read, consider the following questions:

1. According to Peterson, what was the program completion rate in Cleveland?
2. In the author's view, what population should be targeted for boot camp?
3. What services should aftercare programs provide, according to Peterson?

Reprinted from Eric Peterson, "Juvenile Boot Camps: Lessons Learned," at www.ncjrs.org/txtfiles/fs-9636.txt, cited December 21, 1997.

In response to a significant increase in juvenile arrests and repeat offenses over the past decade, several States and many localities have established juvenile boot camps. The first juvenile boot camp programs, modeled after boot camps for adult offenders, emphasized military-style discipline and physical conditioning. The Office of Juvenile Justice and Delinquency Prevention (OJJDP) has supported the development of three juvenile boot camp demonstration sites. This viewpoint describes those demonstration projects, their evaluations, and lessons learned that will benefit future boot camp programs.

HIGHLY STRUCTURED PROGRAMS

In 1992 OJJDP funded three juvenile boot camps designed to address the special needs and circumstances of adolescent offenders. The programs were conducted in Cleveland, Ohio; Denver, Colorado; and Mobile, Alabama.

Focusing on a target population of adjudicated, nonviolent offenders under the age of 18, the boot camp programs were designed as highly structured, 3-month residential programs followed by 6 to 9 months of community-based aftercare. During the aftercare period, youth were to pursue academic and vocational training or employment while under intensive, but progressively diminishing, supervision.

OJJDP undertook impact evaluations for all three sites that compared the recidivism rates for juveniles who participated in the pilot programs with those of control groups. The evaluations also compared the cost-effectiveness of juvenile boot camps with other dispositional alternatives. Reports of the three impact evaluations are available. The evaluations of the Mobile and Cleveland programs are interim reports that present data from the earliest cohorts. As neither program had stabilized when the data were collected, OJJDP is considering expanding the evaluation to include the remaining cohorts. The Denver program is no longer active.

SUCCESS AND FAILURE

Most juvenile boot camp participants completed the residential program and graduated to aftercare. Program completion rates were 96 percent in Cleveland, 87 percent in Mobile, and 76 percent in Denver.

At the two sites where educational gains were measured, substantial improvements in academic skills were noted. In Mobile approximately three-quarters of the participants improved their performance in reading, spelling, language, and math by one grade level or more. In Cleveland the average juvenile boot camp participant improved reading, spelling, and math skills by approximately one grade level.

In addition, where employment records were available, a significant number of participants found jobs while in aftercare.

The pilot programs, however, did not demonstrate a reduction in recidivism. In Denver and Mobile, no statistically significant difference could be found between the recidivism rates of juvenile boot camp participants and those of the control groups (youth confined in State or county institutions, or released on probation). In Cleveland pilot program participants evidenced a higher recidivism rate than juvenile offenders confined in traditional juvenile correctional facilities. It should be noted that none of the sites fully implemented OJJDP's model juvenile boot camp guidelines, and that some critical aftercare support services were not provided.

LESSONS LEARNED

Several significant lessons have emerged from the pilot programs:

The appropriate population should be targeted. Boot camps should be designed as an intermediate intervention. At one site, youth who had been previously confined were significantly more likely to recidivate, while youth with the least serious offenses were also more likely to recidivate.

Facility location is important. Cost issues and community resistance were major obstacles to securing residential and aftercare facilities. To increase attendance and reduce problems, aftercare facilities should be located in gang-neutral areas accessible by public transportation.

Staff selection and training needs are critical. To reduce staff turnover, fill gaps in critical services, and ensure consistent programming, the screening, selection, and training of juvenile boot camp and aftercare staff must be sensitive to the programmatic and operational features of a juvenile boot camp. This is particularly important with regard to youth development issues.

THE IMPORTANCE OF AFTERCARE

Moreover, continuous treatment between the residential and aftercare phases should be integrated philosophically and programmatically, particularly through staffing.

Aftercare programs are challenging to implement. Successful aftercare programs require attention at the outset to develop a comprehensive model with the flexibility to respond to local needs and concerns. Aftercare programs are unlikely to succeed if their participants fail to receive the full range of services prescribed for them. Aftercare programs must be broad-based and flexible enough to meet the particular educational, employment, counseling, and support needs of each participant. The aftercare component should form dynamic linkages with other community services, especially youth service agencies, schools, and employers.

RESULTS FROM A FLORIDA BOOT CAMP

Some statistics from a Department of Juvenile Justice study of the first five platoons in 1994 and 1995 to go through the Leon County, Florida, Boot Camp:

- Typical age of a boot camp graduate: 16
- Average number of court cases before admission to camp: 11.3
- 46 percent of graduates were committed for felony property offenses; 30 percent for felonies against persons; 10 percent for drug felony crimes.
- As a group, boot camp graduates increased approximately one grade level in reading; one grade and three months in both math and language.
- 43 percent of graduates were employed after release from boot camp, most in fast-food chains and retail and grocery stores.
- 71 percent of the graduates were re-arrested within one year of graduation, a slightly lower rate than a comparable group of non-camp juvenile offenders, whose rate was 75 percent.

Chris Poynter, *Tallahassee (Fla.) Democrat*, February 23, 1997.

Coordination among agencies must be maintained. All three sites experienced difficulties in maintaining coordination among the participating agencies. Considerable attention should be paid to building and maintaining a consensus among participating organizations concerning the program's philosophy and procedures.

EVALUATING THE RESULTS

Effective evaluation begins with planning. To assess the program's successes and failures, quantifiable data should be collected about participation in treatment by juveniles in the boot camp and in the control group. Measures of program success should include a broad spectrum of outcomes. Recidivism measures should capture all subsequent delinquent activity, not simply the first new adjudication, and data on new offenses should include information on the origin and circumstances of the complaint to determine whether there is a monitoring effect, in which the intensity of the supervision causes an increase in recorded offending.

When boot camps are used as an alternative to confinement, savings can be achieved. Communities often implement juvenile boot camps, in part, to reduce costs. The experience of the pilot sites indicates that when boot camps are used as an alternative to traditional confinement, costs can be reduced considerably because of the significantly shorter residential stay. However, if boot camps are used as an alternative to probation, savings will not be realized.

Juvenile boot camps embrace a variety of objectives: reducing recidivism, improving academic performance, cutting the cost of treating juvenile offenders, and inculcating the values of self-discipline and hard work. In attempting to reach these objectives, OJJDP is collaborating with the Office of Justice Programs (OJP) to enhance program models, policies, and practices of juvenile boot camps. As a result, many of the lessons learned from OJJDP's three demonstration sites have been incorporated in the OJP Boot Camp Corrections Program.

> "Juvenile boot camps will neither reduce crime nor save on prison costs."

JUVENILE BOOT CAMPS DO NOT REDUCE TEENAGE CRIME

Margaret Beyer

In the following viewpoint, Margaret Beyer argues that military-style boot camps for young offenders will not reduce juvenile crime. These camps are ineffective because they fail to provide nurturing or promote independence, Beyer contends. In addition, she asserts, boot camps ignore teenagers' desire for fairness and their resistance to imposed structure. Beyer claims that approaches to juvenile crime that focus on empowering and encouraging youths are preferable to boot camps. Beyer is a psychologist based in Washington, D.C., who works with juvenile delinquents and their families.

As you read, consider the following questions:

1. What are Paul DeMuro's criticisms of boot camps, as cited by Beyer?
2. According to the author, what is the recidivism rate of the boot camps in Florida and Ohio?
3. Why is young people's rejection of unfair and punitive adults a strength, in Beyer's view?

A lthough juvenile crime is not on the rise, the public, misinformed by politicians and the press, insists on increasingly cruel methods to punish young offenders.

There are more adolescents in the population so there are more juvenile arrests, but this does not justify giving up on rehabilitative approaches. Overall juvenile crime has been decreasing since 1992. Based on 1992 data, the Department of Justice (DOJ) acknowledged that juveniles are not responsible for most of the increase in violent crime. "If juvenile violence had not increased between 1988 and 1992, the U.S. violent crime rate would have increased 16 percent instead of 23 percent." In fact, the arrest rate for juveniles actually dropped slightly between 1991 and 1993: 16,036 per 100,000 were arrested in 1989, 16,893 per 100,000 were arrested in 1991, and 16,681 per 100,000 were arrested in 1993. Juvenile arrest rates for property offenses decreased while juvenile arrest rates for violent offenses increased between 1989 and 1993.

BOOT CAMPS DO NOT SAVE MONEY

Since 1980, younger and younger teenagers have been treated as adult criminals. Boot camps for juveniles are the latest in this dangerous trend and will be as ineffective as wholesale incarceration of youth in adult facilities. Yet the message has not gotten out to state legislatures and corrections departments that juvenile boot camps will neither reduce crime nor save on prison costs.

There have been surprisingly few voices against juvenile boot camps. Paul DeMuro, an independent consultant in Montclair, New Jersey, wrote the 1995 unpublished report on juvenile boot camps, "Where Do We Go from Here?" for the Annie E. Casey Foundation. DeMuro has drawn attention to deaths in boot camps, the use of military discipline to disguise staff mistreatment particularly of minority youth, and the absence of followup supports when youth return to their communities. He has predicted an increase in adult court referrals as youth who fail to complete boot camps or are rearrested after their release are no longer viewed as eligible for juvenile court. Dale Parent, a senior analyst at ABT Associates in Massachusetts, demonstrates through statistical analysis that juvenile boot camps cannot save money unless they have hundreds of beds and the stay is limited to three months—conditions all agree would make the programs pointless. His report, "Planning a Boot Camp," was written for the Department of Justice, Office of Justice Programs Boot Camp Technical Assistance Workshop, held April 1, 1995. Furthermore, Parent emphasizes that juvenile boot camps are widening the net by including youth who previously would not have been locked up—boot camps could only reduce correctional costs if participants are selected from the population already qualified for incarceration. David Altschuler, a professor and researcher at Johns Hopkins Institute for Policy Studies, is directing a long-term study of aftercare for juveniles leaving secure facilities. The study is funded by the DOJ's Office of Juvenile Justice and Delinquency Prevention (OJJDP). Altschuler has argued that incarceration is only as effective as the reintegration services supporting youths to avoid their former criminal lifestyle when they return home. He points out that juvenile boot camps are limited to "shock incarceration" and keep costs down by leaving aftercare to overloaded probation and parole officers. Without any documentation that boot camps decrease delinquency—and, in fact, reports that two early juvenile boot camps (in Florida and Ohio) had recidivism rates of 70 percent—millions of federal and state dollars are going into juvenile boot camp construction and operation.

THE REASONS BOOT CAMPS FAIL

Since the observations of prominent juvenile justice experts and the absence of positive outcome studies have not deterred incarceration-minded politicians, perhaps we should consider educating the public about the dangers of juvenile boot camps through their experiences as parents. Parents search for a wise balance of love and limits to meet their teenagers' needs. The adult criminal system in general, and boot camps in particular, fail the basic test of balancing nurturing and opportunities for independence. Everyone who has been the parent of a teenager knows that boot camps cannot be effective because they violate the basic principles of adolescent development:

• *Teenagers are fairness fanatics:* Operating successful group programs for this age group is difficult because most adolescents are moralistic and intolerant of anything that seems unfair. They especially see group punishment as unfair.

• *Teenagers reject imposed structure:* Although they benefit from limits, adolescents object to being forced to adhere to structure in which they did not have a voice. "Authority problems" in schools and correctional programs can be, at least in part, attributed to insistence on controlling youth who are accustomed to running their own lives. Many youth who have been physically or sexually abused or exposed to substance abuse or domestic violence in their families react especially negatively to imposed outside controls.

• *Teenagers respond to encouragement:* Although youth may alter their behavior momentarily to avoid adverse consequences, attitudes and behaviors seldom change as a result of punishment.

BOOT CAMPS ARE NOT CONSIDERED EFFECTIVE

In 1995, the National League of Cities (NLC) published its annual survey of municipal officials. "Assuring public safety" was among the three highest priorities of the 383 elected municipal officials (drawn from a random sample in cities with populations of 10,000 or more) who responded to the survey. . . .

The most preferred policy—"strengthening and supporting family stability, selected by 64 percent—reflects a growing sentiment that public safety needs to be considered in a much broader context than traditional anti-crime solutions."

The policies and programs believed by municipal officials in the NLC survey as most likely to reduce crime are:

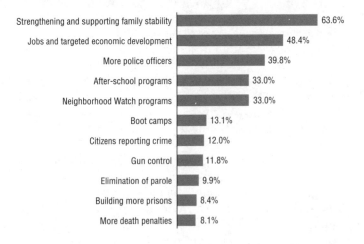

Strengthening and supporting family stability	63.6%
Jobs and targeted economic development	48.4%
More police officers	39.8%
After-school programs	33.0%
Neighborhood Watch programs	33.0%
Boot camps	13.1%
Citizens reporting crime	12.0%
Gun control	11.8%
Elimination of parole	9.9%
Building more prisons	8.4%
More death penalties	8.1%

Richard A. Mendel, *Prevention or Pork? A Hard-Headed Look at Youth-Oriented Anti-Crime Programs,* 1995.

Given their reaction against unfairness, imposed structure, and punishment, it is not surprising that young people reject what might be offered as assistance when they mistrust the adults in charge as unfair, controlling, and punitive. This rejection of "help" is a strength—it is the way that young people have survived the adversity of poverty and racism. If this mistrust of unfair, controlling, and punitive adults is subdued, it undermines the very survival technique that has allowed these youths to make it as far as they have.

PROGRAMS THAT WORK

Ironically, as states build juvenile boot camps that are likely to fail, the ingredients for services that enable delinquents to invest in noncriminal futures are well-known. Delinquents change their behavior when services build on their strengths and meet their needs. Programs such as Associated Marine Institutes in Florida and other states, Youth Advocacy Program in Pennsylvania, Children's Trust Neighborhood Initiative in Washington, D.C., Alternative Rehabilitative Communities (ARC) in Pennsylvania, Kaleidoscope in Illinois, and the family treatment program at the Medical University of South Carolina have high success rates with delinquents. These programs have several characteristics in common:

• *They meet each youth's need to feel competent at something.* These programs provide opportunities for success and celebrate each youth's competence. Recognizing that school and noncriminal employment have been inaccessible, these programs offer youths real preparation for self-respecting work.

• *They meet each youth's need to be in charge.* These programs emphasize making choices and encourage genuine youth involvement in designing the daily routine and carrying out tasks.

• *They meet each youth's need to appreciate the strengths of their families.* These programs empower families and support young people in identifying with the positive characteristics of family members and making peace with the disappointments and hurt from their families.

• *They meet each youth's need to belong.* These programs offer a nonviolent group as desirable as a gang that gives recognition and encouragement and is hopeful about the future.

Programs that are effective with serious juvenile offenders recognize that if the young people do not want what we think they need, little will change in their lives. However well meaning the staff, young people will react against the imposed structure, punishment, and unfairness of juvenile boot camps. Even when they have committed serious crimes, young people have different needs than adults.

"[Kids] settle disagreements or conflicts violently because they haven't been taught to do it non-violently."

PEACE EDUCATION CAN HELP REDUCE TEENAGE VIOLENCE

Colman McCarthy

Courses in peace education can reduce violence in schools, asserts Colman McCarthy in the following viewpoint. He maintains that youths are not naturally wild but that they use violence to solve conflicts because they have not been taught nonviolent methods. Learning nonviolent conflict resolution is just as important as learning math and science, McCarthy contends. He also claims that society's attitudes and responses toward violence need to change in order for peace education to succeed. McCarthy is a syndicated columnist.

As you read, consider the following questions:
1. Why did Walter Annenberg focus on youth violence, as quoted by the author?
2. According to McCarthy, how many of the high school students he spoke to learned peacemaking in grade school?
3. What measures directed toward reducing youth violence does McCarthy criticize?

Reprinted, with permission, from Colman McCarthy, "Peace Education," Liberal Opinion Week, January 3, 1994; ©1994, The Washington Post Writers Group.

In Walter Annenberg's statements accompanying his $500 million gift to help reform public education, the philanthropist focused on one issue: youthful violence. Unless countered, he said at a White House ceremony, it "will not only erode the educational system but will destroy our way of life." To halt "this tragedy" of violence, "education is the most wholesome and effective approach."

Annenberg has been heeding some enlightened advisers. To decrease violence by and among the young, he has directed his generous sum—the largest gift ever to public education—to classroom reforms, not metal detectors, hallway cops, playground police or prisons. A sizable portion of the $500 million is to be devoted to curriculum improvement. Agonizing searches aren't needed on where best to begin: the creation or expansion of academically rigorous courses on non-violent conflict resolution, mediation and peace studies.

Ignorance Leads to Violence

Kids aren't shooting or beating each other, or their teachers, because they're inherently unruly but because they're academically uninformed. They settle disagreements or conflicts violently because they haven't been taught to do it non-violently. Ignorance, not evil, is the problem.

When speaking before college audiences, I ask students for a show of hands on two questions. How many attended a high school that offered courses on conflict resolution? Rarely is a hand raised. Question two: How many went to a high school where courses on math and science were taught? Every hand goes up.

It's the same at high school assemblies: How many went to a grade school that taught courses in peacemaking? None. And math and science courses? All.

If it's considered useful for children to know about trapezoids and nitric oxide—knowledge that may or may not be relevant in their adulthoods—then why not educate them in the art of non-violent conflict resolution, which they'll always need? They'll be having conflicts all their lives—at home, the workplace and most points between—and the solutions to them will be either violent or non-violent.

Society Teaches Violence

Even if taught non-violence, children are saturated by lessons in violence by other teachers beyond the classrooms: fathers or mothers who may be physically or emotionally abusive at home, actors who prostitute their talents in gun movies, fistfighting athletes in football, hockey and baseball games, presidents who send troops to bomb people in Third World conflicts, politicians and attorneys general who back the death penalty, pro-choicers who champion the killing of fetal life as a right, military contractors whose arms dealing has made the United States the world's leading weapons seller, hunters who take pleasure in killing animals.

A SUCCESSFUL MEDIATION PROGRAM

Some school-based prevention programs are centered around mediation. In such programs, students are trained by teachers to be mediators who work with their fellow students in negotiating the settlement of disputes. One such program is the Resolving Conflict Creatively Program (RCCP), which seeks to create a climate of nonviolence in schools. The program started in New York in 1985 and can be found in the Anchorage school districts (Alaska), the New Orleans public schools (Louisiana), the South-Orange Maplewood School District (New Jersey), and the Vista United school districts (California). The program stresses the need for nonviolent alternatives for dealing with conflict, negotiation, and other conflict resolution skills. The lessons involve role playing, interviewing, group dialogue, brainstorming, and other experiential learning techniques. An important aspect of the program is parent training through a Parent Involvement Program component. This consists of a team of two or three parents per school, who are trained for sixty hours in family communication and conflict resolution.

Evaluation of the program indicates that teachers are enthusiastic about the program, and they report decreased levels of violence among the students in the program. Students in the program report that they are now able to resolve their conflict without violence, and they have fewer fights and name-calling.

Janice Joseph, Black Youths, Delinquency, and Juvenile Justice, 1995.

Against that onslaught—much of it legal, socially acceptable or politically popular—schools that might be given Annenberg money to put peace education into the curriculum will be bucking stiff headwinds. But what other choice is present? Give up? Hope the Brady bill does it?

If the current pattern holds, kids in school today—from first grade to 12th grade—will be dealing with their conflicts in a few years, or sooner, by swinging their fists or shooting their guns. Then Congress will pass another crime bill with billions for new prisons, the Department of Education will issue another study on school violence, church leaders will call for prayer days and the networks will carry specials on kids who attacked their teachers.

THERE ARE SOLUTIONS

At the White House ceremony with Walter Annenberg, President Bill Clinton said, "Nearly every problem has been solved somewhere by somebody." On school violence, he's right. Such proven peace educators as Fran Schmidt in Miami, Neil Katz in Syracuse, Timothy Shriver in New Haven, Michael Nagler in California, Ian Harris in Milwaukee and many others have been in classrooms teaching both the techniques of non-violence and the literature of peacemaking.

Solutions to violence exist and can be studied, absorbed and practiced in the nation's 28,000 high schools and 78,000 grade schools. How much of the Annenberg gift eventually goes to peace education will tell whether this is a serious or cosmetic reform.

"Hundreds of grassroots leaders . . .
have shown how the same
mechanisms that are a conduit for
drugs and crime can be used to
import productive, healing
activities."

COMMUNITY-BASED EFFORTS CAN HELP REDUCE TEENAGE VIOLENCE

Robert L. Woodson Sr.

In the following viewpoint, Robert L. Woodson Sr. argues that community-based programs are more effective than national strategies in solving youth violence. Woodson contends that the people who lead these grassroots efforts earn the trust and respect of young people and show youths how to serve their families and communities. Strategies that focus on incarceration backfire, he maintains, because prisons actually breed further violence. Woodson is the president and founder of the Washington, D.C.-based National Center for Neighborhood Enterprise.

As you read, consider the following questions:
1. According to Woodson, what are "wolf pack" attacks?
2. How many Americans are in gangs, according to the author?
3. What is the "bridge program," as described by Woodson?

Reprinted from Robert L. Woodson Sr., "National Youth Gang Strategy Inadequate," *Headway*, December 1996, by permission of *Headway*.

D uring the summer of 1983, the city of Philadelphia was paralyzed with fear as small gangs of marauding black youths arbitrarily targeted citizens on the streets and in shopping malls. In what police termed as "wolf pack" attacks, the victims were knocked to the ground and stripped of rings, watches, gold chains, wallets and purses. A virtual reign of terror spread as reports of the attacks were published and other youths joined in the melee.

A Solution in Philadelphia

Because these robberies were not connected to organized gangs and occurred sporadically, police and law enforcement officials found it impossible to predict or contain the rash of attacks. Neither increased police patrols or emergency funding to traditional social service institutions had any impact on the problem.

As the City was held hostage in this crime wave, movie theaters closed early, stores and shopping centers shut down, and many civic events were canceled. Public officials were at a point of hopelessness when two grassroots leaders stepped forward and suggested a unique strategy. Within one day of the implementation of their plan, the attacks ceased and never again resumed.

The identities of these leaders and how they accomplished this feat contain valuable lessons for addressing a current epidemic of youth crime and gang violence. David and Falaka Fattah were well-known veteran black activists who had discovered that one of their own six sons was an active gang member. At that time, Philadelphia was known as the youth gang capital of the nation. Newspapers published weekly gang violence victim statistics next to the death tolls of the Vietnam War.

In responding to their son's gang activity, the Fattahs reached out to embrace his circle of friends rather than trying to isolate him from them, inviting 13 of the youths to come to live with them in their small row house in West Philadelphia. This informal arrangement blossomed into a gang rescue program called the House of Umoja.

Creating a Peace Pact

Word of the safe-haven soon spread on the streets and the number of young gang members seeking asylum steadily increased. Within a few years, the influence of the Fattah's outreach spread throughout the entire city, and they were able to coordinate a city-wide peace pact that dramatically reduced the annual number of gang-related homicides.

The Fattahs brought this established reputation and foundation of trust and respect with them when they came to the table to address the crisis of the wolf-pack attacks. Their first step was to call in the "experts" with invaluable street experience, former gang members—the "Old Heads" or "Ogs"—they had worked with. This group suggested a collaborative effort with their counterparts who were incarcerated at the local prison, "the House of Correction."

When the call went out for help in stopping the violence, more than 130 inmates signed up to join a crime-prevention task force. The prisoners identified young people who were influential on their "corners" in their neighborhoods who were invited to a conference at the prison the following Saturday.

The response was overwhelming. On the day of the conference, buses ferried more than 300 youths to the prison. After hearing presentations from the inmates on personal responsibility and moral obligation, the group broke up into smaller work shops and discussion groups focused on ending the violence. The following day peace prevailed.

A LACK OF SUPPORT

Although the Fattahs and their group received official recognition from the mayor, the acknowledgement of their unique ability to reach the city's young people was more ceremonial than substantive. When funds were later allocated for crime prevention or youth services, they were designated for conventional social service programs and for increased police patrols. The Fattahs were applauded but then ignored.

Our national strategy, likewise, has failed to provide substantial support for alternative grassroots responses to youth crime and gang activity, in spite of the undeniable effectiveness. While plaques may be bestowed on numerous successful neighborhood-based anti-gang efforts, there has been no effort to develop structures that can harness the capacities of grassroots initiatives in order to sustain and expand their impact. Instead, as in the case of the Fattahs, massive funding has been channeled to conventional social programs, therapeutic intervention, and police interdiction and incarceration.

One definition of insanity is to keep doing the same thing, but to expect different results. As budgets for conventional, failed programs have expanded, the crisis has continued to mount. We are now at a point where, in the words of Attorney General Janet Reno, "Gang violence has spread to every corner of America."

A nationwide survey has reported that gang membership in

the United States has grown to more than 650,000 members who are involved in 25,000 gangs. Youth crime is taking America hostage, one community, one industry at a time. Like the shopping plazas of Philadelphia, one internationally acclaimed mall in Minnesota has considered instituting a curfew because of an onslaught of gang fights.

PRISONS WORSEN VIOLENCE

In response, a massive crackdown was launched by the FBI, the Safe Streets Initiative, which created 133 task forces that resulted in 92,000 arrests and 35,000 convictions nationwide throughout a four-year period. Yet, in the words of one corrections director in Illinois—a state where half of the 38,000 prison population has been identified as gang members—"The problem does not go away. When the community gets rid of its gang problem that problem is then transferred to the correctional institution. In fact, it becomes more intensified."

NO MORE EXCUSES

Two excuses I've grown particularly weary of hearing over the years are these: (1) there's no guarantee that your efforts will result in saving a kid, and (2) you can't save everybody. As general statements, both of those are undeniably true; as excuses, both of them are shamefully lame. Of course there are no guarantees. But we can guarantee what will happen if we *don't* get involved. Kids will keep selling crack to mothers. They will keep screwing up their own lives and those of their friends and relatives. They will keep terrorizing the neighborhoods. They will keep killing each other. Guaran-damn-teed. And of course you can't save everybody. But why should that prevent you from saving *somebody*? . . .

There are no more excuses if you genuinely want the homies to live, because now you know. You might not know about budgets and buildings and meeting agendas but you know that you have to be there for the kids; that you have to help them deal with their anger, fear, and pain; that you have to provide them with the knowledge they need to recognize and steer clear of risky behavior; that you have to give them positive rules for living.

Joseph Marshall Jr. and Lonnie Wheeler, *Street Soldier: One Man's Struggle to Save a Generation—One Life at a Time,* 1996.

In short, rising rates of incarceration of youthful offenders have turned our prisons into breeding grounds of violence and mayhem, which are now being exported back again into the community. Shocking evidence has emerged of gang recruitment and the formation of inter-gang alliances even within prison walls, and chains of command from the prisons to the streets remain undisturbed.

In Washington, D.C., for example, an investigation revealed that Rayful Edmonds, the head of a notorious drug ring who is currently serving a life sentence, has been coordinating a drug trafficking operation from his prison cell which is far more expansive and lucrative than the dynasty he ruled when he was on the outside. From Connecticut to California, homicides have been traced to death orders issued by inmates.

In spite of the daunting scale of this crisis, remedies do exist—in a multitude of replications of the Philadelphia model. Throughout the country, hundreds of grassroots leaders, who have earned the trust and respect of thousands of people they have served, have shown how the same mechanisms that are a conduit for drugs and crime can be used to import productive, healing activities and life-transforming experiences.

SUCCESS STORIES

In Washington, D.C., a group of six ex-offenders formed the Alliance of Concerned Men, an organization dedicated to recognizing and utilizing the capacities of inmates and establishing links through which men who are incarcerated can continue— or begin—to serve their families and communities. As one of ACM's founders, Tyrone Parker explains, "We believe that a man does not relinquish his responsibilities upon incarceration."

Using strategies similar to the Fattahs', the Alliance established a "bridge program" which facilitates prison visits and communication between incarcerated men and their children, and a unique "Adopt-a-Block" program, through which groups of inmates use their influence on the streets to keep their neighborhoods violence free.

From coast to coast, similar efforts are underway, utilizing indigenous community networks and gang structures to constructive ends. In Los Angeles, Leon Watkins tirelessly worked with one young gang leader until he established the trust that led to his transformation. Working together, they then brought hundreds of other youths through that same threshold of opportunity.

In Hartford, Conn., through the investment of one man, Carl Hardrick, five former leaders of the city's most notorious gangs are now working daily to spread the message of peace, productive community service, and prospects for young entrepreneurs. This small group of neighborhood leaders with street names like "Big Bird," "Book," and "Chan," are responsible for dramatically reducing the level of street violence in their city.

The problems of gang violence and youth crime now threaten us as an "American Chernobyl" that is ready to explode. Remedies do exist, but if we are to substantiate the hope they offer, we must be willing to re-channel our investments in past failures to risk success with new strategies implemented by unconventional experts. A virtual army of healers is ready to be mobilized.

PERIODICAL BIBLIOGRAPHY

The following articles have been selected to supplement the diverse views presented in this chapter. Addresses are provided for periodicals not indexed in the *Readers' Guide to Periodical Literature*, the *Alternative Press Index*, the *Social Sciences Index*, or the *Index to Legal Periodicals and Books*.

Awake!	"Protecting Our Children from Gangs," April 22, 1998. Available from Watchtower Bible and Tract Society of New York, 25 Columbia Heights, Brooklyn, NY 11201-2483.
Christian Science Monitor	"Juvenile Justice: Trying to Break Cycle of Crime," July 29, 1996.
John J. DiIulio Jr. et al.	"Crime Solutions: 18 Things We Can Now Do to Fight Back," *American Enterprise*, May-June 1995.
Craig Donegan	"Preventing Juvenile Crime," *CQ Researcher*, March 15, 1996. Available from 1414 22nd St. NW, Washington, DC 20037.
Issues and Controversies On File	"Teen Curfews," August 30, 1996. Available from Facts On File News Service, 11 Penn Plaza, New York, NY 10001-2006.
Richard Lacayo	"Teen Crime," *Time*, July 21, 1997.
John Leo	"Punished for the Sins of the Children," *U.S. News & World Report*, June 12, 1995.
Paul J. McNulty	"Natural Born Killers? Preventing the Coming Explosion of Teenage Crime," *Policy Review*, Winter 1995.
Kurt S. Olsson	"The Juvenile Justice Dilemma," *Corrections Today*, February 1996.
Mary Ann Perga	"Parents Shouldn't Do the Time When Kids Do the Crime," *U.S. Catholic*, December 1996.
Nina Siegal	"Ganging Up on Civil Liberties," *Progressive*, October 1997.
Atom Clay Thompson	"Organizers," *Third Force*, March-April 1998.
Laurel Shaper Walters	"States to Parents: Pay for Your Children's Crimes," *Christian Science Monitor*, April 1, 1996.
Nancy Watzman	"The Curfew Revival Gains Momentum," *Governing*, February 1994.

CHAPTER 3

How Can Teen Pregnancy Be Prevented?

CHAPTER PREFACE

In Idaho, a 1921 law remains on the books holding that unmarried people who have sex "shall be found guilty of fornication." The statute was essentially defunct until 1996, when Gem County, Idaho, resurrected it as a method to discourage teenage pregnancy. In applying the law, Gem County prosecutor Douglas Varie targets pregnant teenagers and their boyfriends. One such teenager, seventeen-year-old Amanda Smisek, was convicted and sentenced to three years of probation, plus parenting classes.

Among Varie's critics is the American Civil Liberties Union (ACLU). Jack Van Valkenburgh, executive director of the ACLU of Idaho, states, "To the extent that the prosecutions are targeting teenagers, and the law applies to everybody, it is selective prosecution, and it denies equal protection of the law." Moreover, warn opponents, while the law will not keep teenagers from having sex, the threat of arrest could prevent teens from seeking birth control. For this reason, some maintain that the enforcement of fornication laws will actually increase teenage pregnancy.

However, Gem County officials assert that prosecutorial discretion—a prosecutor's freedom to determine which cases to prosecute—allows Varie to apply the fornication law as he sees fit. Furthermore, those who support Varie's approach claim that aggressive measures are justified when it comes to teenage pregnancy. These critics contend that since children born out of wedlock are more likely to end up in prison, on drugs, poor, and illiterate, they place a significant burden on society. Varie argues that "the cost [to society] isn't just in welfare. A male child of a single teen mother is three times more likely to go to jail as a child with two parents." Due to the high social costs of teenage pregnancy, Varie and others maintain, prosecuting unmarried teens for having sex is necessary.

Gem County's revival of the fornication statute reflects a nationwide move toward combating teen pregnancy with legislation. In California, for example, adult males who impregnate teenage girls can be prosecuted under statutory rape laws, which prohibit sex between adults and minors. While some laud these measures as effective ways to deter teenage pregnancy, others contend that a punitive approach to teenage pregnancy fails to address its root causes. The following chapter provides diverse views on how teenage pregnancy can be prevented.

| "Parents exercise a powerful influence over their teens' sexual behavior."

TEACHING ABSTINENCE HELPS AVERT TEEN PREGNANCY

Maggie Gallagher

Maggie Gallagher argues in the following viewpoint that encouraging teenagers to abstain from sex can help prevent teenage pregnancy. Furthermore, she asserts, parents have a great deal of influence over whether their teenagers remain virgins. Gallagher is a nationally syndicated columnist.

As you read, consider the following questions:

1. According to the study cited by Gallagher, what three factors help parents discourage their teens from having sex?
2. In the author's words, how likely are teenagers to remain virgins if their parents discourage them from having sex?
3. What is the single biggest influence on whether or not teens have sex, in the author's opinion?

From Maggie Gallagher, "Straight Talk About Sex Education," *The Washington Times*, January 29, 1997. Reprinted by permission of Universal Press Syndicate. All rights reserved.

W hen responsible adults talk to teen-agers about sex, what should we say?

Sex education is now as American as apple pie. On the importance of honest and open sexual communication with kids, Americans are agreed. But what we don't quite know, in our heart of hearts, is just what we should communicate: Do we push abstinence, contraceptives or both?

Programs pushing abstinence only remain highly controversial in some places, the subject of lawsuits by groups like Planned Parenthood, which has argued that schools invade teens' privacy if they don't unroll condoms on bananas in classrooms.

MODERN-DAY SEXUAL VALUES

Teens having sex are now considered normal. It's the virgins who have to explain their peculiar behavior. Meanwhile, parents who don't have pillow talks about the pill with their teens (and don't want condoms handed out in schools) face what can only be called social stigma.

Dana Mack, author of the book *The Assault on Parenthood*, relates the experience of one parent who stood up at a school board meeting to voice her opposition to condom distribution: "It's parents like you that are the reason why we need these machines," a school board member sneered back.

In the face of the MTVing of America, parents with traditional sexual values are apt to feel quaint, if not overwhelmed and impotent. That's too bad. Because several surprising studies suggest that protecting your teens from premature sex is hardly an impossible dream.

One study published in the summer of 1996 in *Family Planning Perspectives*, for example, found that even after controlling for various psychosocial factors (including self-esteem), parents exercise a powerful influence over their teens' sexual behavior.

THREE FACTORS IN HELPING TEENS POSTPONE SEX

If parents want to help their teens postpone sex, this study found, three factors are important: (1) Maintain a good, warm relationship with your child (children are far more likely to accept family values if they feel valued by their family). (2) Let your teens know openly and honestly you expect them not to have sex. And (3) avoid discussing birth control.

Separately each factor about doubles the likelihood that a teen will choose to postpone sex. Put them together, and the power of parents multiplies: A teen who has all three things going for him—warm parents who push abstinence and who don't push contraception—is *twelve-and-a-half times* more likely to remain a virgin than a teen who has none of these things.

And this is not only true of white middle-class families. This study investigated 751 African-American teens and their mothers in Philadelphia, proving that strong moms can protect their kids, even in places, such as urban black neighborhoods, that too many Middle Americans write off.

PARENTS CAN MAKE A DIFFERENCE

"I think one important message is that parents can make a difference," the study's principal author, James Jaccard, a psychology professor at SUNY-Albany, told the *Philadelphia Inquirer*. "Many parents think adolescence is a time of parental rejection and that they have little influence on teen-agers. It becomes very important for parents to open the communication channels because they can have an impact."

ABSTINENCE IS A REALISTIC GOAL

With the widespread failure of conventional sex ed and the growing success of abstinence education, advocates are poised to smash a paralyzing misconception about teenage sex: Although most parents would like their children to delay sex until marriage, they have been convinced that teenage sexual activity is inevitable and uncontrollable. This may come as a surprise to many, but raising teenagers to be sexually abstinent is a realistic goal. All the best research shows that parents are the single most important influence on whether their teens become sexually active. By some estimates, unfortunately, just 10 to 15 percent of today's youth have discussed sex with their parents, even though more than half of sexually active teens, according to a Roper Starch Survey, wish they could.

Kristine Napier, *Policy Review*, May/June 1997.

Research like this may not end the controversy over how we teach sex ed in schools (indeed, the study authors believe their findings aren't relevant to that debate). But at the very least they do suggest that parents with traditional values are not, as experts routinely portray them, an obstacle in the war against teen pregnancy, but one of our most powerful weapons.

One hopeful message to parents comes through loud and clear: Despite TV, despite peer pressure, despite hormones, the single biggest influence on whether or not your teen has sex is you.

And don't let any "expert" convince you otherwise.

| "*Abstinence is a highly risky philosophy in which to put our entire trust.*"

TEACHING ABSTINENCE PUTS TEENS AT RISK OF PREGNANCY AND SEXUALLY TRANSMITTED DISEASES

M. Joycelyn Elders

In the following viewpoint, former U.S. surgeon general M. Joycelyn Elders maintains that sexual education programs promoting abstinence fail to recognize that most teenagers are having sex and therefore need protection against pregnancy and sexually transmitted diseases. The refusal to educate teens about condoms, she claims, places teenagers at a serious risk of contracting AIDS and other sexually transmitted diseases.

As you read, consider the following questions:

1. According to statistics cited by Elders, how many children and youths died of AIDS in 1996?
2. In Elders's opinion, why is abstinence a "highly risky philosophy"?
3. According to the author, why do European teenagers have lower rates of sexually transmitted diseases than teens in the United States?

Reprinted from Call to Arms, "Respect Your Elders!" by M. Joycelyn Elders, POZ, December 1997, by permission of POZ Publishing, New York, N.Y.

These days we confuse ignorance with innocence. Many adults believe (wrongly) that children are asexual, have no sexual thoughts, feelings or desires and shouldn't become aware of sex in any way before puberty. But in fact, sexual expression is coming earlier to teens, not because of loose morals or lack of values, but because children reach menses and puberty at an increasingly younger age. Yet by leaving them in the lurch rather than helping them understand the changes in their bodies, we punish our youth for what is literally beyond their control.

Few children today receive accurate, comprehensive health education at home; their mostly uninformed and anxious parents can't offer it. However, almost all children go to school, and it is there that they could most likely be prepared for a sexually healthy life. For we are losing our children and youth to disease, and it is time to act.

TEENS ARE DYING OF AIDS

Consider these global statistics: In 1996, 1.5 million people, including 350,000 children and youths, died of AIDS. Of the 30 million people infected with HIV, 2.6 million—nearly one in 10—are adolescent or younger. Most new infections occur in people under 25, and about 80 percent of all adult infections occur through unprotected sexual intercourse—yet condom is still a naughty word in the United States.

Abstinence has been widely endorsed and heavily financed by the federal government. The Sexuality Information and Education Council of the United States (SIECUS) reported that all 50 states filed applications for their share of $50 million in federal funds for the welfare reform bill's abstinence-only education program. So while we refuse to support sexuality education, we try to legislate morals. But abstinence is a highly risky philosophy in which to put our entire trust. In his book *Solving America's Sexual Crisis*, sociologist Ira Reiss puts it best when he writes, "Vows of abstinence break more easily than do condoms."

ABSTINENCE PROGRAMS WILL NOT PREVENT NEW HIV INFECTIONS

Preventing new infections in the United States by promoting abstinence alone may never be accomplished, since three-quarters of all teen pregnancies are fathered by adult males. One study reveals a related—and very disturbing—trend: More adolescent girls than boys are diagnosed with HIV. According to the Centers for Disease Control and Prevention (CDC), 90 percent of the AIDS cases under age 20 are among girls. And these infections are acquired in childhood or early adolescence. These girls are generally not getting HIV from teen-age boys. In fact, many of the men responsible for infecting them are relatives.

Dan Wasserman ©1992 Boston Globe. Distributed by the Los Angeles Times Syndicate. Reprinted by permission.

It has been estimated that one in three girls is sexually abused by age 18, and one in four by age 14. These preteens—who cannot "just say no"—likely feel a special sense of shame and despair when their teachers emphasize that the only appropriate method for birth control and disease prevention is abstinence. Let's face it: Teen-agers are having sex, and they need condoms.

In 1997, Shari Lo, a California sophomore, won a trophy at her high school science fair for a project measuring condom reliability. She was on her way to the regional science-fair competition when the school superintendent disqualified her project, explaining that "because it is on condom reliability, it encourages safe sex. Our philosophy is abstinence, not safe sex."

THE NEED FOR COMPREHENSIVE SEX EDUCATION

It's true—albeit rarely stated so bluntly—that as a nation, we care more about philosophy than the lives of our youth. That's why U.S. teens have the highest rates of pregnancy, childbirth, abortion and HIV in the developed world—even though adolescent sexual activity and the age of initial sexual contact in other countries is similar to ours. Adolescents in countries such as Sweden, the Netherlands, Britain and France have much lower rates of Sexually Transmitted Diseases (STDs) and HIV than our own. Why? For one thing, all other developed nations have comprehensive health and sexuality education from kindergarten to grade 12. Discussion of contraception—including condoms—is widespread in the media, and universal health care makes birth control available and affordable. Finland's government sends out a brochure to every 16-year-old on his or her birthday that presents a positive depiction of adolescent sexuality, talks about responsibility and comes with a latex condom.

While our young are dying, we are quibbling over methods. Nationwide, one million teenage girls became pregnant in 1996, and half that number gave birth; three million youths got STDs. HIV infections and AIDS cases are both increasing fastest among adolescents.

Abstinence works for many of our youth. However, I'm not willing to just throw away all the rest for whom it does not work for one reason or another. We are at a low point in our nation's history in terms of caring for our children. We've tried legislating morals, and that didn't work. We've tried just saying no, and that didn't work. We've tried ignorance, and that didn't work. Why don't we try education? Let's end this shameful era by standing up and stepping out to save our precious children.

"If ... young girls were reliably
protected against pregnancy ...
young women would reach legal
adulthood prepared to make their
own reproductive choices in a more
mature way."

LONG-TERM CONTRACEPTIVE DEVICES CAN HELP PREVENT TEEN PREGNANCY

Margaret P. Battin

In the following viewpoint, Margaret P. Battin argues that placing adolescent girls on long-term contraceptive devices would avert all unintentional teenage pregnancies. One such device is Norplant, a contraceptive that is surgically placed in the arm and protects against pregnancy for up to five years. The use of Norplant or other long-term contraceptive devices, Battin contends, would effectively immunize girls against pregnancy until they made the choice to have children. Battin is a professor of medical ethics at the University of Utah School of Medicine.

As you read, consider the following questions:

1. In Battin's opinion, what is the present approach to the problem of teenage pregnancy?
2. How is the use of long-term contraception similar to an immunization against disease, in the author's opinion?
3. According to the author, what are the current means available for long-term contraception?

Reprinted from Margaret P. Battin, "A Better Approach to Adolescent Pregnancy," *Social Science and Medicine*, vol. 41, no. 9, 1995, by permission of Elsevier Science.

For all young women, pregnancy and childbearing is physiologically riskier in the earliest postpubescent years than later. Very early pregnancy is associated with higher rates of both maternal and infant morbidity and mortality. In many cultures, pregnancy in early adolescence is regarded as socially disruptive, especially when no father is known or present and the young mother is the child's sole means of support; it is seen as perpetuating a cycle of poverty. Early pregnancy is often associated with higher rates of malnourishment and inadequate schooling for the child, less education and less economic independence for the mother and higher rates of disturbance in the home.

. . . The individual, social and global risks of very early childbearing are substantial. Given the very large number of adolescent pregnancies that occur annually and the multiple grounds on which postponement of them may seem desirable, we must ask whether there may not be a better strategy for prevention or reduction of unplanned adolescent pregnancy. I would like to propose a thought-experiment—a conjecture—about a better way of approaching the matter of adolescent pregnancy. This may seem outrageous; but because it reveals so much about our current attitudes, I think it is important to have it carefully considered.

USING EDUCATION TO PREVENT TEENAGE PREGNANCY

Clearly, what is done now does not work, at least not everywhere. The prevention of teenage pregnancy, at least in those countries which attempt it, is currently approached mainly by education: adolescent girls are informed of the benefits of avoiding pregnancy and warned of its risks, and are provided with information about the behavioural and contraceptive means of doing so. . . . If education about pregnancy prevention is adequate, it is assumed, teenagers will remain abstinent, or provide themselves with contraceptives or insist that their partners do so.

In some countries, this works well: in the Netherlands and Sweden for example, the rate of teenage pregnancy is very low. In other countries, such as the United States, it is less successful: the rate of teenage pregnancy is high, the highest in the developed world. This is often attributed to differences in sex education: in the United States, unlike the northern European countries, formal sex education is often grossly inadequate . . . and cultural pressures . . . often favour rather than discourage teenage pregnancy.

In some countries, adolescent pregnancy is effectively prevented not by education but by rigid sex-segregation and severe sanctions if it occurs. In other countries, especially in the developing world, pregnancy during adolescence is common.

In many cultures in sub-Saharan Africa, for instance, traditional cultural patterns encourage very early marriage and immediate childbearing. . . . Pregnancy during adolescence varies widely among cultures but it is nevertheless frequent on a global scale. . . .

Is there a better way to approach adolescent pregnancy, given its consequences, its risks and its ubiquitousness—a better way than ineffectual reliance on education or rigid sex segregation? . . . What if it were arranged that adolescent girls, from puberty through 17 (or, in most places, legal adulthood), could not become pregnant unless they made a deliberate, conscious choice to do so? How would this change their prospects, their offspring's prospects and the prospects of their families, societies and the world?

THE BENEFITS OF LONG-TERM CONTRACEPTION

This is conjecture only in one sense: we are probably politically incapable of making it happen. But it is not merely a thought-experiment in another sense: after all, we already have the technology available now that would make this possible. This technology, not usually distinguished from its predecessors, involves long-term contraception which is 'automatic' in its function: it works all the time regardless of what the user does. Unlike short-term modalities such as the condom, the diaphragm, the sponge, and various herbal potions and powders, true 'automatic' long-term contraception provides continuous pregnancy prevention without any further action on the part of the user: without having to obtain it, store it, apply it or activate it, ingest it or insert it, either beforehand or at the time of sex—indeed, without having to do anything at all. (It is this feature of user-independence that makes true long-term contraception ideal for young or inexperienced users.)

Such a strategy would be like immunising youngsters against other health risks: tetanus, diphtheria, pertussis, polio—except that long-term contraception is not permanent and can be immediately reversed when the user wishes. Nor does such contraception in any way interfere with adult reproductive capacity; it is just that adolescents do not become pregnant unless they actively choose to do so. . . .

CURRENT TECHNOLOGIES IN LONG-TERM CONTRACEPTION

At the moment, there are just two contraceptives for women which are sufficiently long-term to remain effective throughout adolescence but nevertheless permit a complete and immediate return to fertility if the user wishes—the subdermal, levonorgestrel implant (Norplant) and the intra-uterine device (IUD). . . . Norplant is effective for years; the contemporary IUD is effective for eight to ten years. Both have excellent reliability and safety records, though both involve some disadvantages, including side effects and culturally unacceptable consequences like altered bleeding patterns or invasion of modesty. There are no reliable, safe, long-term contraceptive technologies yet available for males. . . . Other long-acting female contraceptives now on the market, such as Depo-Provera and, when taken continuously, the Pill, still require user co-operation: this means remembering and obtaining repeat applications, not a foolproof expectation for teenagers.

THE USE OF NORPLANT WOULD REDUCE TEEN PREGNANCIES

Abstinence is the best goal of social policy. But the harsh fact is that we have neither the social will nor the practical tools to achieve it. Meanwhile, each year teenagers have another 400,000 abortions, and 300,000 babies out of wedlock. . . .

Norplant's very effectiveness would lead to a marginal increase in sexual activity among teens, and thus to a concomitant increase in sexually transmitted diseases (which Norplant does not prevent). But on the other side of the social ledger, widespread use of Norplant would sharply reduce the number of abortions and babies born out of wedlock.

Douglas J. Besharov, *National Review*, August 9, 1993.

But this conjecture . . . is not limited to the currently available technologies. Improvements in the two current truly 'automatic' technologies, Norplant and the IUD, and other newly developing modalities allow us to imagine a world in which reliance on educational strategies of variable (but generally low) effectiveness for preventing teen pregnancy is no longer necessary. . . . Every adolescent has [protection], just as every adolescent is immunised against polio whether they expect to be exposed or not. Indeed, the use of such contraception would be entirely independent of sex: initiated at puberty, it would simply be a basic protective feature of their lives. Of course, sexually active adolescents would still need to concern themselves about sexually transmitted diseases, and use condoms if appropriate in addition, but they would not need to worry about unwanted pregnancy.

Of course, adolescents could still have children if they wished to do so. Pregnancy would simply require a positive choice to have the contraceptive device neutralised or removed. Nevertheless, up to the time of legal adulthood, adolescents would be protected from incurring pregnancy in involuntary, inadequately informed, impulsive or unthinking ways—just the ways in which many, perhaps most, adolescent pregnancies occur.

Think about this conjecture carefully. Consider the physical and psychological costs of unwanted, unplanned adolescent pregnancy to the young girls themselves, to their partners, families and social groupings; then consider the larger social costs to their societies, and finally consider the strains in terms of global population and resource pressures. Of course there are often benefits to early pregnancy. But if it were routine that young girls were reliably protected against pregnancy they did not intend, many of the costs would disappear, the benefits could be maintained for those who chose them, and in general, young women would reach legal adulthood prepared to make their own reproductive choices in a more mature way. This would have incalculable repercussions for gender equality; it could alleviate social friction over the issue of abortion, since pregnancy would all be by choice; and it would have a very favourable impact on poverty-perpetuating and population pressures—all without violating any woman's right to have the number of children she wished.

Too bad we aren't developing fully reliable, perfectly safe, side-effect-free long-term contraceptive technologies for both women and men at a faster rate. This would permit a change in human reproduction control from reliance on short-term methods to the routine use of long-term 'automatic' contraception: it would, so to speak, change the default mode in human reproduction—choices about reproduction would no longer be negative choices to avoid children, but positive choices to have them. This simple change—from a negative choice to prevent pregnancy (which is what our sex-education programmes ask of teenagers now) to a positive choice to seek pregnancy—may seem a very minor change in decisional structure, based on a small difference in contraceptive technology, but it is one with incalculable consequences for women, men and the world.

> "To [implant Norplant in teenage girls] would be to . . . state publicly that there are no social standards or sanctions with respect to the sexual activity of young people."

LONG-TERM CONTRACEPTIVE DEVICES PROMOTE TEEN PROMISCUITY

Richard John Neuhaus

In the following viewpoint, Richard John Neuhaus responds to a proposal by Douglas J. Besharov to grant teenagers easy access to the contraceptive Norplant, a long-term contraceptive device that is surgically implanted in the arm and retains its effectiveness for up to five years. Neuhaus maintains that granting access to Norplant would send a message to teenagers that sex is expected of them, thereby vastly increasing teen promiscuity. Neuhaus is the religion editor for *National Review*, a conservative monthly magazine.

As you read, consider the following questions:

1. How does Norplant reduce teenagers' incentives to remain virgins, according to Neuhaus?
2. In Neuhaus's words, what message does the use of Norplant send to teenagers in the inner cities?
3. According to the author, what are the dangerous effects of teenage promiscuity?

M r. Douglas J. Besharov [in his proposal to grant teenagers easy access to Norplant] asks us, "Which is worse: the possibility of a marginal increase in sexual activity? Or losing the opportunity to reduce abortions and out-of-wedlock births by 10, 20, or even 30 per cent? To ask the question is to answer it." I have asked the question, and it is by no means answered. The alternatives he poses are misleading.

Given the figure of a million teenage pregnancies, a 10 per cent reduction by the use of Norplant would require 100,000 implantations. In either case, it's an ambitious program. Presumably the program is voluntary and hundreds of thousands of teenage girls (the proposal does put all the responsibility on the girls) would want to have a minor surgical procedure that would contraceptively equip them for sexual intercourse. Presumably also, the parents would have some say in this and would agree to having their daughters thus equipped. Presumably yet further, one result would be "the possibility of a marginal increase in sexual activity."

A Substantial Increase in Teenage Sex

I suggest that the result would be the near certainty of a substantial increase in sexual intercourse among teenagers. If so, that would mean also an increase in abortions and single-parent children. The problems that the proposal intends to resolve would be greatly exacerbated.

Of course we do not know for sure until it is tried. There are many perilous things that should not be tried. We should not under public auspices try implanting Norplant in teenage girls. To do so would be to try something that possibly no society has tried before: to state publicly that there are no social standards or sanctions with respect to the sexual activity of young people. It might be objected that we are already making that statement by distributing condoms in public schools. Just so. Which is why condom distribution is a dumb idea, and far from settled policy in most schools.

Giving Up on Discouraging Teen Promiscuity

Mr. Besharov says that abstinence is the best goal "for younger teens especially." (At 15 you can't do it but at 16 you can?) He adds, "But the harsh fact is that we have neither the social will nor the practical tools to achieve [the goal of abstinence]." I do not know what he means by "practical tools," but presumably we do not have means of discouraging and encouraging certain behaviors among young people. Parents have never succeeded in controlling totally the behavior of their children, which is just as well. But if Mr. Besharov is suggesting that parents—and churches and schools—should give up on discouraging sexual promiscuity and encouraging abstinence, his is even more of a counsel of despair than I had at first thought.

The critical reference is to "social will." To whom, one may ask, belong the wills that make up this social will? Teenagers, parents, brothers, sisters, pastors, teachers, school boards, aunts, and uncles—each, one by one, can have a will with respect to teenage sexuality. Or perhaps the suggestion is that most people who are in a position to influence teenagers really do not care about what they do sexually. The survey research data do not support that suggestion. But even if most people did not care, that does not mean that we should adopt public policies premised upon not caring. Mr. Besharov cares. He obviously cares about abortion and out-of-wedlock children, and by implication he cares about teenage fornication (he calls it an evil). I have never met the "social will," but I have met many people who care very much about their children's sexual behavior.

But Mr. Besharov, along with many others, is discouraged about the possibility of encouraging abstinence from sexual intercourse. The discouragement is understandable. Many in the media, entertainment, and educational establishments proclaim that abstinence is unnatural, chastity is unattainable, and virginity is a form of sexual deviance. And yet, in such a social climate, at least one half of teenage girls are virgins. It seems quite remarkable. Many in the other half have had sex only once or twice, while many more, those who have been very "sexually active," know that what they have done is not right.

ENCOURAGING TEENS WHO WANT TO ABSTAIN

Let us stipulate for argument's sake that 25 per cent of teenage girls are sexually promiscuous and think there is nothing wrong with that. Why should we agree with them by adopting policies that declare that the sexual behavior of young people is a matter of public indifference? Why should we not, rather, encourage the 75 per cent who want to do the right thing, even if they do not always behave as they know they ought? When it comes to doing the right thing, incentives and disincentives are always in fragile balance. Those who want to do the right thing need all the support that they can get. Girls in particular need support in resisting predatory males.

Consider 16-year-old Thelma who has her Norplant in place. Her reasons for saying no are sharply reduced. She is equipped for sex. Her school and, presumably, her parents have said that they *expect* her to have sexual intercourse. Saying no seems arbitrary, irrational, and downright unfriendly. If through public policy we declare that we expect teenagers to be sexually promiscuous, that it is the normal thing, it is reasonable to suppose that more teenagers will be sexually promiscuous. If, on the other hand, we make it clear that we expect abstinence, chastity, and self-command, virtue might be given a helping hand.

CONTRACEPTION SHOULD NOT REPLACE EDUCATION

[Norplant's] magic technology replaces individual decision-making and discourages responsible attitudes regarding sexual behaviour, not least on the part of men.

This is undesirable both from an ethical and practical point of view. In the absence of [sexual] education, for example, why suppose that behavioural patterns formed when it was not necessary to assume responsibility for reproductive choices will automatically be replaced by mature behaviour when the long-term contraceptive is withdrawn? How would women have been prepared to make mature choices in the absence of education?

Rosa N. Geldstein and Edith A. Pantelides, *Reproductive Health Matters*, November 1, 1996.

Or we can give up. We can, perhaps implicitly but with a powerful social effect, agree with the minority (maybe the small minority) of teenagers who are sexually promiscuous and think there is nothing wrong with that. But, it might be objected, Norplant would be used selectively. It would not be a general statement of approval with respect to teenage promiscuity since it would be given only to those girls who already are "sexually active."

Anyone who takes that objection seriously has been on a long vacation from American reality. Norplant would be administered, as it is said, on a non-discriminatory basis, meaning there is no room for discriminations between good and bad, right and wrong. There must be, as policy guidelines would make clear, no "judgmental" connotation attached to getting a Norplant—the rules of self-esteem require that. In sum, great effort would be expended in making sure it is understood that Norplant and the sexual promiscuity it is intended to facilitate are perfectly acceptable.

RACIST CONNOTATIONS OF NORPLANT POLICIES

To be sure, many Americans think it is more acceptable for "their" teenagers than for ours. The racist caricature of inner-city black teenagers as incorrigibly rutting animals is no part of Mr. Besharov's argument, but it is an undeniable part of the public discussion of Norplant, condom distribution, and related policies. Those who live at the bottom margin of society, where the fragility of behavioral norms is most pronounced, are most in need of encouragement. What they do not need is a message from the larger society, conveyed through public policies such as the use of Norplant, that nothing better is expected of them.

There are other considerations that Mr. Besharov does not address adequately. He touches all too lightly, for example, on the epidemic of venereal diseases (now called sexually transmitted diseases or STDs). Some 65 per cent of STDs are found among teenagers, some of them resulting in sterility or even in death. Norplant is of no help in resisting STDs, and the sexual behavior that it facilitates is the very means of infection. Mr. Besharov also neglects the documented relationship between sexual promiscuity among teenagers and failing grades, drug and alcohol abuse, increased suicide rates, and other "at risk" behavior. The entire society has a large stake in teenagers growing up to form stable and healthy marriages. Policies that have the effect of "normalizing" promiscuity make that goal much less likely.

Mr. Besharov notes the explosion of abortion rates after the 1973 *Roe vs. Wade* decision. Abortion is legal, many thought, therefore abortion is all right and therefore abortion rates soared. But policies and their consequences can move in other directions. For instance, we know that, in states that require parental consent for abortion, both teenage abortion rates and teenage pregnancy rates fall dramatically. What changes once can be changed again. "Each year," Mr. Besharov writes, "teenagers have another 400,000 abortions and 300,000 babies out of wedlock." There is nothing inevitable about that. It was not the case 25 years ago and it need not be the case ten years from now.

The Norplant proposal leans in one direction, aiming to contain the damage of the allegedly inevitable, and I suggest we should lean in the other, determined to reduce both abortions and out-of-wedlock births by challenging the sexual license that is the source of both.

"In the case of teen-age pregnancies, all that is needed is thorough and systematic enforcement of laws pertaining to statutory rape."

ENFORCING STATUTORY RAPE LAWS CAN HELP REDUCE TEEN PREGNANCY

Ralph deToledano

Statutory rape laws prohibit adults from engaging in sex with minors and, in some cases, forbid teenagers from having sex with each other. In the following viewpoint, Ralph deToledano promotes the vigorous enforcement of these laws as an effective way to reduce the incidence of teenage pregnancy. If males knew they faced fines or imprisonment for having sex with teenage girls, he contends, a significant number of teenage pregnancies would be averted. DeToledano is a syndicated columnist.

As you read, consider the following questions:

1. In the author's opinion, if a teenage girl becomes pregnant, what should she be required to do?
2. According to deToledano, what should the government require of males who father illegitimate children?
3. How does deToledano characterize the "New Morality"?

Reprinted from Ralph deToledano, "Teen-Age Mothers: Lots of Talk, Little Action," *Conservative Chronicle*, August 28, 1996, by permission of Ralph deToledano and Creators Syndicate.

Teen-age pregnancies, as well as those of women 19–23, continue to be both a social problem and a drain on federal, state and municipal budgets. The annual rate of these pregnancies continues to zoom—some 5 percent a year—but all that Congress and state legislatures have done about it is to wring their collective hands. Now there will be more viewing with alarm as a 24-member bipartisan congressional [committee] ponders the situation, seeking to throw more laws and more money at the problem.

"The explosion of out-of-wedlock teen births is a moral crisis that threatens to undermine our nation," says Rep. Nita Lowry, a leader of the Congressional Advisory Panel to the National Campaign to Reduce Teen-Age Pregnancy. But Robert Rector, an analyst at the Heritage Foundation, adds: "The reality is, most of out-of-wedlock births occur to women age 19 to 23—and this is what cuts into the taxpayer's pocket the most."

So we will get more talk, but little action. And the fact is that out-of-wedlock pregnancies could be cut down dramatically without passage of a single new law.

ENFORCING STATUTORY RAPE LAWS

In the case of teen-age pregnancies, all that is needed is thorough and systematic enforcement of laws pertaining to statutory rape. A girl of 16 and under has, by law, been raped, whether she consented to or even initiated the sex act. She should be required to name and testify against the male, of any age, who should be prosecuted for rape and given the maximum penalty. Once upon a time, this was done routinely, but the liberal bleeding hearts have tied the hands of police, prosecutors and the government agencies that handle and subsidize these pregnancies.

If these predatory males knew for certain that they would face prison and fines for every casual roll in the hay, you would see a tremendous decline in the teen-age pregnancies that result. In addition to fines and imprisonment, these men can be compelled to support their illegitimate offspring, which would free government from becoming surrogate parents.

As for the women in the 19 to 23 age range, they too can be required to name the father of their child, to the attending physician. An unwed mother who goes on welfare should be required to name the father of her child, and he could be traced through his Social Security number if he became a fugitive from his parental responsibility. He cannot be made to marry the woman he has made pregnant, but he can be compelled to support his child. With this over their heads, men would be less prone to indulge in casual and irresponsible liaisons. The financial burdens of out-of-wedlock sex would pass from the welfare system to the individual involved.

A RETURN TO RESPONSIBILITY

One would think that the women's-fibbers and the organized feminists would be gung-ho for the enforcement of now-existent laws to protect girls and young women from what is largely their victimization. It would do far more for the status of women than the campaign against domestic violence.

ADULT MEN ARE CAUSING TEEN PREGNANCIES

The problem with teen sex is not simply that teens are having sex. Adults, in disturbing numbers, are having sex with teens. . . . Federal and state surveys suggest that adult males are the fathers of some two-thirds of the babies born to teenage girls. According to the Alan Guttmacher Institute, 39 percent of 15-year-old mothers say the fathers of their babies are 20 years old or older. For 17-year-old teenage moms, 55 percent of the fathers are adults; for 19-year-olds, it is 78 percent.

Joseph P. Shapiro, *U.S. News & World Report*, August 14, 1995.

But we live in a time, brought on by liberal ideology, in which all the talk is of rights and none of responsibilities. In the past, men and women flouted the moral and social standards of the community. But if it ended in trouble, they did not go running to a governmental Daddy to bail them out. If a man got a woman pregnant, there were social pressures to make him marry her or to provide for the child. That is, if the man could not push the woman into having an abortion.

THE "NEW MORALITY"

But the New Morality, stemming from Havelock Ellis, Freud and feminist "liberationism," has cheapened human relations and made sex about as significant as chewing gum. People have a "right" to act as irresponsibly as they wish—and then to send the bill to the government. Men and women are "entitled" to having society pay for their carelessness—and the cost be damned.

To do otherwise is to destroy the individual's "self-esteem." To listen to the New Moralists, social restraints are a form of fascism—and to be concerned over what people do in the privacy of the bedroom or the parked car, no matter what the cost to society or to the individuals involved, is unconstitutional and a violation of the Rights of Man.

So we will have congressional commissions and perhaps hearings by Senate and House Committees. There will be much alarmist talk. But nothing will be done to enforce the laws now on the books for fear that it will upset the American Civil Liberties Union, Hillary Clinton and the liberal media. And the incidence of out-of-wedlock pregnancies, paid for by your taxes and mine, will increase.

And the wringing of hands, the viewing with alarm, will go on, ad infinitum and ad nauseam, until people begin really to care.

> *"As a remedy for teen pregnancy, . . .*
> *the crusade against statutory rape is*
> *. . . impractical."*

ENFORCING STATUTORY RAPE LAWS WILL NOT REDUCE TEEN PREGNANCY

Catherine Elton

Enforcing statutory rape laws, which prohibit adults from having sex with minors, has been promoted by some as an effective method for deterring teenage pregnancy. In the following viewpoint, Catherine Elton asserts that the enforcement of statutory rape laws would only avert a small percentage of teenage pregnancies. Furthermore, she contends, cases of statutory rape are nearly impossible to prosecute because teenage girls are often reluctant to testify against their older boyfriends. Elton is a writer for the *New Republic*, a weekly magazine that offers opinions on political and social issues.

As you read, consider the following questions:

1. According to statistics cited by Elton, how many fifteen- to seventeen-year-old unmarried teenage girls have babies fathered by men at least four years older?
2. What does Elton propose as an appropriate alternative in some cases to enforcing statutory rape laws?
3. Why do advocates for teen mothers worry about the enforcement of statutory rape laws, in the author's opinion?

Reprinted from Catherine Elton, "Jail Baiting," *The New Republic*, October 20, 1997, ©1997 The New Republic, Inc., by permission.

When a Wisconsin prosecutor charged 19-year-old Kevin Gillson with sexual assault for impregnating his 15-year-old girlfriend, it was widely seen as a case of prosecutorial discretion gone awry. "The insanity of this so-called abuse prosecution speaks for itself," the *St. Petersburg Times* editorialized. Noting that Gillson's name would be entered into a national registry for sex offenders even though he planned to marry his girlfriend and help raise the child, *The Milwaukee Journal Sentinel*, like many observers, pleaded "for judicial mercy."

But while the Gillson case was extreme, it was nonetheless emblematic of a new trend: fighting teen pregnancy through tougher statutory rape laws. California, Delaware, Florida, and Georgia have all passed legislation beefing up existing laws prohibiting sex with girls under the age of consent. In his State of the State address, Republican California Governor Pete Wilson declared, "It's not macho to get a teenager pregnant, but if you lack the decency to understand this yourself we'll give you a year to think about it in county jail." Wilson has dedicated $8.4 million to the Statutory Rape Vertical Prosecution program, which now boasts 827 convictions. (Prior to this, one California official told me, prosecuting statutory rape "just wasn't happening.") The federal government has jumped on the bandwagon, too: the 1996 Welfare Reform Act contained a provision calling for states to "aggressively enforce statutory rape laws," while the attorney general has called the issue a "high priority."

AN "EPIDEMIC" OF ADULT MEN PREYING ON TEENAGE GIRLS

The trend's genesis lies in a handful of studies, published in 1995 while the nation was knee-deep in the welfare reform debate, which revealed that as many as two-thirds of teenage girls who became pregnant did so by adult men. As the two-thirds number became famous, politicians suggested what they thought was an obvious remedy: prosecute the "predatory males," not merely to set an example but also to keep them from striking again. But applying this theory has proven far more difficult than the politicians ever imagined. There are clearly cases in which relationships between older men and younger women are inappropriate, but determining which relationships fall into that category requires moral judgments about which Americans are sincerely, and deeply, divided. Even in the most egregious cases, criminalizing the behavior may be too extreme a response.

To understand why, go back to the studies for a moment. They did not really show—as many politicians seemed to think—that there was an epidemic of older men preying upon school-aged girls. According to a study by the Urban Institute, a well-respected authority on these matters, 62 percent of teen pregnancies (births to 15- to 19-year-olds) involve 18- or 19-year-old mothers. What's more, only 27 percent of babies born to girls who are 15, 16, or 17 are fathered by men at least five years older; 23 percent of the pregnant 15- to 17-year-olds with partners five or more years older are married when they give birth. The Urban Institute concluded that "only 8 percent [of teen pregnancies] involved unmarried women aged 15 to 17 and men who were at least five years older," and that only 13 percent of all pregnancies to unmarried 15- to 17-year-olds are fathered by men at least four years older.

STATUTORY RAPE LAWS ARE APPLIED UNEQUALLY

Law enforcement officials apply the [statutory rape] law principally against two groups: men, frequently older, who have sex with girls from "good homes"; and minority men, who are punished if they commit the crime of having sex with white women or impregnate a woman of color under circumstances that add to the welfare rolls.

Richard Delgato, *ABA Journal*, August 1996.

Even within this small group, prosecutors are finding it hard to get convictions, for it's often not clear whether the girls are really "victims." "Juries have trouble with these cases because they think teenagers lie, they think she manipulated him, and jurors think she looks older," says Sharon Elstein, coordinator of a forthcoming American Bar Association (ABA) study on the issue. "They wonder why the court is wasting its time."

While the relationship between, say, a 15-year-old girl and a 21-year-old man may strike a prosecutor as inherently coercive, it doesn't instantly resonate as criminal among a jury of peers. "When you meet the 20-year-old and the 13-year-old you are surprised," says Mike Males, an author of one of the first studies to pinpoint the two-thirds figure. "Thirteen-year-olds are portrayed as gum-chewing, braces-wearing twits and the 20-year-olds are supposed to be more mature. Very often this is not the case."

Of course, many times the girls don't see themselves as victims, and this is enough to scare off many prosecutors: it's hard to convict when the victim blows kisses to the defendant or leaves the courtroom holding his hand. But the ABA found that one-quarter of prosecutors it surveyed would pursue action regardless. Rick Trunfio, an assistant district attorney in Syracuse,

New York, is one such prosecutor: he had been aggressively taking on these cases even before it became fashionable in the media. In a community of 500,000, his office prosecutes 100 to 150 cases per year; 80 percent of the time, he wins some kind of a conviction (sometimes to a lesser crime). Not prosecuting because of uncooperative victims is, in Trunfio's eyes, a "cop-out." "That's what subpoenas are for," he says without hesitation, noting that he's willing to subpoena not just a victim but her diaries and her love letters, too.

ENFORCING STATUTORY RAPE LAWS IS IMPRACTICAL

Trunfio and other zealous prosecutors liken their cause to the fight against domestic violence. There was, after all, a time when society would refuse to prosecute a man who beat his wife because the victim did not want to cooperate. But in some teen sex cases, it's probably more appropriate to encourage the "victim" to marry the older male—and get out of her parents' unstable home—than to prosecute the father. During the summer of 1996, for example, in Orange County, California, social service workers and a juvenile court even recommended a pregnant 13-year-old marry her 20-year-old boyfriend because it provided more stability than her current lifestyle of skipping school and abusing drugs. "We are hearing these guys are exploitative, opportunistic predators," says Elstein, "but it's not all like that. Sometimes this is the best thing that's ever happened to her."

Perhaps, as Trunfio argues, there is something inherently exploitative about a relationship between an older man or boy and a young teenage girl. But advocates for teen mothers also worry that, if the state really begins to crack down on statutory rape, girls will stop coming in for prenatal care because they fear somebody might report their boyfriends.

And then, of course, there is the concern about disproportionate punishment for men. Since statutory rape is a sex crime, many of those convicted must register as sexual offenders. But is it really fair to lump a 20-year-old who got a 15-year-old pregnant together with child molesters? As a political rallying cry, prosecuting statutory rape offered politicians a chance to attack a modern-day problem with a traditional sounding solution. As a remedy for teen pregnancy, however, the crusade against statutory rape is not only impractical, but it often has a far different impact than intended. "[T]hanks to the court system," Gillson's young fiancée said in a statement read into the court record, "I have lost the love of my life and the father of my unborn baby."

| "Welfare is illegitimacy's economic life support system."

ENDING WELFARE WILL HELP REDUCE TEEN PREGNANCY

William J. Bennett and Peter Wehner

William J. Bennett and Peter Wehner argue in the following viewpoint that the welfare system encourages out-of-wedlock births, many of which are to teenage mothers. If welfare benefits were eliminated, the authors maintain, the number of young single women having babies would fall dramatically. Bennett is a codirector of Empower America, a free market political advocacy organization, and the author of *The Book of Virtues*. Wehner is the director of policy at Empower America.

As you read, consider the following questions:

1. According to the authors, what important moral principle is behind the proposed policy to end welfare?
2. What evidence do Bennett and Wehner offer for the failure of the welfare system?
3. In the authors' opinion, what should be the point of welfare reform?

Reprinted from William J. Bennett and Peter Wehner, "Let's Outlaw Welfare for Unmarried Mothers," *Newsday*, February 3, 1994, by permission of the authors.

Republicans should propose legislation that ends welfare for anyone having a child out of wedlock. Our preference is to end, one year after the legislation is passed, all forms of economic support for single mothers who have new children. [The Welfare Reform bill of 1996 required that teenage mothers live at home or attend school in order to collect welfare benefits, but did not abolish temporary aid to single mothers.]

These would include Aid to Families with Dependent Children, subsidized housing and food stamps, an end to all forms of assistance for those single mothers currently on welfare, an end to visitation rights for illegitimate fathers and a change in tax codes to make them more favorable to marriage and children. The specifics are less important than the end game; somewhere soon we want welfare to end, and when it does we can judge these policies, and their broad social consequences, against reality.

HAVING CHILDREN OUT OF WEDLOCK IS WRONG

These proposed policy changes are based on an important moral principle: Having children out of wedlock is wrong—not simply economically unwise for the individuals involved or a financial burden on society, but morally wrong.

Even Secretary of Health and Human Services Donna Shalala, she of impeccable liberal credentials, said in an interview: "I don't like to put this in moral terms, but I do believe that having children out of wedlock is just wrong."

By the year 2000, according to the most reliable projections, 40 percent of all American births and 80 percent of minority births will be illegitimate. These numbers have frightening social implications. Welfare may not cause illegitimacy, but it does make it economically practical. There is hardly any question illegitimacy rates would fall—probably dramatically—if aid-to-dependent-children payments were stopped. Welfare is illegitimacy's economic life support system.

THE WELFARE SYSTEM SHOULD BE ENDED

Social scientist Charles Murray, in a 1993 *Wall Street Journal* article, went beyond the unwed-mother issue. He called for ending the current welfare system outright. His views had an explosive effect, and set off a chain reaction that transformed the welfare debate. We are now at one of those rare political moments when a fundamental, even radical, and positive change in public policy is possible.

That reform of this magnitude is possible can be explained

largely by widespread acceptance of overwhelming empirical evidence: The current welfare system is a complete failure. Over the last three decades, we have spent enormous sums of money on welfare programs, and what do we have to show for it? An underclass that is much larger, more violent and more poorly educated and consisting of many more single-parent families.

Reprinted by permission of Chuck Asay and Creators Syndicate.

Reaction to Murray's article was overwhelmingly favorable, including positive reaction from some unlikely places. Here is what President Bill Clinton said in an interview about welfare's fiercest and most prominent critic:

"[Murray] did the country a great service. He and I have often disagreed, but I think his analysis is essentially right. . . . There's no question that [ending welfare payments to single mothers] would work. The question is . . . is it morally right?"

Clinton's embrace of the Murray analysis means the intellectual debate over welfare policy is essentially over; we are now debating the relative merits of changing the current system vs. dismantling it. . . .

Welfare Encourages Illegitimacy

The point [of welfare reform] is not to ensure tougher work provisions and job training; rather, it is to go after a system that fosters illegitimacy and its attendant social pathologies. Making adoption easier is an essential and compassionate part of this effort. Adoption is the best alternative we have to protecting a child's interest in a post-welfare world. The demand for adoption is virtually unlimited, but society has made adoption exceedingly difficult. Lifting restrictions on interracial adoption and easing age limitations for adoptive parents will help ensure that large numbers of children will be adopted into good, stable, loving homes. And for older children, we must invest generously in the kind of orphanages and group homes that provide order and care.

Ending welfare in this way is prudent, humane and politically smart. It would be prudent because the social science evidence is in: Illegitimacy is the surest road to economic poverty and social decay. And welfare subsidizes and sustains illegitimacy. . . .

The current welfare system is the most pernicious government program of the last quarter-century. We have lost large parts of an entire generation because of the human wreckage left in its wake. Enough is enough. It's time to pull the plug.

> "[Eliminating welfare] may have the perverse and unintended consequence of encouraging some of the conditions . . . associated with teen pregnancy—principally poverty and and family dysfunction."

ENDING WELFARE WILL NOT REDUCE TEEN PREGNANCY

Kristin A. Moore

In the following viewpoint, Kristin A. Moore contends that abolishing the welfare system will do nothing to prevent teenage pregnancy. In fact, the author claims, as welfare benefits have been scaled back, teenage pregnancy has increased—a statistic that defies the notion that welfare encourages teen pregnancies. Moore is executive director of Child Trends, Inc., a research organization dedicated to studying children, youth, and families.

As you read, consider the following questions:

1. According to Moore, what four factors promote teenage pregnancy?
2. What does the author cite as two consequences of cutting welfare to teenage mothers?
3. In the author's opinion, how should long-term welfare dependency of teenage mothers be discouraged?

Reprinted from Kristin A. Moore, "Welfare Bill Won't Stop Teenage Pregnancy," *The Christian Science Monitor*, Opinion/Essays, December 18, 1995, by permission of the author.

Among the most controversial [issues in the United States] is the question of what role welfare plays in encouraging teenage pregnancy and childbearing. About one-half of women on welfare were teens when they had their first child. In general, teenage mothers are much less likely than their childless peers to complete high school and much more likely to need long-term support.

Does this mean welfare promotes teen pregnancy? Those who say yes argue you get more of what you subsidize. But if this were the case, one would expect teen birth rates to have declined in recent years, as welfare benefits have shrunk. Instead, births to teenagers have increased. The argument that welfare encourages teen births also suggests that European countries, which offer more generous benefits than the US, should have higher rates of teenage childbirths. Yet they don't.

WHAT PROMOTES TEEN PREGNANCY?

So if welfare doesn't promote teen pregnancy, what does? Overwhelmingly, evidence points to four underlying factors, none of which are addressed by cutting welfare to teenage parents. These factors are: 1) early school failure, 2) early behavior problems, 3) poverty, and 4) family dysfunction. Study after study finds a strong link between these four conditions and early sexual activity, teenage pregnancy, and adolescent parenthood.

As early as elementary school, children who have trouble in school often become frustrated and exhibit behavior problems. As school success becomes less attainable, they may see little value in playing by the rules that help other students get ahead. Over time, some grow susceptible to dangerous influences in their neighborhoods and schools and to negative messages in the news media and popular culture. Too often, the results are drug and alcohol use, violence, and early and unprotected sex, which can lead to teen pregnancy.

Poor children, in particular, may feel less hopeful about the future and may therefore see less reason than more-affluent children to delay childbearing until after marriage—or at least until they are financially able to support a child. Data on teen pregnancy and childbearing consistently show that adolescents in poor families and communities tend to initiate sexual intercourse at a younger age, to use contraceptives less effectively, and to have more unintended pregnancies.

Finally, children in dysfunctional families are at higher risk of early pregnancy. Their parents often fail to provide adequate supervision, to communicate effectively with their children, to teach strong values, and to educate them about how and why to delay sex and parenthood. Most dramatically, severely dysfunctional families may fail to protect their daughters from unwanted sexual advances. Increasingly, studies indicate many girls' initial sexual experiences are coercive. A majority of girls whose first sexual experiences occurred before age 15 report that these incidents were not voluntary.

CUTTING WELFARE WILL NOT INFLUENCE TEEN BEHAVIOR

If you have ever spent time around adolescents, you know that long-range planning is not one of their strong points. It is ridiculous to believe that denying welfare benefits to [teenage] mothers . . . will cut the rate of illegitimate births.

Cynthia Tucker, *Liberal Opinion*, January 30, 1995.

As the nation turns again to the difficult question of how to discourage welfare dependency, these findings have at least two important implications. First, cutting welfare to teenage parents will probably do little to discourage teen sex, pregnancy, and childbearing. Second, it may have the perverse and unintended consequence of encouraging some of the conditions research shows are associated with teen pregnancy—principally poverty and family dysfunction.

What, then, can we do to discourage long-term welfare dependency? Research suggests a very different set of proposals than those under discussion.

HOW SHOULD WELFARE DEPENDENCY BE DISCOURAGED?

First, start early, to ensure that children enter school with the skills they need to succeed. Second, support parents in the tough job of raising and protecting their children. Third, focus on males as well as females, including men in their 20s, since they are the sexual partners of a large proportion of teenage girls. Fourth, encourage abstinence, but also provide contraceptive information to kids who do have sex. (Research indicates that the most effective sex education programs combine the teaching of abstinence with information on contraception.) Most important, invest time and resources in teens so they will perceive opportunities for themselves and realize the value of staying in school and building a positive future.

Cutting welfare benefits to teen mothers may "end welfare as we know it," but it won't end the underlying problem of teenage pregnancy and childbearing. Meeting that challenge will require a broader and more sustained effort.

PERIODICAL BIBLIOGRAPHY

The following articles have been selected to supplement the diverse views presented in this chapter. Addresses are provided for periodicals not indexed in the *Readers' Guide to Periodical Literature*, the *Alternative Press Index*, the *Social Sciences Index*, or the *Index to Legal Periodicals and Books*.

James Brooke — "Idaho County Finds Way to Chastise Pregnant Teen-Agers: They Go to Court," *New York Times*, October 28, 1996.

William F. Buckley Jr. — "Zounds! Enforcing the Law in Idaho!" *National Review*, August 12, 1996.

Arthur J. Delaney — "The Grotesque World of Today's Sex Education," *New Oxford Review*, May 1996. Available from 1069 Kains Ave., Berkeley, CA 94706.

Elizabeth Gleick — "Putting the Jail in Jailbait," *Time*, January 29, 1996.

Ellen Goodman — "The Revival of 'Shotgun' Marriage," *Liberal Opinion Week*, September 23, 1996. Available from PO Box 880, Vinton, IA 52349-0880.

Debra W. Haffner — "What's Wrong with Abstinence—Only Sexuality Education Programs?" *SIECUS Report*, April 1, 1997. Available from 130 W. 42nd St., Suite 350, New York, NY 10036-7802.

David J. Kalke — "It's Our Duty to Give Away Condoms," *New York Times*, July 8, 1995.

Jane Mauldon and Kristin Luker — "Does Liberalism Cause Sex?" *American Prospect*, Winter 1996.

Ellen Perlman — "The Mother of All Welfare Problems," *Governing*, January 1997.

John Sheffield — "WARNING: Your Theology May Be Fatal to Your Kids," *U.S. Catholic*, July 1996.

Kathleen Sylvester — "Preventable Calamity: How to Reduce Teenage Pregnancy," *USA Today*, March 1997.

Gerald Unks — "Will Schools Risk Teaching About the Risk of AIDS?" *Clearing House*, March 13, 1996. Available from Customer Service, 1319 18th St. NW, Washington, DC 20036.

WHAT ROLE DO THE MEDIA AND GOVERNMENT PLAY IN THE PROBLEM OF TEEN SUBSTANCE ABUSE?

CHAPTER PREFACE

Since the 1980s, drug education programs have become commonplace throughout American schools. The most popular of these programs is DARE (Drug Abuse Resistance Education), which is offered in nearly 75 percent of the nation's school districts. In the DARE program, taught primarily to fifth- and sixth-grade students, a specially trained police officer comes to a classroom once a week for seventeen consecutive weeks. Students are given lessons that include information about the dangers of drug use, role-playing exercises, and group discussions. Variations of the curriculum are taught from kindergarten through high school.

Although DARE is popular, many people question its effectiveness. For example, journalist Jeff Elliott argues that the statistics presented in the lessons are inaccurate. In addition, he contends, the role-playing lessons are not realistic: "When Maggie [a student] role-plays saying no to Officer Campbell, she reinforces her skills at turning down drugs from a uniformed policeman. Not a likely real-life scenario."

The result, these critics assert, is that DARE fails to reduce juvenile drug use. As evidence, they cite reports such as the 1997 *Monitoring the Future Study*, which indicates that drug use among high school seniors has risen since 1994. In that year, 38 percent of high school seniors reported that they had used marijuana or hashish sometime during their life. In 1997, half of all seniors had used marijuana. Being a DARE graduate may even increase the likelihood of drug use, critics maintain. They cite one study that shows DARE graduates are more likely than nongraduates to use marijuana.

Although some studies question DARE's effectiveness, others have indicated positive results. A 1995 evaluation in South Carolina concluded that 77 percent of DARE graduates in one county were not using drugs four years after receiving instruction. Even critics maintain that DARE can succeed. A 1994 study by the Research Triangle Institute (RTI) found that DARE deterred alcohol, tobacco, or drug use in only 3 percent of its participants. However, RTI praised the program's organization and community support and concluded that with some modifications, including more interactive methods, the program can be effective.

Drug education programs are only one factor influencing teen drug use. Other variables include government antidrug efforts and media portrayals of drug use. These and related issues are examined in the following chapter.

| "Material legitimizing drugs can be found in music, film, television, the Internet and mass market outlets."

THE MEDIA ENCOURAGE TEEN SUBSTANCE ABUSE

Barry R. McCaffrey

In the following viewpoint, Barry R. McCaffrey argues that the substance abuse problem among teenagers is due in part to the influence of the media. McCaffrey asserts that sophisticated pro-drug messages are imparted to youths through music, television, the Internet, and other media. He maintains that while free speech must be protected, the media have the obligation to present the dangerous consequences of drug use accurately. McCaffrey is the director of the Office of National Drug Control Policy.

As you read, consider the following questions:
1. How many millions of Americans use drugs regularly, according to the author?
2. In McCaffrey's view, how does the speed of mass communication affect news reporting on the drug abuse issue?
3. According to McCaffrey, what is the biggest challenge faced by those who are combatting the irresponsible portrayal of drugs in the media?

Reprinted from Barry R. McCaffrey, "Mass Manipulation of Young Minds," Los Angeles Times, January 2, 1997.

In our national effort to combat substance abuse, the entertainment industry has often been targeted unfairly as the creator of a popular culture that sends inappropriate drug messages to youth. The truth is, Hollywood writers, producers and directors are parents, community leaders and educators—in the best sense of the word—just like the rest of us. Culture is a joint product that the media reflect as much as invent. In fact, most mass media mirror an America envied around the globe. Recent studies show that we do have a problem in terms of rising adolescent drug use, but blame should not be focused on one industry.

One study found that youngsters are less likely to turn to addictive drugs if they have a concerned adult spending time with them. In the wake of shattered families and the need for two-parent wage earners, the adults talking to our children frequently reach them through TV, film, video games, radio, music, the Internet and advertising. We call on the mass media to honor the highest ideals that make the creative arts the repository of our collective cultural heritage.

THE GROWTH IN SUBSTANCE ABUSE

While overall drug use in America has declined for the last 15 years, from 23 million regular users to 12 million, substance abuse among young people has grown since 1992. One-third of eighth-graders report the use of illicit drugs, including inhalants. About 15% admit to having drunk more than five alcoholic beverages in a row during the previous two weeks. The National Survey on Drug Abuse found that marijuana was used by 77% of current drug users (9.8 million of the estimated 12.8 million Americans who used an illicit drug during the month prior to being interviewed). The report, "Cigarettes, Alcohol, Marijuana: Gateways to Illicit Drug Use," showed that children who used marijuana were 85 times more likely to use cocaine. Heroin use among adolescents has doubled. There are 3.6 million Americans hooked on cocaine, heroin, methamphetamines and new "designer" drugs.

In facing the challenge of drug abuse, the media have never been less monolithic. Fragmentation is rampant in the entertainment business. Vertical integration of media conglomerates adds pressure to the marketplace and the creative process. Cable television now cuts into network territory, and competition among stations means that less free air time is available for public service announcements to combat drug use. The number of these has dropped. Commercial forces work against children's programming, where positive role models can be presented, because advertising targets viewers aged 18 to 49 as the prime consumer market.

Changes in viewer habits have also worked against drug education. Channel surfing on a remote control leads TV watchers away from public service announcements.

THE SOPHISTICATION OF PRO-DRUG MEDIA

In general, the speed of mass communication mitigates against exploring an issue carefully as people's attention span decreases in correlation with shorter, rapid-fire presentation. ABC's Ted Koppel has noted that sound bites in news broadcasts have gone down from an average of 22 seconds to eight seconds. Furthermore, pro-drug messages are communicated to our children through the most sophisticated, multimedia techniques while anti-drug forces typically fight back with bumper stickers: that is, with one-dimensional approaches.

The intensification of media effects such as virtual reality has been coupled with a thirst for heightened experience and risk-taking in our culture. Exaggerated proportions and greater degrees of violence are related to this trend. This mentality provides the context for drug use either as a "high" beyond normal experience or as an instant solution to discomfort in a now-oriented society. The glamorization of drugs in "heroin chic" fashions encourages their use. Technology has made America stronger and faster in every respect; the demand for intensity and "speed" through drugs is a negative counterpart to these industrial changes.

THE MEDIA ARE COMPLACENT

The media must share the blame for the fact that so many kids today don't know the perils of drug abuse. When today's teenagers were toddlers, I personally produced two prize-wining television specials about the curse of drug abuse. . . .

These days, no one is clamoring for TV shows or magazine articles about drug abuse. "Been there, done that" is the prevailing attitude.

Carl Rowan, *Liberal Opinion Week*, September 9, 1996.

There have been excellent initiatives such as the push for three hours a week of educational programming, some of which can be devoted to drug education. Mediascope, a nonprofit organization that promotes social and health issues, published a nationwide study of media violence. A similar, quantified study of drugs in the media would be useful. In addition there has been considerable interest in media literacy so that children and parents alike will understand how subtle messages influence viewers. ABC, HBO and the Academy of Television Arts and Sciences are developing excellent antidrug campaigns. Programs like ER and NYPD Blue usually depict public health issues accurately, showing the results of destructive behavior. However, the biggest challenge we face today is a willingness by some in the entertainment industry to produce whatever sells.

THE MEDIA'S INFLUENCE

Unfortunately, material legitimizing drugs can be found in music, film, television, the Internet and mass market outlets. Fortunately, consumers are reacting to objectionable messages, and chains like Wal-Mart and Blockbuster Video have decided not to stock CDs and tapes with offensive content.

The influence of the media should not be underestimated. By mid-adolescence, kids have watched about 15,000 hours of television—more time than they spend with teachers in school. Add to that figure the hours devoted to video games, watching tapes on the VCR, listening to the radio and attending movies, and the media's impact becomes primary.

Concerns have arisen periodically in this country over media content. In the continuing dialogue, extremes have been presented on both sides. Free speech as guaranteed in the 1st Amendment to the Constitution must be protected. However, the news and entertainment industries owe it to our youth to portray realistically the dangerous consequences of illegal drug use. Writers and producers of comedy series might think about the impact of "wink and nod" acceptance of illegal drugs as well as blatant pro-drug messages that put teens at risk. A spirit of cooperation is the key to a constructive partnership between the media and the public. The Office of National Drug Control Policy offers support and elicits help in our national challenge to beat back the problem of illegal drugs that threaten America's children.

"Contrary to the official/media
script, . . . drug abusers are not
getting younger and younger, but
older and older."

THE MEDIA EXAGGERATE THE EXTENT
OF TEEN SUBSTANCE ABUSE

Mike Males

The press misstates the true extent of America's drug problem,
Mike Males claims in the following viewpoint. Males contends
that teenage drug use is not a serious problem; instead, he
maintains, the actual drug crisis is among adults. According to
Males, adults over age thirty-five represent a significant percentage of overdose deaths and emergency room admittances. In
contrast, he maintains, only a small percentage of teenagers use
illegal drugs. Males argues that the media are too eager to help
politicians blame youths for the nation's drug problem instead
of focusing on the dangers of adult drug use. Males is the
author of *The Scapegoat Generation: America's War on Adolescents.*

As you read, consider the following questions:

1. According to statistics cited by Males, what percentage of
   heroin-related emergency room cases in 1995 were due to
   drug use by patients over age thirty-five?
2. What percentage of youths do not use cocaine or heroin,
   according to the author?
3. What does Males think is the scariest aspect of the media's
   failure to acknowledge the adult drug problem?

Reprinted from Mike Males, "Another Anti-teen Fix," *Extra!* November/December 1996,
by permission of *Extra!*

With all the obedient indignation of *Pravda* blaring an official diatribe against enemies of the state, the U.S. media has thundered with headlines repeating the official line of an "exploding teenage drug crisis."

The Media Is Anti-Youth

At least the old Soviet journalists could claim they had no better source of information than state propaganda. What made the American media's anti-youth rampage so reprehensible was that the press did have better information right in reporters' hands. The officials who orchestrated the latest press frenzy actually distributed the excellent 1995 Drug-Related Emergency Department Episodes report by the Drug Abuse Warning Network (DAWN) and the 1995 National Household Survey on Drug Abuse by the U.S. Department of Health and Human Services—confident that few in the press would actually read them.

This official smugness was justified. The press ignored what the reports said and reported only what drug-war interests said the reports said. Shrieking headlines of skyrocketing teen-drug use dutifully ensued, as they do on schedule most every August and December when politicians dispense the latest survey. The media's Teen Armageddon theme was founded in the 1995 Household Survey's finding that 8.2 percent of 12–17-year-olds said they had used marijuana in the previous month, up from 1992's level of 3.4 percent.

Had reporters taken minimal time to examine the data with care (instead of charging out to assess how the hullabaloo affected the Bob Dole–Bill Clinton race), they would have unearthed far more startling and disturbing facts about America's real drug malaise. Contrary to the official/media script, the new reports reconfirmed that drug abusers are not getting younger and younger, but older and older. Said the Household Survey in an ignored finding on "the aging cohort of drug users" whose "severe drug problems" dominate the statistics: "In 1979, 12 percent of patients with cocaine episodes were age 35 and older. By 1985, the percentage was 19, and by 1995 it was 43." For heroin, 55 percent of the emergency room cases in 1995 were over age 35, up from 40 percent just seven years earlier.

The DAWN report revealed that in 1995, the rate of ER treatments for cocaine, heroin and marijuana abuse was about the same for teens and young adults (ages 12–25) as it was in the late '80s—despite all the press nostalgia for Nancy Reagan's "just say no" crusades. But during the last seven years, drug emergencies rose by 150 percent among those over age 35. A whopping 96 percent of the 140,000 hospital ER episodes for cocaine, heroin and marijuana in the first half of 1995 involved adults, and four-fifths involved adults over age 26.

STABLE TEENAGE DRUG USE

Rates of teenagers going to ER for drugs were low and stable in 1995, while those of adults were high and rising—exactly the opposite of what the press reported. The reason for the confusion: Officials cleverly released the new Household Survey at the same time they resurrected DAWN's three-month-old survey of hospital emergency treatments for drug abuse. Their evident hope was that reporters would mix the two surveys up, blame rising teen drug use for rising hospital admissions and ignore the much worse adult problem. The hoax worked like a charm.

Newsweek's eight-page cover-story spread (8/26/96) juxtaposed a chart of drug usage by eighth graders with one showing rising ER visits for heroin. USA Today's (8/20/96) lead sentence read: "Teenage drug abuse has risen sharply since 1992, accompanied by increasing visits to hospitals for drug-related emergencies." Stories in the New York Times (8/21/96) and Los Angeles Times (8/30/96) both linked the rise in drug ER trips to increased teen drug use.

The New York Times story asserted that the "steep decline" in adult drug abuse means fewer modern teens are scared away from drugs by the spectacle of debilitated adult addicts and quoted University of Michigan surveyor Lloyd Johnston: "This generation doesn't know about the dangers of drugs the way the last did." Read the reports! This generation of youths is seeing more drug abuse among its elders—14,000 deaths, half a million ER cases, and 1 million adults undergoing addiction treatment in 1995—than any generation since the late 1960s.

MOST YOUTHS DO NOT USE DRUGS

That may be exactly why the 1995 survey found that nine in 10 youths were not currently illegal drug users, and 99 percent were not users of harder drugs such as cocaine or heroin. The survey documented the low rate of heavy drug use among students as well as long-term studies showing that occasional marijuana use rarely evolves into more serious drug habits (Journal of Abnormal Psychology, 1/88; American Psychologist, 5/90).

The survey demolished the oft-repeated contention that using pot is the "gateway" to harder drugs. The survey reported that 65 million Americans age 12 and older, a legion including 100 percent of the occupants of the Oval Office and House Speakership, had tried marijuana—but only two million were current users of cocaine, crack, heroin or speed. That is, even if every hard-druggie started out smoking marijuana, fewer than 3 percent of marijuana smokers become hard-drug patrons.

Teenage marijuana use, past or present, was hardly a topic to generate headline clarions of doom. So routine is the experience in post-1960 America that Clinton's drug policy chief, Barry McCaffrey, admonished politicians jockeying to exploit drug hysteria to lay off berating their opponents' youthful drug use—the better to unite in berating today's youthful drug use.

ADULTS ARE THE GREATER DRUG RISK

Drug emergency room visits compiled by Drug Abuse Warning Network, 1993

Age	Cocaine	Heroin	Marijuana	Total	Rate*
6–11	7	2	na	9	< 0.1
12–17	1,583	282	4,293	6,158	29.8
18–25	22,077	7,912	9,656	39,645	133.7
26–34	52,715	21,127	9,342	83,184	215.0
35–44	37,477	25,792	4,540	67,809	170.0
45–54	7,669	6,561	959	15,189	55.4
55+	1,789	1,289	376	3,454	6.5
Total	123,317	62,965	29,166	215,448	92.8

*Drug-related ER episodes per 100,000 population in each age group.

Source: Substance Abuse and Mental Health Services Administration, *Preliminary Estimates of Drug-Related Emergency Department Episodes*, December 1994.

Nor, the reports showed, is the problem exclusive to aging "60s druggies." True, Clinton's older Baby Boom cohort, now age 45–54, suffered a skyrocketing death rate from abuse of harder street drugs (such as cocaine and heroin), which is now 13 times higher than found among 1995 high schoolers. But Bob Dole's generation of 55–75-year-olds, who supposedly abstained in their 1940s and 1950s youth, now display death tolls from cocaine and heroin more than double that of today's teens—and escalating rapidly.

If the media wanted to honestly examine the relatively low rate of teenage drug use and even lower rate of drug abuse, they would have focused on medical drugs, not street drugs. The media continue to omit the fascinating fact that in 1995, four times more teenagers received emergency drug treatment after ingesting aspirin or aspirin substitutes (such as Tylenol or Advil) than for all street drugs put together.

No Evidence of Heavy Drug Use

It would be worrisome if solid evidence showed that the young are taking up hard drugs such as barbiturates or heroin, or mixing them with another deadly hard drug, liquor—killer cocktails that sent tens of thousands to early graves in the '60s drug crisis. California, which has the nation's largest drug toll, provides detailed records. In 1970, a shocking 43 percent of California's drug overdose deaths were ages 10–24—nearly all from heroin, pills or dope with booze chasers (*California Vital Statistics,* 1970–94). Proof that when lots of young people abuse hard drugs, lots die.

But there is no indication, either from surveys, ER records, addiction treatment admissions or morgues, that today's young are indulging in the hard stuff in any significant numbers. In 1994, just 5 percent of California's drug overdose dead were under age 25.

But with a servile press, who needs evidence? Recent media have been awash in screams that a heroin craze is ensnaring teens and young adults en masse, including a *USA Today* article (7/19/96) that would embarrass the *National Enquirer.* The piece featured *Sassy* magazine editor Caroline Lettieri's intimation that every 14-year-old in Los Angeles was smoking black-tar smack. (If so, heroin must be safer than Tylenol: L.A. hospitals reported a total of 3,724 heroin emergency treatments in the most recent year, only 14 of which involved teens. But 330 L.A. teens wound up in [the] ER for Tylenol's effects).

USA Today's article brimmed with avowals by so-called "experts" that "heroin is the pot of the '90s" and that "smoking or snorting smack is as commonplace as beer for a younger generation." Right. Reporter Elizabeth Snead failed to cite the Household Survey's finding that only 0.2 percent of youths used heroin in the month before the survey—1/100th of the number who drank beer.

The Real Age of Heroin Users

Newsweek's (8/26/96) cover was graced by a 21-year-old former addict and proclaimed: "Heroin . . . Are Teens at Risk?" The story spent six pages terrorizing parents who "are right to be scared" that hordes of youths are primed by "pop culture images" to follow heroin-plagued celebrities over the cliff—absent evidence that anything of the sort was occurring. In truth, the story admitted in a couple of brief sentences, "kids on dope are still rare" and "most heroin users today are still old-timers."

The drug war's government/corporate fountain of disinformation, the Partnership for a Drug-Free America, launched a new campaign (and unabashed pitch for bucks) painting heroin as a youth scourge (*L.A. Times*, 7/30/96). None of the media hyperventilation mentioned the Household Survey's finding that the only age group to show a significantly "increasing rate of heroin smoking" is "adults age 35 and older." Nor Centers for Disease Control studies showing that much of contemporary heroin abuse is among Vietnam veterans whose postwar traumas were neglected by authorities (*Journal of the American Medical Association*, 2/13/87).

The real story is both the rarity of heroin abuse and the evolution of what was once a young man's drug into a 30-40-50-something peril. In 1995, 55 percent of heroin emergency cases involved persons over age 35. The most dramatic rise by far has been among this older group—up 175 percent since 1990. California, which accounts for nearly half the nation's heroin deaths, exemplifies the astonishing trend. In 1970, 44 percent of its heroin deaths involved victims under age 25; in 1994, just 3 percent did. Not one California teenager died of a heroin overdose in the entire year, as did only 17 adults age 20–24—compared to 485 over age 25.

Designated Scapegoats

The most striking feature of major media drug stories is their formulaic sameness—indeed, all were scripted by the same few officials and "experts." The media have embraced politicians' tacit ground rule that adolescents are Campaign '96's designated scapegoats, a free-fire zone to be blasted at will. Any politician or interest group may depict youth problems as mushrooming to boost their public images and win funding for their plans to meet the "crisis"; when they want to portray youth problems as declining, the press allows the same interests to grab credit. It's no-lose.

The scariest aspect is that the past half century suggests that epidemics of adult drug abuse forecast similar behaviors among the young. The late-1960s heroin and barbiturate crisis among young adults was preceded by a mushrooming toll of barbiturate addiction, overdose and suicide among grownups of their parents' generation, beginning in the late 1950s and fueled by irresponsible prescriptions issued by physicians. Then as now, officials ignored and denied the adult drug crisis, damaging both parents and their children. As a result, there may be a youth hard-drug crisis on the 1990s horizon as well—one promoted by official dereliction and the media's refusal to expose it, not occasional teen pot smokers.

The media hero of the 1996 drug furor is none other than Bush-era drug czar Bill Bennett, recovering nicotine addict and author of the 1989 National Drug Control Strategy, which ignored the plight of drug addicts and hard-drug abusers and instead demonized casual marijuana smokers (*Newsweek*, 8/26/96). None of the media mentioned the irony that the Clinton era has fully implemented Bennett's age- and race-tainted policy. During the 1992–94 period, arrests of teens for simple marijuana possession skyrocketed. Federal health and FBI Uniform Crime Reports (1994) show that a black teenager is only one-fifth as likely to die from drug abuse as a white adult, but is 10 times more likely to be arrested for drugs.

No matter. The media chastise Clinton for being soft on druggie kids and trumpet "Back to War" (*Newsweek*, 8/26/96). The latest round of stories featured reporters angrily denouncing teenagers: "What can you do when children just won't listen?" ABC News scolded in its August 20, 1996, lead story. A better question: What can you do when a free press just won't do its job?

"I'm convinced that the resurgence [in teen drug use] stems in part from the disappearance ... of effective national leadership in the fight against drug use."

An Inadequate Government Antidrug Effort Has Contributed to the Problem of Teen Drug Abuse

Rob Portman

In the following viewpoint, Rob Portman argues that the federal government is to blame for the growing problem of teenage drug use. He contends that, instead of reducing the extent of teen drug use, the actions taken by the federal government in the early 1990s worsened the problem. Due to this failure in national leadership, according to Portman, the problem must be dealt with at the community level. He maintains that members of Congress should encourage their constituents to work together on this issue. Portman is a Republican congressman from Ohio.

As you read, consider the following questions:

1. According to the author, what actions taken by President Bill Clinton led to a rise in teenage drug use?
2. Why does Portman want businesses involved in community coalitions?
3. In the author's view, what role can the federal government play in fighting drug abuse?

Abridged from Rob Portman, "Addicted to Failure," *Policy Review*, September/October 1996, by permission of *Policy Review*.

In 1995, a 16-year-old constituent of mine, Jeff Gardner, died from a lethal combination of "huffing" gasoline and smoking marijuana. After Jeff's death, his mother, who was aware of a much larger drug problem in the community, called a parent's meeting at the local high school. No one came. She told me her story and asked how her representative in Congress was going to help address the growing drug problem. It was a fair question, but I was not satisfied with the response I could give her.

GOVERNMENT LEADERSHIP IS NEEDED TO REDUCE DRUG USE

Members of Congress take seriously their responsibility to represent their constituents in Washington—by legislating, by voting, and when appropriate, by securing federal funding for state and local concerns. Despite spending $13 billion annually on drug-control programs, however, drug abuse is rising dramatically among our youth (see chart).

A big part of the problem has been President Bill Clinton's failure to show any leadership on this issue (until his wise appointment of General Barry McCaffrey as the new drug czar). In fact, President Clinton hurt the antidrug effort by cutting the Office of National Drug Control Policy from 147 to 25 full-time positions, by hiring a surgeon general who advocated legalization of drugs, by cutting funding for interdiction efforts, and by sending confusing messages about the stigma of illegal drug use. It is no surprise, then, that after dramatic reductions in drug use during the decade before Clinton took office, drug use has nearly doubled among teenagers during his administration. The evidence shows that national leadership is critical in reducing drug abuse.

Jeff's mother wanted that leadership, but in a manner that would help her in Goshen, Ohio. Spending more federal dollars on drug-control programs was unlikely to directly touch this mother's life. Neither would it encourage other parents in her community to address the drug problem. How could I really help? By rolling up my sleeves and providing leadership where it matters most—at the local community level.

Members of Congress are in a unique position to mobilize people in their own communities. By the nature of our jobs, we deal with every sector of the districts we represent. We can also bring statewide and nationwide expertise and resources to bear on a problem. And we can draw the attention of news media that is so critical to educating and mobilizing neighborhoods to solve their toughest social problems. What I've initiated—and what I'm challenging my colleagues in Congress to embrace—is a new model of governance that recognizes the limitations of Washington-based solutions, while drawing on the resources of citizens locally.

CAUSE FOR ALARM

If there is any public-policy area that demands a new, more effective approach, it is drug abuse. Recent Gallup polls show that crime and drugs are Americans' top concerns. When you ask parents and children what is the most serious issue facing youth today, both groups cite drug abuse.

National statistics show there is indeed cause for alarm. After a decade of progress in the war on drugs, the number of young people using drugs began to increase in 1992; use among young kids showed the sharpest increase. LSD use is now at its highest level since 1975, when it was first measured. Since 1992, the number of children between 12 and 17 using marijuana has nearly doubled. To put the problem in perspective, in the average class of 25 eighth-graders (13- and 14-year-olds), five are now using marijuana. And drug abuse is implicated in other social problems—violent crime, dropout rates, and domestic violence, to name a few.

Greater Cincinnati has a drug problem that mirrors the startling national statistics. This region of the country experienced a similar decline in drug use in the 1980s. But by the early 1990s, it began to skyrocket. Why?

I'm convinced that the resurgence stems in part from the disappearance both of effective national leadership in the fight against drug use and of the media attention that usually follows such leadership. This attention is vital to teaching children that drug abuse is both dangerous and wrong.

COMMUNITY ACTIVISM IS CRUCIAL

No one makes this point more authoritatively than Jim Burke, the chairman of the Partnership for a Drug-Free America. It was Burke's group in the 1980s that launched the most extensive and successful public-service campaign in the country. Burke also believes strongly that, while the message must emanate from our national leaders and engage the opinion shapers at every level, this issue is best addressed at the community level.

I decided we could not afford to wait for another tragedy to prompt us to action. Since 1995, I have spearheaded an effort to establish the Coalition for a Drug-Free Greater Cincinnati. This effort is not about flashy press conferences and slick brochures. It's a serious, long-term initiative that brings together for the first time community activists already involved in the antidrug effort, key business figures, religious leaders, the media, parents, young people, law enforcement officials, and others. Our aim is to develop and implement a comprehensive, community-based strategy to reduce drug abuse in our region.

How do you start a coalition? First, you do a lot of listening at all levels—to kids and parents, grass-roots activists, and state and national leaders in the field. Over an 18-month period, we led or helped organize countless meetings in all sorts of settings, from living rooms to classrooms, and from boardrooms to community centers. . . .

LOSING THE WAR AGAINST ADDICTION

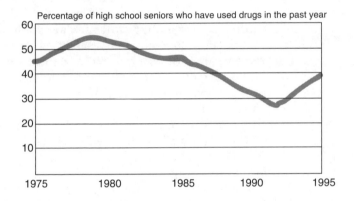

Percentage of high school seniors who have used drugs in the past year

Source: Monitoring the Future Study, University of Michigan, December 1995.

Work is a good place to find parents who need counsel on dealing with teenage drug use. So we had to engage businesses. . . .

We also brought the National Parents' Resource Institute for Drug Education (PRIDE), a premier national parents' group, to one of our school districts to train more than 600 parents in taking practical steps to keep their kids drug free. . . .

The list of initiatives proposed by the local community, brought to the coalition by state and national leaders, and facilitated by congressional leadership, goes on and on. . . .

FINDING A NEW APPROACH

The public rightly expects the federal government to do something about drug abuse, which diminishes and threatens the lives of so many of our young people. And the federal government clearly has an important role in combating drug abuse:

protecting our borders and interdicting drugs from other countries, strengthening our federal criminal-justice system, and providing federal assistance for the best prevention and treatment programs.

Despite a significant federal effort, however, our country is still seeing dramatic increases in drug use among our teenagers. In the last two years alone, use of illegal drugs has increased 50 percent. We need a new approach.

Many of my colleagues are beginning to agree. At least 15 other members of Congress are establishing, or supporting, similar community coalition efforts in their regions. The entire House of Representatives—in an unusual show of election-year bipartisanship—recently endorsed this community-based initiative.

That's a much more significant step than cynics imagine. Although the public has become disenchanted with the federal government's ability to address our worst social problems, there's still an abiding faith in a community's ability to fashion solutions close to the needs of ordinary people. And members of Congress can still be a catalyst. Although the public seems to distrust Congress as a whole, individual members are generally well respected in their districts.

The point is that members of Congress *can* and *should* inspire citizens to action. We've heard about the need to revitalize civil society. Well, here's a concrete example of how members of Congress can do that in a way that actually touches people's lives—not by passing more laws in Washington, but by using their bully pulpits to engage their communities back home. This is how we as national leaders can best exert—and sustain—national leadership over the long haul.

And for the sake of the Jeff Gardners in our communities, we'd better get started.

| "You wonder just how much impact federal drug policy has on a teenager's propensity to smoke a joint."

AN INADEQUATE GOVERNMENT ANTIDRUG EFFORT IS NOT RESPONSIBLE FOR TEEN DRUG ABUSE

Jacob Sullum

Many conservative politicians have blamed the rise of teenage drug use on the government's lack of effort in fighting the problem. In the following viewpoint, Jacob Sullum contends that this argument is unconvincing because government antidrug efforts have intensified, as evidenced by the fact that arrests for drug offenses are increasing. Sullum argues that the real reason teenage substance use has risen is that government antidrug efforts—including drug education programs and antidrug advertising campaigns—are ineffective in altering the behavior of teenagers. Sullum is a senior editor at *Reason*, a monthly libertarian magazine.

As you read, consider the following questions:

1. What cultural indicators does the author believe reflect the increase in teenage drug use?
2. According to Sullum, how many drug arrests were there in 1994?
3. How do adolescents define "cool," according to the author?

Reprinted, with permission, from Jacob Sullum, "Drug Charge," *Reason*, March 1996. Copyright 1996 by the Reason Foundation, 3415 S. Sepulveda Blvd., Suite 400, Los Angeles, CA 90034; www.reason.org.

Teenage drug use is up and Orrin Hatch says it's Bill Clinton's fault. "President Clinton has been AWOL—absent without leadership—on the drug issue," the chairman of the Senate Judiciary Committee said at a December 1995 press conference. "Ineffectual leadership and failed federal policies have combined with ambiguous cultural messages to generate changing attitudes among our young people and sharp increases in youthful drug use."

It's tempting to dismiss Hatch's remarks as partisan posturing. But history teaches us to be on guard when politicians start warning that the nation's youth are in peril. After all, parental alarm helped set off the wave of anti-drug hysteria that swept the nation in the 1980s.

THE TEENAGE DRUG CULTURE

And Hatch is right about one thing: Drug use by teenagers seems to be rising. In the 1992 National Household Survey on Drug Abuse, 4 percent of respondents in the 12-to-17 age group reported using marijuana during the previous month. That figure rose to 4.9 percent in 1993 and 6 percent in 1994. The increase in marijuana use was the main reason for the rise in past-month illegal drug use, which went from 6.1 percent in 1992 to 8.2 percent in 1994. Those figures follow a 13-year decline, and they are still less than half the peak levels seen in 1979. But the rise seems to be more than a blip. The trend can also be observed in cultural indicators such as the movie *Dazed and Confused*, caps embroidered with cannabis leaves, the popularity of the pot-obsessed rap group Cypress Hill, and the *Saturday Night Live*–inspired catch phrase, "you can put your weed in there."

Hatch's explanation for the trend—Clinton's lack of enthusiasm for the war on drugs—is unconvincing. For one thing, Clinton, like his Republican predecessors, has requested ever-escalating anti-drug budgets. Hatch says more of that money should be spent on interdiction. But a wide range of drug policy specialists, including congressional researchers and scholars at the RAND Corporation, have concluded that beefing up interdiction is not a cost-effective way to raise retail prices or reduce availability.

HARSHER GOVERNMENT POLICIES

Hatch also charges Clinton with neglecting enforcement. Yet during his administration the number of Americans in state and federal prisons surpassed 1 million for the first time, largely because of harsh sentences for drug offenses, and the United States now has the highest incarceration rate in the world. The total number of drug arrests reached a record 1 million in 1994, about 43 percent more than in 1991. Nearly half of those arrests were for marijuana, most for simple possession. Says Allen St. Pierre, deputy national director of the National Organization for the Reform of Marijuana Laws, "These data confirm that the federal government's war on marijuana consumers has gotten significantly tougher under Clinton's regime."

DRUG EXPERIMENTATION DOES NOT CAUSE ADDICTION

The vast majority of kids who experiment with dope will not become drug addicts. . . .

Contrary to anti-drug propaganda, you can experiment with illicit drugs and still go on to live a successful and productive life. Contemplating the latest report [on the rise in adolescent drug use], we ought to keep in mind the reassuring certainty that most of the teen-age users won't still be using drugs a decade from now.

Stephen Chapman, *Conservative Chronicle*, September 4, 1996.

Which makes you wonder just how much impact federal drug policy has on a teenager's propensity to smoke a joint. Another puzzle: The same surveys that find an increase in teenagers' use of marijuana and LSD also find an increase in their use of tobacco and alcohol. In the Household Survey, for example, the percentage of 12-to-17-year-olds who reported smoking cigarettes during the previous month rose from 9.6 in 1992 to 18.9 in 1994. Past-month alcohol use rose from 15.7 percent in 1992 to 21.6 percent in 1994. In proportional terms, marijuana use increased more than alcohol use but less than cigarette use. Enforcement of the laws forbidding sales of tobacco and alcohol to minors has never been very effective, but there's no reason to believe it has been especially lax in recent years.

FAILED PROPAGANDA

On the other hand, during the last decade both legal and illegal drugs have been the targets of pervasive propaganda, much of it government-sponsored, aimed at convincing kids to stay away from them. Posters and TV ads depict smokers as disgusting, inconsiderate, and antisocial. Drug Abuse Resistance Education (DARE) communicates an all-or-nothing, "Just Say No" message to elementary-school students. A typical fifth-grader exposed to DARE at a Los Angeles school where my wife taught wrote an essay in which she pledged never to drink beer or smoke pot, because she wanted to attend college, get married, and raise a family—accomplishments that exposure to alcohol or marijuana would make impossible. Commercials from the Partnership for a Drug-Free America portray pot smokers as lazy, stupid, and unattractive. Their vivid images (the fried egg/brain, the diver jumping into an empty pool) warn of disastrous consequences from experimenting with illegal drugs.

Those scare tactics may work over the short term, but they tend to backfire as kids get older. For one thing, teenagers discover through personal observation that much of what they've been told about drugs is nonsense. (Drug warriors are alarmed that the percentage of high school seniors who think smoking marijuana poses a "great risk" has dropped, but the truth is that smoking marijuana *doesn't* pose a great risk.) Perhaps more important, many adolescents define *cool* as whatever most offends adults. Which may explain why tobacco's popularity has increased the most.

| "Saving our children from a lifetime addiction is going to take all of us. . . . from business to government at the Federal, State and local levels; to young people themselves."

THE GOVERNMENT SHOULD COMBAT TEEN SMOKING

Donna E. Shalala

Donna E. Shalala is the secretary of the U.S. Department of Health and Human Services. In the following viewpoint, she argues that teenage smoking is a growing and critical problem that needs to be tackled with government actions and community assistance. Shalala advocates restrictions on advertising so that parents, not tobacco companies, will be the ones to educate children about smoking. This viewpoint is taken from a speech given by Shalala on May 29, 1996, at the National Tobacco Control Conference in Chicago. Some of the proposals mentioned in the viewpoint, such as restrictions on tobacco advertising, were later included in a settlement reached between the tobacco industry and the attorneys general of forty states. As of this writing, the terms of the settlement had not been approved by Congress. However, R.J. Reynolds Tobacco Company agreed to stop using Joe Camel in its advertisements by September 1998.

As you read, consider the following questions:

1. At what age does the average smoker start smoking, according to Shalala?
2. What is the goal of the Clinton administration's proposals, according to the author?
3. What does Shalala believe the entertainment industry can do to reduce teenage smoking?

Reprinted from Donna E. Shalala, "Smoking and Youth," a speech delivered at the National Tobacco Control Conference, May 29, 1996, Chicago, Illinois.

Fifty years ago, an ad appeared in *Life Magazine* proclaiming, "More doctors smoke Camels than any other cigarette."

That was then. This is now: Television and radio airwaves no longer carry commercial jingles touting the "pleasures" of smoking and smokeless tobacco. And parents and children are now armed with powerful information in the battle to save their health and maybe even their lives.

THE TOBACCO WAR IS UNFINISHED

Yes, we have "come a long way, baby." But our journey is not over.

Not when more than 90 percent of 6-year-olds can identify Joe Camel as a symbol of smoking.

Not when 77 percent of high school students who tried were able to buy cigarettes in stores—without showing proof of age.

Not when smoking among high school students has climbed about 25 percent since 1992.

Not when the smoking rates for African American males in high school have almost doubled since 1992.

Not when 45 percent of white male high school students use smokeless tobacco or cigarettes.

And not when the average smoker starts at age 14½ and becomes a daily smoker before age 18.

Smoking is a pediatric disease—that must be stopped.

YOUNG PEOPLE SPEAK OUT

Just listen to what our young people have to say:

This from a 16-year-old girl: "I'd like to be a model. Smoking burns off a lot of calories."

A teenager says: "My nerves are bad. Smoking calms me down."

One girl started smoking at 14 because, "All these really cool girls were doing it. I thought they looked so cool."

Every time a child lights up a cigarette, the future of our country hangs in the balance.

Every time a child lights up a cigarette, who knows what brilliant minds and bright dreams will fade into the bleak backdrop of disease and premature death? Future world-class athletes, future computer giants, future educators, and maybe even future Presidents.

Every young person we can save today is another smoke-free adult tomorrow.

The tobacco culture has essentially functioned as a "third parent" for American children: Enticing them with attractive images, playing upon their desire to be glamorous, luring them with T-Shirts and trinkets, and giving them easy ways to obtain cigarettes from vending machines and even free giveaways.

GOVERNMENT TAKES A STAND

There is not a parent in America who wants their children to endure the suffocating death grip of emphysema or lung cancer.

That's why we're working with you to implement the Synar regulations [legislation named after Congressman Mike Synar that requires states to enforce their bans on tobacco sales to minors or lose federal anti-drug abuse funding]—and help states flash a red light on the sale of cigarettes to minors.

That's why we are helping support local community-based groups through the National Cancer Institute and the Centers for Disease Control and Prevention.

And that's why we're continuing to support research that sheds light on why children start smoking—and what we can do to help stop them.

But now, we have an opportunity to stand with parents and do even more.

We have an opportunity to strike a big blow—a winning blow—against underage smoking in this country.

Never before in history. Let me repeat: Never before in history has a President had the courage and conviction to take on the fight against tobacco—in the name of public health and the name of our children. I am proud of that—and I know you are too.

THE PRESIDENT'S PROPOSAL

Overall, our goal is to reduce smoking among children and adolescents by 50 percent within seven years. And, to do that, President Bill Clinton has offered some of the boldest public health proposals this country has ever seen:

To reduce the access and appeal of tobacco to children, we propose to limit all the easy ways that children get tobacco, keep tobacco billboards at least 1,000 feet from our children's schools, take the Marlboro Man and Joe Camel out of publications read by millions of children, and prohibit tobacco companies from using the allure of their name brands in sponsoring events.

Some might say: "Can't parents take care of their children?" The answer is, "Of course they can."

That's precisely the point of our proposal: To make sure that parents—not the tobacco culture—are in control when it comes to educating children about an addiction that could take years off their lives.

Our proposal is about putting power back into the hands of parents—where it belongs. And, it's all part of our comprehensive strategy to help parents steer their precious children away from all the dangerous minefields like drugs, tobacco, pregnancy, AIDS and violence—and towards healthy, productive futures.

Are these important steps? Absolutely.

Source: Rob Rogers. Reprinted with permission from United Feature Syndicate.

With the Food and Drug Administration proposed rule, we would reduce kids' access to tobacco and the substantial appeal created by $6 billion of advertising and promotion.

The President has put forth a comprehensive and effective proposal to reduce children's use of cigarettes and smokeless tobacco.

The President's mark is the right one.

I know some of you may be wondering about the possibility of finding a legislative solution to this problem.

In August 1995, in the East Room, the President said he would rather put these restrictions into law immediately through legislation than wait for a long regulatory proceeding.

An Inadequate Response

The President has reiterated this point, by saying: "If the tobacco companies will voluntarily accept legislation containing limits that will be as effective as what we propose, I will say, again, we believe it's better to have the companies come forward and ask for legislation."

Let me be clear: When we are shown a bill that is as effective and meaningful as the measures the President has proposed, we will enthusiastically work with Congress.

But Philip Morris and United States Tobacco's proposal falls short of that mark. For example, under their proposal, the Marlboro Man would still ride the billboard prairies and rope our children in.

Our children would still be able to walk into stores and grab a pack of cigarettes from a self-service display. And Joe Camel would still pop up in magazines read by lots of children—offering concert tickets in exchange for a lifetime of addiction.

That is not good enough.

If the companies seriously engage Congress, and Congress gets to work on legislation that meets the President's mark, he is ready. Meanwhile, we will continue to work on the President's initiative.

SUPPORT IS VITAL

We will not—let me repeat—we will not retreat from our commitment to the health of our children. And, I know you won't either.

But government cannot do it alone—and we shouldn't ever try.

It's going to take leaders who speak to children every day—from the family rooms to the classrooms, and from the televisions to the soccer fields.

We need to reach children where they live, where they learn, and where they hang out—with words and images they understand.

That's why we're teaming up with leaders throughout the media and entertainment industries—from daytime talk show hosts to TV producers to the editors of popular magazines.

Some people say that we're wasting our time trying to work with the entertainment industry. They say that the industry will never change and that the proper role for government is merely to shake a finger at them. But, I strongly disagree.

I don't have the luxury or the desire to give up on people who speak to millions of children each day.

You're looking at a huge movie fan—and I know that this industry is savvy and talented enough to create characters who are cool enough not to smoke.

That's the challenge I brought to industry leaders when I visited California in April 1996—to use their enormous power the right way. And, that's the message we need to send to role models all over America: "Our children are watching your example." The question is, what lessons will they learn?

From the PTA, parents are learning how they can act today to help their children avoid tobacco and addiction tomorrow.

From Major League Baseball and Oral Health America, they're learning about the tragic effects of smokeless tobacco.

From the American Medical Association, the American Cancer Society, the American Lung Association, the American Heart Association, the American Academy of Pediatrics, and others, communities are learning how to protect children from tobacco—school by school, block by block, home by home.

And, from the U.S. National Women's Soccer team, they're learning that like oil and water, tobacco and fitness just don't mix.

FIGHTING SMOKING AT THE COMMUNITY LEVEL

Saving our children from a lifetime addiction is going to take all of us. From parents to teachers; from coaches to clergy; from business to government at the Federal, State and local levels; to young people themselves.

Because, the battle against underage smoking will only be won at the community level by leaders like you—leaders who forge strong partnerships. And leaders who marry vision with action to stop smoking before it even starts.

I want you to know that our Administration remains 100 percent committed to the effective work you do at the State, local and community levels. And we must continue to support your community-based initiatives now and into the future.

With your leadership, we have an opportunity to return power to parents and communities.

We have an opportunity to change the course of deadly diseases.

We have an opportunity to help children avoid the shadow of nicotine addiction—protecting our best and smartest investment for the future.

And, if we win this battle, we have an opportunity to fundamentally change the course of history—and do something that historians will no doubt record as the most important public health triumph of our time.

It can be done. It must be done. And, working together, it will be done.

"We all agree underage teenagers shouldn't smoke; that's not the issue. The issue is whether the FDA should launch yet another extravagant regulatory crusade."

GOVERNMENT EFFORTS TO COMBAT TEEN SMOKING ARE UNNECESSARY AND WASTEFUL

Part I: Edwin Feulner; Part II: D. T. Armentano

In Part I of the following two-part viewpoint, Edwin Feulner argues that the tobacco regulations proposed by the Food and Drug Administration (FDA) in an attempt to reduce teenage smoking are counterproductive. He contends that the regulations could actually entice teenagers to smoke by making smoking seem rebellious. In Part II, D. T. Armentano maintains that restrictions on tobacco advertising are unnecessary because teen smoking is a less extensive problem than the FDA claims. Feulner is the president of the Heritage Foundation, a conservative Washington-based think tank. Armentano is professor emeritus of economics at the University of Hartford in Connecticut. Some of the FDA's proposals cited in the viewpoint became part of a settlement reached in June 1997 between the tobacco industry and the attorneys general of forty states; however, as of this writing, Congress had not approved the settlement.

As you read, consider the following questions:

1. According to Feulner, who is better qualified than the FDA to address the issue of teenage smoking?
2. In Armentano's view, what would be the actual impact of the tobacco regulations?

Part I: Reprinted from Edwin Feulner, "FDA: The Smoking Police," at
http://seldy.townhall.com/heritage/commentary/of-ef14.html, cited March 4, 1998,
by permission of the author. Part II: Reprinted from D.T. Armentano, "Teen Smoking: The
New Prohibition," The Freeman, January 1997, by permission of The Freeman.

I

Is the government supposed to protect us from everything that could possibly harm us? Or are there some areas where we should be responsible for taking care of ourselves?

RESTRICTIONS ON TEEN SMOKING

Take teenagers and smoking. The Food and Drug Administration (FDA) and its Commissioner David Kessler are getting ready to pounce on America with a litany of new regulations aimed at stopping teens from smoking.

The FDA's proposed restrictions include:
- Banning cigarette vending machines and self-service displays in stores;
- Requiring tobacco companies to launch a $150 million-per-year nationwide TV ad campaign to discourage under-age smoking;
- Banning the use of tobacco brand names on T-shirts, hats, keychains and lighters; and
- Banning brand-name sponsorship of sporting events, such as the Virginia Slims tennis tournament.

Of course, we all agree underage teenagers shouldn't smoke; that's not the issue. The issue is whether the FDA should launch yet another extravagant regulatory crusade whose nuisance value will likely outweigh any benefits.

UNNECESSARY RAIDS

Remember: this is the FDA that conducted the 1991 raid that captured 24,000 half-gallons of Citrus Hill "fresh choice" orange juice, all because the agency didn't like the way the o.j. was labeled! Are the food and drug police now going to swoop down on every mom and pop grocery store to make sure teen employees aren't smoking in the boy's room?

Apparently so. Since 1990, the FDA's staff has grown from 7,600 to 8,700, and its budget has ballooned from $598 million to $760 million. They've got to do something with all that extra manpower and money.

So, now they're going to send out an army of regulators whose job will be to make sure mom and pop conceal cigarettes from view—as if this ever stopped a teenager from doing something he or she was determined to do. Store workers will have to take time out to deal with every tobacco transaction, since cigarettes will only be sold from behind the counter and not from self-service displays. The watchdogs will probably even send in teenagers paid to test the system. If something slips through the cracks, out come the handcuffs!

REGULATIONS LEAD TO REBELLION

Come on. American University student and former Heritage Foundation intern Jennifer Murray may have said it best in an essay when she accused President Bill Clinton of forgetting what it's like to be a teenager. "Formula-One racing cars painted with tobacco company logos, billboards at sports events, advertisements in magazines (particularly of those men on horseback)— none of these had anything to do with my [former] tendency to light up," Jennifer confessed. "The main contributor was something President Clinton's 'solutions' would only encourage: rebellion." The new federal regulations, far from preventing teens from smoking, "by focusing additional attention on the forbidden, could actually entice them," Jennifer warns.

Isn't there someone more qualified than the FDA orange juice police to address this issue? Such as parents?

Let's get real. As Jennifer pointed out, "Banning cigarette ads and vending machines will do more for President Clinton's wavering image than it will for teens." Does anyone really believe the president is lying awake at night worrying about teen smoking? I kinda doubt it. But he is worried about being popular.

Smoking sure isn't as popular as it used to be. And everybody cares about kids.

You do the math.

II

The expressed goal of the Clinton Administration's proposed regulations on cigarettes and smokeless tobacco products is to reduce adolescent consumption by one half. Roughly three million American juveniles smoke and an additional one million young males use smokeless tobacco. Putting aside (for the moment) all of the other difficulties with the new regulations, can they possibly accomplish their objective?

NO DIRECT RELATIONSHIP

The government proposes severe new restrictions on the advertising of cigarettes under the mistaken assumption that there is a direct relationship between advertising and the decision to begin smoking. But there is little reliable evidence in the literature to support this contention and plenty of evidence to contradict it.

Juvenile smoking actually increased in Finland after a complete ban on tobacco advertising was implemented in 1978.

Norway, which completely prohibited tobacco advertising in 1975, has a higher percentage of juvenile smokers than does the United States. And black teens in the United States, presumably exposed to the same "persuasive" advertising as white teens, have far lower smoking rates.

Do Not Discriminate Against Smokers

Smokers have become disenfranchised and dehumanized; they are non-people. To talk about them would pollute the moral purity of the anti-smoking crusade. Smoking is unhealthy; lowering it among teens would be good. But how much is society entitled to punish adult smokers to protect teens? How much should society discriminate against a large class of people (smokers) whose behavior offends—but does not threaten or impoverish—the larger public? And how much can society change teens, who consistently defy what their elders think best?

Robert J. Samuelson, *Washington Post*, February 25, 1998.

It is widely acknowledged (outside of Washington) that the decision to start using tobacco products is influenced primarily by culture, family, and peer pressure, not corporate advertising. So banning brand-name event sponsorships, or limiting cigarette brand logos on race cars and drivers' uniforms, will have no measurable effect on any ten-year-old's decision to light up.

Teenage Smoking Has Decreased

Food and Drug Administration (FDA) Commissioner David Kessler would have us believe that billboards near playgrounds and the use of cigarette brand names on t-shirts (which would all be prohibited under the new regulations) have created a teen-smoking health epidemic. Nonsense. The marginal increase in teen smoking recorded since 1991 is easily swamped by the longer-term steadily downward trend.

Listening to the FDA one would never know that the percentage of high school seniors who smoke daily has fallen from over 28 percent in 1977 to less than 20 percent in 1994. Heavy smoking (half a pack or more per day) among high school seniors had declined from 17.9 percent in 1975 to approximately 11 percent today. Yet the Administration now proposes to restrict tobacco advertising in teen-oriented magazines to a black-and-white, text-only format even though there is no evidence that such publishing censorship would impact teen cigarette consumption.

The bottom line is that these new regulations have little to do with changing cigarette consumption by teenagers. What they will do, however, is hurt certain advertisers, promoters of sporting events, tobacco manufacturers and their employees, and vending machine owners. Even more importantly, they will enhance the power of government bureaucrats to exercise additional control over private markets and lifestyles. And that's what the antismoking crusade is really all about.

TOBACCO REGULATIONS ALREADY EXIST

Make no mistake about it. The FDA would like to severely restrict the sale of *all* cigarettes in the United States. The Administration knows that total prohibition is politically impractical at the moment so it starts the crusade with regulations that aim to "protect the children." And when these fail, as they must, the regulators will return with stronger recommendations and sterner controls.

But controls are already a way of life in this industry. Laws addressing tobacco sales to minors are on the books in every state and the District of Columbia. Dozens of governmental agencies, including the Department of Health and Human Services, the Federal Trade Commission, and the Bureau of Alcohol, Tobacco and Firearms, already police and regulate the industry. Every state taxes cigarettes and most lump a sales tax on top of the excise tax. Cigarettes are already among the most taxed and regulated products in America.

The Administration has invited public comment, so it should be told that its new regulations will not affect teen smoking but will, instead, reduce employment and income in tobacco-related industries. It should also be told that its contrived rationale to regulate cigarettes as a "medical device" is as phony as a three-dollar bill. Finally, it should be told that freedom and persuasion, not censorship or regulation, are the primary social values that we choose to pass on to our children . . . whether they smoke or not.

PERIODICAL BIBLIOGRAPHY

The following articles have been selected to supplement the diverse views presented in this chapter. Addresses are provided for periodicals not indexed in the *Readers' Guide to Periodical Literature*, the *Alternative Press Index*, the *Social Sciences Index*, or the *Index to Legal Periodicals and Books*.

James Bovard	"Unsafe at Any Speed," *American Spectator*, April 1996.
Stephen Chapman	"Washington Cannot Solve the Drug Problem," *Conservative Chronicle*, September 4, 1996. Available from PO Box 37077, Boone, IA 50037-0077.
Sarah Glazer	"Preventing Teen Drug Use," *CQ Researcher*, July 28, 1995. Available from 1414 22nd St. NW, Washington, DC 20037.
Daniel R. Levine	"Drugs Are Back—Big Time," *Reader's Digest*, February 1996.
Mike Males	"High on Lies: The Phony 'Teen Drug Crisis' Hides the Deadly Truths of the 'War on Drugs,'" *Extra!*, September/October 1995.
Barry R. McCaffrey	"Prevention Programs Work," *Vital Speeches of the Day*, November 15, 1996.
Lance Morrow	"Kids and Pot," *Time*, December 9, 1996.
New York Times	"The Attack on Teen-Age Smoking," August 11, 1995.
Rob Portman and Bob Dole	"Preventing Teen Drug Abuse," *Christian Science Monitor*, February 27, 1996.
Carl Rowan	"Who's to Blame for Drug Use, Smoking?" *Liberal Opinion Week*, September 9, 1996. Available from PO Box 880, Vinton, IA 52349-0880.
Jacob Sullum	"Weed Whackers," *Reason*, November 1996.
Wall Street Journal	"Drugs and God," March 6, 1996.
Christopher S. Wren	"Marijuana Use by Youths Rebounding After Decline," *New York Times*, February 20, 1996.
Mortimer B. Zuckerman	"Great Idea for Ruining Kids," *U.S. News & World Report*, February 24, 1997.

FOR FURTHER DISCUSSION

CHAPTER 1

1. Of the factors discussed in this chapter, which do you think contributes most to teen problems? Explain your answer. What factors not mentioned by the authors might put teens at risk?

2. Mona Charen argues that media violence encourages teens to engage in violent behavior. Mike Males maintains that real violence, not media violence, is to blame. Whose argument do you find more convincing, and why?

3. Edward Grimsley contends that adults' inconsistent messages about morality confuse teenagers. What examples of mixed messages does he provide? Do you agree with Grimsley's assertion that adults are hypocritical about issues of morality? Why or why not?

CHAPTER 2

1. Roger L. Conner is the executive director of an organization that seeks to balance individual liberties and community responsibility. George Brooks is a jail chaplain in Chicago. How do you think their affiliations influence their views on the rights of gang members? Explain.

2. Margaret Beyer bases her argument that juvenile boot camps are a failure partly on evidence that such programs do not reduce recidivism. Eric Peterson acknowledges that boot camps do not decrease recidivism, but he cites statistics showing that boot camps can improve participants' educational skills and increase employment. Can these camps be considered successful if they do not reduce the number of repeat offenders? Why or why not? If increased academic achievement and employment for these teenagers is desired, which programs do you think are more effective—boot camps or the programs described in Beyer's viewpoint? Explain your reasoning.

3. The authors in this chapter offer a variety of solutions to the problem of teenage crime and violence. Which solution(s) do you believe is most effective? What other approaches do you think might work? Explain your answers.

CHAPTER 3

1. The authors of the viewpoints in this chapter discuss four different methods for preventing teenage pregnancy. Which methods do you feel would help reduce teenage pregnancy?

Which would be ineffective? Support your answers with references to the viewpoints.

2. Maggie Gallagher maintains that parents can successfully encourage teenagers to abstain from sex. M. Jocelyn Elders, on the other hand, contends that most teens have sex and therefore need to be educated about preventing pregnancy and sexually transmitted diseases. Which argument do you find more convincing, and why? Is it inevitable that teenagers will have sex? Why or why not?

3. Ralph deToledano argues that the enforcement of statutory rape laws can reduce teen pregnancy. Catherine Elton disagrees. How do these authors view relationships between adult males and teenage girls? How do their differing views about these relationships influence their opinions about enforcing statutory rape laws?

CHAPTER 4

1. Barry R. McCaffrey contends that the media popularize and legitimize drug use. He asserts that the media should present the destructive results of substance abuse. Do you find his argument convincing? Why or why not?

2. Rob Portman argues that teen drug use should be combated on a community level, claiming that the federal effort has been inadequate. Jacob Sullum contends that the federal government has intensified its antidrug efforts but that those efforts fail because they place too great an emphasis on inaccurate propaganda. Should teenage substance abuse be fought on a federal or local level? What are the advantages and disadvantages of both approaches? Explain your answers.

ORGANIZATIONS TO CONTACT

The editors have compiled the following list of organizations concerned with the issues debated in this book. The descriptions are derived from materials provided by the organizations. All have publications or information available for interested readers. The list was
compiled on the date of publication of the present volume; the information provided here may change. Be aware that many organizations
take several weeks or longer to respond to inquiries, so allow as much
time as possible.

Advocates for Youth
1025 Vermont Ave. NW, Suite 200, Washington, DC 20005
(202) 347-5700 • fax: (202) 347-2263
info@advocatesforyouth.org
web address: http://www.advocatesforyouth.org

Advocates for Youth believes young people should have access to information and services that help prevent teen pregnancy and the spread
of sexually transmitted diseases and enable youth to make healthy decisions about sexuality. The organization publishes brochures, fact
sheets, and bibliographies on adolescent pregnancy, adolescent sexuality, and sexuality education.

The Alan Guttmacher Institute
120 Wall St., New York, NY 10005
(212) 248-1111 • fax: (212) 248-1951
e-mail: info@agi-usa.org • web address: http://www.agi-usa.org

The institute works to protect and expand the reproductive choices of
all women and men. It strives to ensure people's access to the information and services they need to exercise their rights and responsibilities
concerning sexual activity, reproduction, and family planning. Among
the institute's publications are the books *Teenage Pregnancy in Industrialized
Countries* and *Today's Adolescents, Tomorrow's Parents: A Portrait of the Americas* and
the report "Sex and America's Teenagers."

American Civil Liberties Union (ACLU)
132 W. 43rd St., New York, NY 10036
(212) 944-9800 • fax: (212) 869-9065
e-mail: aclu@aclu.org • web address: http://www.aclu.org

The ACLU is a national organization that works to defend Americans'
civil rights as guaranteed by the U.S. Constitution. It opposes curfew
laws for juveniles and others and seeks to protect the public-assembly
rights of gang members or people associated with gangs. The ACLU's
numerous publications include the briefing papers "Reproductive
Freedom: The Rights of Minors," "Point of View: School Uniforms,"
and "Equality in Education."

Children's Defense Fund (CDF)
25 E St. NW, Washington, DC 20001
(800) CDF-1200 • (202) 628-8787
e-mail: cdfinfo@childrensdefense.org
web address: http://www.childrensdefense.org

The Children's Defense Fund advocates policies and programs to improve the lives of children and teens in America. CDF's Safe Start program works to prevent the spread of violence and guns in schools, and Healthy Start works for universal health care for children. The fund publishes a monthly newsletter, *CDF Reports*, as well as on-line news and reports such as "Children in the States: 1998 Data" and "How to Reduce Teen Violence."

Drug Policy Foundation
4455 Connecticut Ave. NW, Suite B-500, Washington, DC 20008-2302
(202) 537-5005 • fax: (202) 537-3007
e-mail: dpf@dpf.org
web addresses: http://www.dpf.org or http://www.drugpolicy.org

The foundation is dedicated to studying alternatives to the war on drugs. It supports legalization of drug use, though not for minors. It publishes the quarterly *Drug Policy Letter*.

Family Research Council
801 G St. NW, Washington, DC 20001
(202) 393-2100 • fax: (202) 393-2134
e-mail: corrdept@frc.org • web address: http://www.frc.org

The council seeks to promote and protect the interests of the traditional family. It focuses on issues such as parental autonomy and responsibility, community supports for single parents, and adolescent pregnancy. Among the council's numerous publications are the papers "Revolt of the Virgins," "Abstinence: The New Sexual Revolution," and "Abstinence Programs Show Promise in Reducing Sexual Activity and Pregnancy Among Teens."

The Heritage Foundation
214 Massachusetts Ave. NE, Washington, DC 20002
(800) 544-4843 • (202) 546-4400 • fax: (202) 546-0904
e-mail: pubs@heritage.org • web address: http://www.heritage.org

The Heritage Foundation is a public policy research institute that supports the ideas of limited government and the free-market system. It promotes the view that the welfare system has contributed to the problems of illegitimacy and teenage pregnancy. Among the foundation's numerous publications is its Backgrounder series, which includes "Liberal Welfare Programs: What the Data Show on Programs for Teenage Mothers," the paper "Rising Illegitimacy: America's Social Catastrophe," and the bulletin "How Congress Can Protect the Rights of Parents to Raise Their Children."

**The National Center on Addiction and
Substance Abuse at Columbia University (CASA)**
152 W. 57th St., 12th Fl., New York, NY 10019-3310
(212) 841-5200 • fax: (212) 956-8020
web address: http://www.casa.columbia.org

CASA works to combat all forms of substance abuse and to study the links between substance abuse and other societal problems, including crime, homelessness, and teen pregnancy. The center publishes reports and surveys on the cost, impact, and prevention of substance abuse, including "Substance Abuse and the American Adolescent," "Rethinking Rites of Passage: Substance Abuse on America's Campuses," and the CASA 1997 Back to School Survey, all of which are available on-line.

National Council on Alcoholism and Drug Dependence (NCADD)
12 W. 21st St., New York, NY 10010
(800) 622-2255 • (212) 206-6770 • fax: (212) 645-1690
e-mail: national@ncadd.org • web address: http://www.ncadd.org

In addition to helping individuals overcome addictions, NCADD advises the federal government on drug and alcohol policies and develops substance abuse prevention and education programs for youth. It publishes fact sheets and pamphlets on substance abuse, including the titles *Youth and Alcohol* and *Who's Got the Power? You . . . or Drugs?*

National Institute of Justice (NIJ)
810 Seventh St. NW, Washington, DC 20531
(202) 307-2942
e-mail: askncjrs@ncjrs.org
web address: http://www.ojp.usdoj.gov/nij/

NIJ is the primary federal sponsor of research on crime and its control. It sponsors research efforts through grants and contracts that are carried out by universities, private institutions, and state and local agencies. Its publications include the research briefs *Gang Crime and Law Enforcement Recordkeeping* and *Street Gang Crime in Chicago.*

National Institute on Drug Abuse (NIDA)
U.S. Department of Health and Human Services
5600 Fishers Ln., Rockville, MD 20857
(301) 443-6245
e-mail: information@lists.nida.nih.gov
web address: http://www.nida.nih.gov

NIDA supports and conducts research on drug abuse—including the yearly Monitoring the Future Survey—in order to improve addiction prevention, treatment, and policy efforts. It publishes the bimonthly *NIDA Notes* newsletter, the periodic *NIDA Capsules* fact sheets, and a catalog of research reports and public education materials, such as "Marijuana: Facts for Teens."

National School Safety Center (NSSC)

4165 Thousand Oaks Blvd., Suite 290, Westlake Village, CA 91362
(805) 373-9977 • fax: (805) 373-9277
e-mail: june@nssc1.org • web address: http://www.nssc1.org

NSSC is a research organization that studies school crime and violence, including hate crimes. The center believes that teacher training is an effective means of reducing these problems. Its publications include the book *Gangs in Schools: Breaking Up Is Hard to Do* and the *School Safety Update* newsletter, which is published nine times a year.

Office for Victims of Crime Resource Center

810 Seventh St. NW, Washington, DC 20531
(800) 627-9872
web address: http://www.ojp.usdoj.gov/ovc

Established in 1983 by the U.S. Department of Justice's Office for Victims of Crime, the resource center is a primary source of information regarding victim-related issues. It answers questions by using national and regional statistics, research findings, and a network of victim advocates and organizations. The center distributes all Office of Justice Programs publications, including *Female Victims of Violent Crime* and *Sexual Assault: An Overview*.

Office of Juvenile Justice and Delinquency Prevention (OJJDP)

633 Indiana Ave. NW, Washington, DC 20531
(202) 307-5911 • fax: (202) 307-2093
e-mail: askjj@ojp.usdoj.gov
web address: http://www.ncjrs.org/ojjhome.htm

As the primary federal agency charged with monitoring and improving the juvenile justice system, the OJJDP develops and funds programs on juvenile justice. Among its goals are the prevention and control of illegal drug use and serious crime by juveniles. Through its Juvenile Justice Clearinghouse, the OJJDP distributes fact sheets and reports such as "How Juveniles Get to Criminal Court," "Gang Suppression and Intervention: Community Models," and "Minorities and the Juvenile Justice System."

Partnership for a Drug-Free America

405 Lexington Ave., 16th Fl., New York, NY 10174
(212) 922-1560
web address: http://www.drugfreeamerica.org

The Partnership for a Drug-Free America is a private, nonprofit coalition of professionals from the communications industry. Based on the belief that changing attitudes is the key to changing behavior, the partnership's mission is to reduce demand for illegal drugs by changing public attitudes about drugs through the media. The partnership's website includes an on-line database of drug information, news about media efforts to stop drug abuse, and other resources for parents and teens.

Suicide Awareness\Voices of Education (SA\VE)
PO Box 24507, Minneapolis, MN 55424-0507
(612) 946-7998
e-mail: save@winternet.com • web address: http://www.save.org

SA\VE works to prevent suicide and to help those grieving after the suicide of a loved one. Its members believe that brain diseases such as depression should be detected and treated promptly because they can result in suicide. In addition to pamphlets and the book *Suicide: Survivors—A Guide for Those Left Behind*, the organization publishes the quarterly newsletter *Afterwords*.

Suicide Information and Education Centre
#201 1615 Tenth Ave. SW, Calgary, AB T3C OJ7, CANADA
(403) 245-3900 • fax: (403) 245-0299
e-mail: siec@nucleus.com • web address: http://www.siec.ca

The Suicide Information and Education Centre acquires and distributes information on suicide prevention. It maintains a computerized database, a free mailing list, and a document delivery service. It publishes the quarterly *Current Awareness Bulletin* and the monthly *SIEC Clipping Service*.

BIBLIOGRAPHY OF BOOKS

Alan Guttmacher Institute	*Sex and America's Teenagers.* New York: Alan Guttmacher Institute, 1994.
S. Beth Atkin	*Voices from the Streets:Young Former Gang Members Tell Their Stories.* Boston: Little, Brown, 1996.
William J. Bennett, John J. DiIulio Jr., and John P. Walters	*Body Count: Moral Poverty . . . and How to Win America's War Against Crime and Drugs.* New York: Simon & Schuster, 1996.
Bureau of Justice Assistance	*Addressing Community Gang Problems: A Model for Problem Solving.* Washington, DC: Bureau of Justice Assistance, January 1997. Available from http://www.ojp.usdoj.gov/BJA.
Phyllida Burlingame	*Sex, Lies, and Politics: Abstinence-Only Curricula in California Public Schools.* Oakland, CA: Applied Research Center, 1997.
Michael Carrera	*Adolescent Sexuality and Pregnancy Prevention: Replication Manual.* New York: Bernice and Milton Stern National Training Center for Adolescent Sexuality and Family Life Education, 1996.
Glenn Alan Cheney	*Drugs, Teens, and Recovery: Real-Life Stories of Trying to Stay Clean.* Hillside, NJ: Enslow, 1993.
Janet Ollila Colberg	*Red Light, Green Light: Preventing Teen Pregnancy.* Helena, MT: Summer Kitchen Press, 1997.
Robert Coles et al.	*The Youngest Parents: Teenage Pregnancy as It Shapes Lives.* Durham, NC: Center for Documentary Studies, 1997.
James E. Cote and Anton L. Allahar	*Generation on Hold: Coming of Age in the Late Twentieth Century.* New York: New York University Press, 1996.
Herbert C. Covey, Scott Menard, and Robert J. Franzese	*Juvenile Gangs.* Springfield, IL: Charles C. Thomas, 1997.
David H. Demo and Anne-Marie Ambert, eds.	*Parents and Adolescents in Changing Families.* Minneapolis: National Council on Family Relations, 1995.
Shirley Dicks, ed.	*Young Blood: Juvenile Justice and the Death Penalty.* Amherst, NY: Prometheus Books, 1995.
Linnea A. Due	*Joining the Tribe: Growing Up Gay and Lesbian in the '90s.* New York: Anchor Books, 1995.
Irving B. Harris	*Children in Jeopardy: Can We Break the Cycle of Poverty?* New Haven, CT: Yale University Press, 1996.

| James C. Howell | *Juvenile Justice and Youth Violence.* Thousand Oaks, CA: Sage, 1997. |

| Yusuf Jah and Sister Shah'Keyah | *Uprising: Crips and Bloods Tell the Story of America's Youth in the Crossfire.* New York: Scribner, 1995. |

| Janice Joseph | *Black Youths, Delinquency, and Juvenile Justice.* Westport, CT: Praeger, 1995. |

| Malcolm W. Klein | *The American Street Gang: Its Nature, Prevalence, and Control.* New York: Oxford University Press, 1995. |

| Kristin Luker | *Dubious Conceptions: The Politics of Teenage Pregnancy.* Cambridge, MA: Harvard University Press, 1996. |

| Barbara S. Lynch and Richard J. Bonnie, eds. | *Growing Up Tobacco Free.* Washington, DC: National Academy Press, 1994. |

| Mike Males | *The Scapegoat Generation: America's War on Adolescents.* Monroe, ME: Common Courage Press, 1996. |

| Joseph Marshall Jr. and Lonnie Wheeler | *Street Soldier: One Man's Struggle to Save a Generation—One Life at a Time.* New York: Bantam Doubleday Dell, 1996. |

| Karin A. Martin | *Puberty, Sexuality, and the Self: Boys and Girls at Adolescence.* New York: Routledge, 1996. |

| Rebecca A. Maynard, ed. | *Kids Having Kids: Economic Costs and Social Consequences of Teen Pregnancy.* Washington, DC: Urban Institute Press, 1997. |

| James B. McCarthy | *Adolescence and Character Disturbance.* Lanham, MD: University Press of America, 1995. |

| Barbara A. Miller | *Teenage Pregnancy and Poverty: The Economic Realities.* New York: Rosen, 1997. |

| Jeffrey L. Morelock | *Drugs in High School: The Disturbing Truth.* St. Petersburg, FL: Guideline, 1995. |

| National Institute on Drug Abuse | *Drug Abuse Prevention for At-Risk Groups.* Washington, DC: U.S. Department of Health and Human Services, 1997. |

| Office of Juvenile Justice and Delinquency Prevention | *Urban Delinquency and Substance Abuse.* Washington, DC: U.S. Department of Justice, March 1994. |

| Gary Remafedi, ed. | *Death by Denial: Studies of Suicide in Gay and Lesbian Teenagers.* Boston: Alyson, 1994. |

| Elizabeth A. Ryan | *Straight Talk About Drugs and Alcohol.* New York: Facts On File, 1995. |

| William B. Sanders | *Gangbangs and Drive-Bys: Grounded Culture and Juvenile Gang Violence.* New York: Walter de Gruyter, 1994. |

Gini Sikes	*8 Ball Chicks: A Year in the Violent World of Girl Gangsters.* New York: Doubleday, 1997.
Judie Smith	*Drugs and Suicide.* New York: Rosen, 1995.
Irving A. Spergel	*The Youth Gang Problem: A Community Approach.* New York: Oxford University Press, 1995.
Lee G. Streetman	*Drugs, Delinquency, and Pregnancy: A Panel Study of Adolescent Problem Behaviors.* New York: Vantage, 1996.
Sharon Thompson	*Going All the Way: Teenage Girls' Tales of Sex, Romance, and Pregnancy.* New York: Hill and Wang, 1995.
Margi Trapani	*Reality Check: Teenage Fathers Speak Out.* New York: Rosen, 1997.
U.S. Senate Subcommittee on Juvenile Justice	*Juvenile Crime: Breaking the Cycle of Violence: Hearing Before the U.S. Senate Committee on the Judiciary, November 29, 1994.* Washington, DC: U.S. Government Printing Office, 1996.

INDEX

Of course we need to confine criminals for their own good and society's, but a process of positive reinforcement must be the means of dealing with criminals and their "crimes." Karpman, one of the proponents of this theory, puts it this way:

> Basically, criminality is but a symptom of insanity, using the term in its widest generic sense to express unacceptable social behavior based on unconscious motivation flowing from a disturbed instinctive and emotional life, whether this appears in frank psychoses, or in less obvious form in neuroses and unrecognized psychoses. . . . If criminals are products of early environmental influences in the same sense that psychotics and neurotics are, then it should be possible to reach them psychotherapeutically.[26]

Let me begin my criticism of rehabilitation by relating a retelling of the Good Samaritan story. You recall that a Jew went down from Jerusalem to Jericho and fell among thieves who beat him, robbed him, and left him dying. A priest and a Levite passed by him but an outcast Samaritan came to his rescue, bringing him to a hotel for treatment and paying his bills.

A contemporary version of the story goes like this. A man is brutally robbed and left on the side of the road by his assailants. A priest comes by but regrets having to leave the man in his condition, in order to avoid being late for the church service he must lead. Likewise, a lawyer passes by, rushing to meet a client. Finally, a psychiatrist sees our subject, rushes over to him, places the man's head in his lap and in a distraught voice cries out, "Oh, this is awful! How deplorable! Tell me, sir, who did this to you? He needs help."

Not all psychiatrists fit this description of mislocating the victim, but the story cannot be dismissed as merely a joke in poor taste. It fits an attitude that substitutes the concept of sickness for moral failure. Let me briefly note some of the problems with the whole theory of rehabilitation as a substitute for punishment. First, this doctrine undermines the very notion of human autonomy and responsibility. Individuals who are not mentally ill are free agents whose actions should be taken seriously as flowing from free decisions.[27] If a person kills in cold blood, he or she

---

26. Benjamin Karpman, "Criminal Psychodynamics," *Journal of Criminal Law and Criminology* 47 (1956): 9. See also B. F. Skinner, *Science and Human Behavior* (Macmillan, 1953), 182–193.

27. I am assuming that the case for free will and responsibility is cogent. For a good discussion see the readings by Harry Frankfurt, Gary Watson, and Peter van

must bear the responsibility for that murder. Rehabilitation theories reduce moral problems to medical problems.

Furthermore, rehabilitation doesn't seem to work. Rehabilitation is a form of socialization through sophisticated medical treatment. While humans are malleable, there are limits to what socialization and medical technology can do. Socialization can be relatively effective in infancy and early childhood, less so in late childhood, while even less effective in adulthood. Perhaps at some future time when brain manipulation becomes possible, we will make greater strides toward behavior modification. Perhaps we will be able to plant electrodes in a criminal's brain and so affect his cerebral cortex that he "repents" of his crime and is restored to society. The question then will be whether we have a right to tamper with someone's psyche in this manner. Furthermore, would a neurologically induced repentance for a crime really be repentance—or would it be an overriding of the criminal's autonomy and personality? And won't that tampering itself be a form of punishment?

Conclusion

Let me bring this part of our work to a close by suggesting that there are elements of truth in all three theories of punishment. Rehabilitationism, insofar as it seeks to restore the criminal to society as a morally whole being, has merit as an aspect of the penal process, but it cannot stand alone. Retributivism is surely correct to make guilt a necessary condition for punishment and to seek to make the punishment fit the crime. Its emphasis on desert is vital to our theory of reward and punishment, and with this it respects humans as rational, responsible agents, who should be treated in a manner fitting to their deserts. But it may be too rigid in its *retrospective* gaze and in need of mercy and *prospective* vision. Utilitarianism seems correct in emphasizing this prospective feature of treatment with the goal of promoting human flourishing. But it is in danger of manipulating people for the social good—even of punishing the innocent or punishing the guilty more than they deserve (for social purposes). One way of combining retributivism and utilitarianism has been suggested by John Rawls in his classic essay, "Two Concepts of Rules." Rawls attempts

Inwagen in *Moral Responsibility*, ed. John Martin Fischer (Ithaca: Cornell University Press, 1986).

to do justice to both the retributive and the utilitarian theories of punishment.[28] He argues that there is a difference between justifying an institution and justifying a given instance where the institution is applied. The question "Why do we have law or system?" is of a different nature from the question "Why are we applying the law in the present situation in this mode?" Applied to punishment: (1) "Why do we have a system of punishment?" and (2) "Why are we harming John for his misdeed?" are two different sorts of questions. When we justify the institution of punishment, we resort to utilitarian or consequentialist considerations: A society in which the wicked prosper will offer inadequate inducement to virtue. A society in which some rules are made and enforced will get on better than a society in which no rules exist or are enforced. But when we seek to justify an individual application of punishment, we resort to retributivist considerations; for example, when someone commits a breach against the law, that person merits a fitting punishment.

So we can operate on two levels. On the second-order (reflective) level we accept rule utilitarianism and acknowledge that the penal law should serve society's overall good. In order to do this we need a retributive system—one that adheres to common ideas of fair play and desert. So rule utilitarianism on the second-order level yields retributivism on the first-order level. As we have noted, some have interpreted this process to entail that there is no noninstitutional or natural desert or justice, but that these things only come into being by social choice. It is more accurate to say that there is a primordial or deontological idea of desert which needs social choice to become activated or institutionalized for human purposes. It is not as though society could rationally choose some other practice, but that, if it is to choose rationally—to promote its goals of flourishing and resolving conflicts of interest—it must choose to reward and punish according to one's desert.

Part II: Capital Punishment

The small crowd that gathered outside the prison to protest the execution of Steven Judy softly sang, "We Shall Overcome" . . . But it didn't seem quite the same hearing it sung out of concern for someone who, on finding a woman with a flat tire, raped and murdered

---

28. John Rawls, "Two Concepts of Justice," *Philosophical Review* (1955).

her and drowned her three small children, then said that he hadn't been "losing any sleep" over his crimes. . . .

I remember the grocer's wife. She was a plump, happy woman who enjoyed the long workday she shared with her husband in their ma-and-pa store. One evening, two young men came in and showed guns, and the grocer gave them everything in the cash register.

For no reason, almost as an afterthought, one of the men shot the grocer in the face. The woman stood only a few feet from her husband when he was turned into a dead, bloody mess.

She was about 50 when it happened. In a few years her mind was almost gone, and she looked 80. They might as well have killed her too.

Then there was the woman I got to know after her daughter was killed by a wolfpack gang during a motoring trip. The mother called me occasionally, but nothing that I said could ease her torment. It ended when she took her own life.

A couple of years ago I spent a long evening with the husband, sister and parents of a fine young woman who had been forced into the trunk of a car in a hospital parking lot. The degenerate who kidnapped her kept her in the trunk, like an ant in a jar, until he got tired of the game. Then he killed her."[29]

Who so sheddeth man's blood, by man shall his blood be shed. (Genesis 9:6)

Proponents of capital punishment justify it from either a retributive or a utilitarian framework, sometimes using both theories for a combined justification. Abolitionists deny that these arguments for capital punishment are sound, because the sanctity of human life which gives each person a right to life is inconsistent with the practice of putting criminals to death.

As we noted in Part I, the retributivist argues (1) that all the guilty deserve to be punished; (2) that only the guilty deserve to be punished; and (3) that the guilty deserve a punishment proportional in severity to their crime. It follows that all those who commit capital offenses deserve capital punishments. This is the idea suggested in the quotation from the Bible at the beginning of this part of our work, assuming that malice aforethought is present.

---

29. Mike Royko, quoted in Michael Moore, "The Moral Worth of Retributivism" in *Punishment and Rehabilitation,* ed. Jeffrie G. Murphy, 3d. ed. (Wadsworth, 1995): 98–99.

A classic expression of the retributivist position on capital punishment is Kant's statement that if an offender, "has committed murder, he must *die*. In this case, no possible substitute can satisfy justice. For there is no *parallel* between death and even the most miserable life, so that there is no equality of crime and retribution unless the perpetrator is judicially put to death (at all events without any maltreatment which might make humanity an object of horror in the person of the sufferer)."

As quoted in Part I, Kant illustrates the doctrine of exact retribution:

> Even if a civil society were to dissolve itself with the consent of all its members (for example, if a people who inhabited an island decided to separate and disperse to other parts of the world), the last murderer in prison would first have to be executed in order that each should receive his just deserts and that the people should not bear the guilt of a capital crime through failing to insist on its punishment; for if they do not do so, they can be regarded as accomplices in the public violation of justice.[30]

For Kant the death penalty was a conclusion of the argument for justice: just recompense to the victim and just punishment to the offender. As a person of dignity, the victim deserves (as a kind of compensatory justice) to have the offender harmed in proportion to the gravity of the crime, and as a person of high worth and responsibility, the offender shows himself or herself deserving of capital punishment.

Let us expand on the retributivist argument. Each person has a right to life. But criminal C violates an innocent person V's right to life by threatening it or by killing V. The threat to V constitutes a grave offense, but taking V's life constitutes a capital offense. Attempting to take V's life, from a moral point of view, is equivalent to taking his or her life. Therefore C deserves to be put to death for the offense.

But the abolitionist responds, "No, putting the criminal to death only compounds evil. If killing is an evil, then the state actually doubles the evil by executing the murderer. The state violates the criminal's right to life. It carries out *legalized murder*." To quote the famous eighteenth-century abolitionist Cesare di Beccaria, "The death penalty cannot be useful because of the example of barbarity it gives to men . . . it seems to me absurd that the laws . . . which punish homicide should themselves commit it."[31]

---

30. Immanuel Kant, *The Metaphysics of Morals*, trans. John Ladd (Indianapolis: Bobbs-Merrill, 1965), 103.

31. Cesare di Beccaria, *Of Crimes and Punishments*, trans. Henry Paolucci (Indianapolis: Bobbs-Merrill, 1963, originally published 1764).

But the abolitionist is mistaken on two counts. First, the state does not violate the criminal's right to life, for the right to life (more precisely, the right not to be killed) is not an absolute right which can never be overridden (or forfeited).[32] If the right to life were absolute, we could not kill aggressors even when it was necessary to defend our lives or those of our loved ones. It is a *prima facie* or conditional right which can be overridden by a more weighty moral reason. Our right to life, liberty and property is connected with our duty to respect the rights of others to life, liberty and property. By violating the right of another to liberty, I thereby forfeit my right to liberty. By violating the right of another to property, I thereby forfeit my property right. Similarly, by violating the right of another to life, I thereby forfeit my right to life. Violating the victim's right to life is a sufficient reason for overriding the criminal's prima facie right to life. The criminal in murdering the innocent victim has made himself vulnerable to the state's authority to use the sword in behalf of justice and self-defense.

On the retributivist account, this forfeiture of the criminal's right to life only tells part of the story. Forfeiture gives the moral and legal authority the right to inflict the criminal with a punishment, but it says nothing about the *duty* of the authority to punish. The principle of just desert completes the theory of retribution. Not only do murderers forfeit their right to life, but they positively deserve their punishment. If they have committed a capital offense, they deserve a capital punishment. If first-degree murder is on the level of the worst types of crimes, as we think it is, then we are justified in imposing the worst type of punishments on the murderer. Death would be the fitting punishment; anything less would

---

32. In this essay I speak of the *forfeiting* or the *overriding* of a right to life as interchangeable, though they are not the same thing. I may forfeit my right to drive by violating laws against drinking alcohol while driving, but my right to drive the family car today may be overridden by my father's need to take it to work. If one thinks of a right not to be killed as natural right which society cannot override, as Kant seems to, the only way it can be morally undermined is by one's own immoral acts. The criminal forfeits his right to freedom or life. A consequentialist or contractualist may argue that the right not to be killed is only a prima facie right that can be overridden for good moral reasons, one of which is the murdering of another person. Since I think that all three theories justify the death penalty for murder, I am not taking sides between them in this work—except to insist that even in utilitarian defenses a retributive core must be present in terms of the criminal doing something to deserve what he or she gets.

indicate that we regarded murder a less serious offense. So the abolitionist is mistaken in holding that killing is always wrong. Killing may be an evil, but, if so, it is a lesser evil when carried out as an act of retributivist justice. A greater evil would be to permit the guilty to go unpunished or improperly punished.

We do know of crimes worse than murder—repeatedly torturing victims over a long period of time and driving them insane is worse than murdering them. A thoroughgoing retributivist might well advocate legal punishment consisting of torturing torturers and rapists (probably using machines so as to distance the retributivist as far as possible from the repulsive nature of the punishment). The ancient biblical *lex talionis,* discussed in Part I, demands an equivalent punishment to that of the crime itself. In the context of purposefully harming others, the passage reads: "Thou shalt give life for life, an eye for an eye, a tooth for a tooth, a hand for a hand, burning for burning, wound for wound, stripe for stripe" (Exod. 21:23–25). Accordingly, the torturer should be tortured exactly to the severity that he tortured the victim, the rapist should be raped, and the cheater should have an equivalent harm inflicted upon him or her. The criminals deserve such punishment, as it reflects the principle of proportionality.

As we argued in Part I, the principle of desert can be overridden by other considerations, and good reasons exist for not always giving the criminal all he or she deserves. How could we punish Hitler, Eichmann, Stalin, or a serial killer in proportion to the gravity of their offenses? There are limits to what punishment can and should do. In some cases, e.g., serial murder, giving the criminal precisely what he deserves is impossible; and since we are under no obligation to do the impossible (*ultra posse nemo obligatur*), we do not always have an obligation to give people what they deserve.[33] Although Hitler and the serial killer surely deserve more than the death penalty, it's hard to say how much more. Our intuitions are unclear on how to determine anything more than the death penalty, so we tend to accept that as the upper limit—even though both retributivism and deterrence might be served by these harsher punishments.

Part of our reluctance to be consistent retributivists may be cultural,

---

33. There is an asymmetry between reward and punishment. A beneficiary of a reward has the right to decline the reward, but the recipient of a deserved punishment has no such option. On the other hand, a more stringent obligation exists to give people what they positively deserve than what they negatively deserve. We can forgive those who trespass against us.

rather than strictly (or objectively) moral. Killing and torturing are vile acts, and we—most educated people in Western society at least—shudder at the thought of doing these things to others, even though we agree they deserve them. As war veterans know, killing, even in a just war, exacts a psychological toll. It may have a "brutalization" effect. Let us call these psychological factors *external considerations* against exacting equivalence of punishment to crime. At any rate, because of a slow trend towards non-violence in much of our society, corporal punishment, torture, and executions have become increasing unpopular. Whippings, burnings, and torture have been declared too vile a response to the criminal. The death penalty is the sole remaining corporal penalty, and we have striven to make it as painless as possible (another paradox for retributivists and deterrentists). The question is whether something less than death would do as well, say, long-term prison sentences. A mild retributivist might allow mercy to enter the picture earlier, perhaps advocating long prison sentences. But for most retributivists, like myself, death seems an appropriate punishment for the worst types of crimes—though, strictly speaking, it may not be anywhere near to the proportion of suffering or evil done by the criminal.[34] Anything more (e.g., torture), though perhaps deserved in some cases, would have unacceptable social costs. Anything less would be a failure to approximate justice and carry out minimally adequate deterrence.

If a society is secure, it might well opt to show mercy and not execute murderers. At this point utilitarian reasons may mitigate retributive judgments, inclining the state towards lesser punishments, not because the criminal doesn't deserve the death penalty, but because a secure society isn't threatened as a whole by occasional murders, heinous though they be. In a secure society (Scandinavian countries, Switzerland, the Netherlands, and Austria come to mind—with crime rates a tiny fraction of that of the United States) capital offenses are not tearing away at the very fabric of the social order.[35] However, given the justice of death as a fitting moral

---

34. Most debates center on whether the death penalty is appropriate for first-degree murder. It is confined to murder and espionage in federal and most state laws. I would consider it for white-collar crimes where powerful government officials or business people abuse their power, betray the public trust, and do irrevocable harm to those beholden to them. For example, bank presidents or executives who embezzle from those who have entrusted to them their savings both deserve and might be deterred by the threat of the death penalty.

35. Perhaps we ought to err on the side of mercy and reform, but there seem

response to capital crimes, the burden of proof for overriding the death penalty in capital offense cases rests with the abolitionist. If the forfeiture of right argument and the desert argument, sketched above, are sound, the murderer has forfeited his right to life and the death penalty is deserved. As such the death penalty is not only a morally permissible act, but a prima facie duty, which may be overridden only for good reasons.

Retributivism and the Rehabilitative Penance Model of Punishment

Recently, several philosophers, including Herbert Morris, Margaret Falls, and Anthony Duff, have put forth a version of retributivism that, as retributive, emphasizes desert, but also appeals to the idea of inherent human dignity to put severe limits on punishment, prohibiting capital punishment. The goal of punishment is penance, not death.

Duff holds that punishment must be a form of communication to the criminal, expressing moral condemnation for the deed and calling the culprit to repent. The criminal's autonomy and dignity must be preserved in the punitive process. A necessary condition for this preservation of dignity and autonomy is that the criminal recognize what he or she has done, acknowledge his or her guilt, and repent of the crime. It follows that we may not put the murderer to death, for that precludes the opportunity for repentance and restoration to the community. The penance model is a sophisticated version of the rehabilitation theory of punishment, discussed in Part I. It is more cogent than the usual rehabilitative theories in that it links retribution with rehabilitation.

One corollary of this view, set forth by Duff, states that if the criminal becomes insane or amnesiac after the crime, he cannot be punished.[36] I find this counterintuitive and a clue as to why this theory is mistaken. Suppose we developed a pill (or a way of using electrodes on parts of

---

to be times when this is not feasible—either because the criminal is beyond the pale of reform or because of the social costs.

"There but for the grace of God go I." I feel this sentiment too. There is some luck in not being evil—for which we should be eternally grateful, and this may mitigate our rage at evildoers, but it should not cancel it altogether. If I did a dastardly act, I would expect you to sympathize ("There but for the grace of God go I") but still execute me. I'm still deserving of the death penalty.

36. Anthony Duff, "Expression, Penance and Reform," in Jeffrie Murphy, ed. *Punishment and Rehabilitation,* 3d. ed. (Wadsworth, 1995), 169–198.

the brain) that would cause selective amnesia. Criminal Charley has just committed cold-blooded murder. Now he takes the pill which will eliminate the memory of his deed (as well as his putting the pill in his mouth). The result: success. Charley no longer remembers what he did. But would he not still deserve severe punishment?

There is no incompatibility between penance and desert. I may repent of my sins and immoral deeds and still acknowledge that I deserve to be punished for them. In fact, the very nature of repenting includes a sense of deserving to suffer for wrongdoing. The convicted murderer Gary Gilmore requested that he be executed for his heinous murders, holding that he deserved nothing less than death.

Perhaps religious people will insist that criminals, no matter how low they sink, still possess the image of God. In this spirit, the Christian philosopher Margaret Falls argues movingly that treating people as moral agents prohibits us from executing them. "Holding an offender responsible necessarily includes demanding that she respond as only moral agents can: by reevaluating her behavior. If the punishment meted out makes reflective response to it impossible, then it is not a demand for response as a moral agent. Death is not a punishment to which reflective moral response is possible. . . . Death terminates the possibility of moral reform."[37]

To Falls's argument that the death penalty makes moral reform impossible, two things must be said: (1) It's false, and (2) it's not an argument for the complete abolition of capital punishment.

(1) Regarding the claim that it's false, the criminal may be given time to repent of his or her offense before execution. It is hard to know when the murderer has truly repented and has been rehabilitated, since faking it is in the murderer's self-interest, but even if he does repent, the heinousness of the deed remains and he should receive his just desert. Indeed, given my Golden Rule argument (discussed below), one would expect the repentant murderer to agree that he or she deserved to die and, as Gary Gilmore did, request execution. (2) Regarding my second claim, even if some offenders were suitably rehabilitated, and even if we had a policy of showing mercy to those who gave strong evidence of having been morally reformed, many criminals may well be incurable, given our present means for rehabilitation and moral reform. Present rehabilitation programs are

---

37. Margaret Falls, "Against the Death Penalty: A Christian Stance in a Secular World," *Christian Century* (December 10, 1986), 1118, 1119.

not very successful. In fact, I doubt whether it is the primary goal of the criminal justice system to engage in rehabilitation. Its primary goal is to protect society and carry out justice, though if it can aid in reforming the prisoner, so much the better. The point is, failure to reform the criminal need not be proof that the system is unjust.

Here is a paradox for the abolitionist: *Either* the murderer is a free being with inherent dignity and so may be held accountable for his crime to the point of being executed for it, *or* the murderer is not a free being with inherent dignity and so does not deserve any special protection as possessing positive value. He may be killed as would be a rabid dog, man-eating tiger, or a dangerous virus. Either way, the death penalty seems fair. Let me elaborate on this paradox.

Elsewhere, I have argued that, although a popular dogma, the secular doctrine that all humans have equal *positive* worth is groundless. The notion of equal worth, perhaps the most misused term in our moral vocabulary, is a derivation from a past religious age (assuming that our age is secular) when people believed that human beings were endowed with a soul possessing the infinite image of God. The statement in the Declaration of Independence that "all men are created equal" entails a Creator, which plays no role in the secularist's theory of justice. We may, of course, be equally worthless, but I know of no account that gives us both a notion of positive worth and an equal distribution of that quality. Some philosophers say that our ability to reason gives us inherent worth, but if it does, then surely we are radically unequal, as anyone who has graded philosophy papers or observed people reasoning knows. We may apply the *principle of impartiality* and judge people by equal laws and by the same moral code, but then the resulting evaluations of people will be vastly different. As in grading students' tests and course work, some will get high marks in the moral-evaluation and some will fail. Generally, we can say that a person's worth is grounded in such things as his or her moral character and contribution to society (it may include the global society, including nonhuman animals).[38]

If our moral status is largely what gives us worth, it would follow that people like Jeffrey Dahmer, Ted Bundy, Steven Judy, Adolf Hitler, Hein-

---

38. See my "A Critique of Contemporary Egalitarianism," *Faith and Philosophy* 8, no. 4 (1991), and my "Theories of Equality: A Critical Analysis," *Behavior and Philosophy* 23, no. 2 (Summer 1995).

rich Himmler, and Joseph Stalin, who are grossly immoral, who sadistically harm others, who with malice aforethought commit or order others to commit violent crimes, are evil. They have *negative* worth. Many criminals, even if they are leaders of nations, may be morally incurable. A tradition, going back at least to Plato, states that even as the life of a person with an incurably diseased body is not worth living, so the life of a person with an incurably diseased soul is not worth living. Speaking of the pilot of a ferry who conveys people across a river to their destination, Plato says:

> [The pilot] knows that if anyone afflicted in the body with serious and incurable disease has escaped drowning, the man is wretched for not having died and has received no benefit from him [the pilot]. He therefore reckons that if any man suffers many incurable diseases in the soul, which is so much more precious than the body, for such a man life is not worth living and it will be no benefit to him if he, the pilot, saves him from the sea or from the law court or from any other risk. For he knows it is not better for an evil man to live, for he must needs live ill.[39]

In the *Laws* Plato says that the execution of an incurable criminal is a double blessing to the community: "It will be a lesson to them to keep themselves from wrong, and it will rid society of an evil man. These are reasons for which a legislator is bound to ordain the chastisement of death for such desperate villainies and for them alone."[40]

I am not arguing for this position, only suggesting that it is a cogent implication not only of a Platonic thesis that some people have evil souls, but also of a secular view of humanity as an animal who has evolved by accident from "lower" animals over time. If humans do not possess some kind of intrinsic value—say the image of God—then why not rid ourselves of those who egregiously violate the necessary conditions for civilized living, our moral and legal codes? How are sadistic murderers of more worth than a rabid dog, a man-eating tiger or the HIV virus?

So my challenge to the abolitionist stands. If the religious view is correct, and we have a dignity that is based on a transcendent trait, then the fact that we have freely killed a child of God leads to the judgment that we deserve to be executed for our malicious act. But if secularism is correct and we have no value apart from our moral character and social function,

---

39. Plato, *Gorgias* 512a (see also *Gorgias* 425c).
40. Plato, *Laws* 862d.

then many criminals manifest a corrupt soul and are the embodiment of evil, so destroying them is good riddance to bad rubbish. It is prudent to destroy what is evil. Besides, it isn't as though we are doing to the criminal anything that will not happen in a few years anyway. In the end we all rot—unless there is something more to life than the secularist supposes.

Either way, it seems we may justifiably execute the murderer.[41] Yet there is another reason why we should favor the death penalty: the value of deterrence.

Deterrence

The utilitarian argument for capital punishment is that it deters would-be offenders from committing first degree murder. Thorstein Sellin's study of comparing states with and without capital punishment concludes that the death penalty is not a better deterrent of homicides than imprisonment.[42] On the other hand, Isaac Ehrlich's study, the most thorough study to date, takes into account the problems of complex sociological data in terms of race, heredity, regional lines, standards of housing, education, opportunities, cultural patterns, intelligence, and so forth, and concludes that the death penalty does deter. His simultaneous equation regression model suggests that over the period 1933–1969 "an additional execution per year . . . may have resulted on the average in 7 or 8 fewer murders."[43] It should be noted that Ehrlich began his study as an abolitionist, but his data forced him to change his position. However, Ehrlich's study has been criticized, largely for technical reasons, so that his conclusion that we have significant statistical evidence that the death penalty deters better than

---

41. The paradox should be qualified. If the criminal has the same status as a rabid dog, we do not have an obligation to kill him. We can isolate him somewhere. But, the question arises, if he, indeed, has no moral status, why waste any resources on him at all? He has no right not to be killed. Some, including Tziporah Kasachkoff and John Kleinig have urged that we ought to adhere to the principle "use no more force than is necessary to get the job done." But I see no reason to adhere to this principle in this sort of case. It may be that with regard to rabid dogs the principle doesn't obtain. Or in cases of criminals, it may be that more, rather than less, force is deserved.

42. Thorstein Sellin, *The Death Penalty* (1959) reprinted in *The Death Penalty in America*, ed. Hugo Bedau (Anchor Books, 1967).

43. Isaac Ehrlich, "The Deterrent Effect of Capital Punishment: A Question of Life and Death," *American Economic Review* 65 (June 1975): 397–417.

prison sentences is not conclusive.[44] The problems seem to be that there are simply too many variables to control in comparing demographic patterns (culture, heredity, poverty, education, religion, and general environmental factors) and that the death penalty isn't carried out frequently enough to have the effect that it might have under circumstances of greater use. One criticism of Ehrlich's work is that if he had omitted the years 1962 to 1969, he would have had significantly different results. David Baldus and James Cole contend that Ehrlich omitted salient variables, such as the rate of migration from rural to urban areas. On the other hand, Stephen Layson's study in 1985 corroborates Ehrlich's conclusion, except that Layson's work indicates that each time the death penalty is applied, the murder rate is reduced by about eighteen murders.[45] A consensus is wanting, so that at present we must conclude that we lack strong statistical evidence that capital punishment deters. But this should not be construed as evidence against the deterrence thesis. There is no such evidence for nondeterrence either. The statistics available are simply inconclusive either way.

Precisely on the basis of this inconclusivity with regard to the evidence, some abolitionists, for example, Stephen Nathanson, argue that deterrence cannot be the moral basis for capital punishment. "The death penalty can be justified as analogous to defensive killing only if it can be shown that it does save lives. Since that has not been shown, one cannot appeal to this protective function as providing a moral basis for executing murderers."[46] I think Nathanson is wrong about this. There is some nonstatistical evidence based on common sense that gives credence to the hypothe-

---

44. See for example David Baldus and James Cole, "A Comparison of the Work of Thorstein Sellin and Isaac Ehrlich on the Deterrent Effect of Capital Punishment," *Yale Law Journal* 85 (1975).

45. Stephen Layson, "Homicide and Deterrence: A Reexamination of the United States Time-Series Evidence," *Southern Economic Journal* (1985): 68, 80.

46. Stephen Nathanson, *An Eye for an Eye?* (Lanham, Md.: Rowman & Littlefield, 1987). See chap. 2 for the abolitionist's argument. Actually Nathanson admits the deterrent effect of the death penalty. On p. 17 he says "I doubt that anyone would deny that the death penalty deters some murderers, if this means only that fewer murders would occur in a situation where the death penalty was imposed than in a situation in which murderers suffered no punishment at all." The question seems to be whether long term imprisonment doesn't do as well. Although I shall take issue with many of the arguments in Nathanson's book, I regard it as one of the best defenses of abolitionism.

sis that the threat of the death penalty deters and that it does so better than long prison sentences. I will discuss the commonsense case below, but first I want to present an argument for the deterrent effect of capital punishment that is agnostic as to whether the death penalty deters better than lesser punishments.[47]

Ernest van den Haag has set forth what he calls the Best Bet Argument.[48] He argues that even though we don't know for certain whether the death penalty deters or prevents other murders, we should bet that it does. Indeed, due to our ignorance, any social policy we take is a gamble. Not to choose capital punishment for first-degree murder is as much a bet that capital punishment doesn't deter as choosing the policy is a bet that it does. There is a significant difference in the betting, however, in that to bet against capital punishment is to bet against the innocent and for the murderer, while to bet for it is to bet against the murderer and for the innocent.[49]

The point is this: We are accountable for what we let happen, as well as for what we actually do. If I fail to bring up my children properly, so that they are a menace to society, I am to some extent responsible for their bad

---

47. Ibid., 31.

48. Ernest van den Haag, "On Deterrence and the Death Penalty," *Ethics* 78 (July 1968).

49. The Best Bet argument rejects the passive/active distinction involved in killing and letting die. Many people think that it is far worse to kill someone than to let him die—even with the same motivation. More generally, they hold that it is worse to *do* something bad than *allowing* something bad to happen. I think people feel this way because they are tacitly supposing different motivational stances. Judith Jarvis Thomson gives the following counterexample to this doctrine. John is a trolley driver who suddenly realizes that his brakes have failed. He is heading for a group of workers on the track before him and will certainly kill them if something isn't done immediately. Fortunately, there is a side track to the right onto which John can turn the trolley. Unfortunately, there is one worker on that track who will be killed if John steers the trolley onto the side track. Now if the passive/active distinction holds, John should do nothing but simply allow the trolley to take its toll of the five men on the track before him. But that seems terrible. Surely, by turning quickly and causing the trolley to move onto the side track John will be saving a total of four lives. It seems morally preferable for John to turn the trolley onto the side track and actively cause the death of one man rather than passively allow the death of five. John is caught in a situation in which he cannot help doing or allowing harm, but he can act so that the lesser of the evils obtains—rather than the greater of the evils.

behavior. I could have caused it to be somewhat better. If I have good evidence that a bomb will blow up the building you are working in and fail to notify you (assuming I can), I am partly responsible for your death, if and when the bomb explodes. So we are responsible for what we omit doing, as well as for what we do. Purposefully to refrain from a lesser evil which we know will allow a greater evil to occur is to be at least partially responsible for the greater evil. This responsibility for our omissions underlies van den Haag's argument, to which we now return.

Suppose that we choose a policy of capital punishment for capital crimes. In this case we are betting that the death of some murderers will be more than compensated for by the lives of some innocents not being murdered (either by these murderers or others who would have murdered). If we're right, we have saved the lives of the innocent. If we're wrong, unfortunately, we've sacrificed the lives of some murderers. But say we choose not to have a social policy of capital punishment. If capital punishment doesn't work as a deterrent, we've come out ahead, but if it does work, then we've missed an opportunity to save innocent lives. If we value the saving of innocent lives more highly than the loss of the guilty, then to bet on a policy of capital punishment turns out to be rational. The reasoning goes like this. Let "CP" stand for "capital punishment":

THE WAGER

	CP works	*CP doesn't work*
We bet on CP	a. We win: Some murderers die & innocents are saved.	b. We lose: Some murderers die for no purpose.
We bet against CP	c. We lose: Murderers live & innocents needlessly die.	d. We win: Murderers live & some lives of others are unaffected.

Suppose that we estimate that the utility value of a murderer's life is 5, while the value of an innocent's life is 10. (Although we cannot give lives exact numerical values, we can make rough comparative estimates of value—e.g. Mother Teresa's life is more valuable than Adolf Hitler's; all things being equal, the life of an innocent person has at least twice the value of a murderer's life. My own sense is that the murderer has forfeited most, if not all, of his worth, but if I had to put a ratio to it, it would be 1,000 to 1.) Given van den Haag's figures, the sums work out this way:

A murderer saved	$+5$
A murderer executed	-5
An innocent saved	$+10$
An innocent murdered	-10

Suppose that for each execution only two innocent lives are spared. Then the outcomes (correlating to the above wager table) read as follows:

a. $-5 + 20 = +15$
b. -5
c. $+5 - 20 = -15$
d. $+5$

If all the possibilities are roughly equal, we can sum their outcomes like this:

If we bet on capital punishment, (a) and (b) obtain $= +10$

If we bet against capital punishment (c) and (d) obtain $= -10$.

So to execute convicted murderers turns out to be a good bet. To abolish the death penalty for convicted murderers would be a bad bet. We unnecessarily put the innocent at risk.

Even if we value the utility of an innocent life only slightly more than that of a murderer, it is still rational to execute convicted murderers. As van den Haag writes, "Though we have no proof of the positive deterrence of the penalty, we also have no proof of zero or negative effectiveness. I believe we have no right to risk additional future victims of murder for the sake of sparing convicted murderers; on the contrary, our moral obligation is to risk the possible ineffectiveness of executions."[50]

A Critique of the Best Bet Argument

The abolitionist David Conway has constructed an instructive, imaginary dialogue about van den Haag's argument in which an opponent (O) objects to this line of reasoning, contending that the gambling metaphor regarding capital punishment (C.P.) is misleading, for it seems to devalue the lives of the guilty. We ought not to gamble with human lives. The issue is between the *possibility* of saving some lives (if deterrence works) and the *certainty* of sacrificing some lives (whether or not it works). Con-

---

50. Ernest van den Haag, "On Deterrence."

way's proponent (P) for van den Haag's argument counters that gambling can be interpreted as doing a cost-benefit analysis with regard to saving lives. Here is a segment of Conway's dialogue:

P: [T]here are other circumstances in which we must gamble with lives in this way. Suppose you were almost, but not quite certain that a madman was about to set off all the bombs in the Western hemisphere. On [your] principle [that we ought not gamble with human life], you would not be justified in shooting him, even if it were the only possible way to stop him.

O: Yes, I suppose that I must grant you that. But perhaps my suppositions that gambling is taking the risk and that gambling with human lives is wrong, taken together, at least partially account for my intuitive revulsion with van den Haag's argument.

P: That may be. But so far, your intuitions have come to nothing in producing a genuine objection to the argument. I might add that I cannot even agree with your intuition that not gambling is taking the sure thing. Don't we sometimes disapprove of the person who refuses to take out life insurance or automobile insurance on the grounds that he is unwisely gambling that he will not die prematurely or be responsible for a highway accident? And he is taking the sure thing, keeping the premium money in his pocket. So, in common sense terms, failure to take a wise bet is sometimes "gambling."

O: You are right again. . . . But that does not change my views about C.P. Once the bet is clarified, it should be clear that you are asking us to risk too much, to actually take a human life on far too small a chance of saving others. It is just a rotten bet.

P: But it is not. As I have said, the life of each murderer is clearly worth much less than the life of an innocent, and, besides, each criminal life lost may save many innocents.

The opponent remains troubled by the notion of evaluating human worth, but finally admits that he is willing to grant that the life of the innocent is worth somewhat more than that of the murderer. Yet he goes on to give his fundamental objection:

O: The basic problem with your wager is simply that we have no reason to think that C.P. does work, and in the absence of such reason, the probability that it does is virtually zero. In general, your proponents seems confused about the evidence. First, you say C.P. deters. Then you are confronted with evidence such as: State A and State B have virtually identical capital crime rates but State A hasn't had C.P. for one hundred years. You reply, for instance, that this could be because State A has more Quakers, who are peace-loving folk and so help to keep the crime rate down. And, you say, with C.P and all those Quakers, State A perhaps could have had an even lower crime rate. Since we do not know about all such variables, the evidence is "inconclusive." Here "inconclusive" can only mean that while the evidence does not indicate that C.P. deters, it also does not demonstrate that it does not.

The next thing we see is your proponents saying that we just do not know whether C.P. deters or not, since the evidence is "inconclusive." But for this to follow, "inconclusive" must mean something like "tends to point both ways." The only studies available, on your own account, fail to supply any evidence at all that it *does* deter. From this, we cannot get "inconclusive" in the latter sense; we can't say that "we just don't know" whether it deters, we can only conclude, "we have no reason to think it does." Its status as a deterrent is no different from, e.g., prolonged tickling of murderers' feet. It could deter, but why think it does? . . .

P: So you demand that we have definite, unequivocal evidence and very high probability that C.P. deters before it could be said to be justifiable.

O: No, I never said that . . . I think the "Best-Bet Argument" shows that the demand is too strong. Given the possible gains and losses, if there is even a strong possibility that it works, I do not think it would be irrational to give it another try. But we should do so in full cognizance of the betting situation. We would be taking lives on the chance that there will be more than compensating saving of lives. And, I also think that it is damned difficult to show that there is even a strong possibility that C.P. deters.[51]

There are several things to say about Conway's dialogue. Like his opponent, you may object that this kind of quantifying of human life is entirely inappropriate. But if you had to choose between saving an innocent person and saving one who had just committed cold-blooded murder, which would you choose? We generally judge that conscientiously moral people are more worthy than viciously immoral ones, that the innocent are more worthy of aid than those who are guilty of squandering aid. Van den Haag's argument only formalizes these comparisons and applies them to the practice of capital punishment. Some humans are worth more than others, and some have forfeited their right not to be killed, whereas most people have not. Our practices should take this into account.

Secondly, you may still have doubts about the validity of putting a value on human life. But ask yourself, "What gives humans value?" or "What gives their lives value?" From a religious perspective they may have intrinsic value, but they still may forfeit a right to life by committing murder.

---

51. David Conway, "Capital Punishment and Deterrence: Some Considerations in Dialogue Form," *Philosophy and Public Affairs* 3, no. 4 (Summer 1974).

But if you accept a secular point of view, isn't it some quality like moral integrity or contribution to the community that at least partly gives us worth? If so, then the murderer has lost a good bit of whatever value his life had. Kant, who set forth the idea that persons have intrinsic worth based on their ability to reason, held that we could forfeit that worth ("obliterate it") through immoral acts, so that the death penalty might well be appropriate.

Thirdly, if we had evidence that there was a 50 percent chance that executing a murderer would bring back the innocent victim, wouldn't you vote for the execution? I would vote for it if there was *virtually any chance* at all. But how different is that bet from the one that says there is a good chance that executing a person convicted of first-degree murder will prevent the murders of other innocent people? If the death penalty does deter, and we have evidence that it does, then we are partly responsible for the deaths of additional innocents by not inflicting that penalty.

Finally, the opponent is wrong in arguing that we have no evidence at all about the deterrent effect of capital punishment, so that it is tantamount to the evidence that tickling murderers' feet deters. We have evidence, though not statistical proof, based on commonsense experience, which makes the case for deterrence even stronger than the Best Bet argument. I now turn to the Argument from Anecdotal Evidence, a commonsense argument.

The Argument from Anecdotal Evidence

Abolitionists like Stephen Nathanson argue that because the statistical evidence in favor of the deterrent effect of capital punishment is indecisive, we have no basis for concluding that it is a better deterrent than long prison sentences.[52] If I understand these opponents, their argument presents us with an exclusive disjunct: Either we must have conclusive statistical evidence (i.e., a proof) for the deterrent effect of the death penalty, or we have no grounds for supposing that the death penalty deters. Many people accept this argument. Just this morning a colleague said to me, "There is no statistical evidence that the death penalty deters," as if to dismiss the argument from deterrence altogether. This is premature judgment, for the argument commits the fallacy of supposing that only two

---

52. Nathanson, *An Eye for an Eye?* Chap. 2.

opposites are possible. There is a middle position that holds that while we cannot prove conclusively that the death penalty deters, the weight of evidence supports its deterrence. Furthermore, I think there are too many variables to hold constant for us to prove via statistics the deterrence hypothesis, and even if the requisite statistics were available, we could question whether they were cases of mere correlation versus causation. On the other hand, commonsense or anecdotal evidence may provide insight into the psychology of human motivation, providing evidence that fear of the death penalty deters some types of would-be criminals from committing murder.[53] Granted, people are sometimes deceived about their motivation. But usually they are not deceived, and, as a rule, we should presume they know their motives until we have evidence to the contrary. The general commonsense argument goes like this:

1. What people (including potential criminals) fear more will have a greater deterrent effect on them.
2. People (including potential criminals) fear death more than they do any other humane punishment.
3. The death penalty is a humane punishment.
4. Therefore, people (including criminals) will be deterred more by the death penalty than by any other humane punishment.

Since the purpose of this argument is to show that the death penalty very likely deters more than long term prison sentences, I am assuming it is *humane*, that is, acceptable to the moral sensitivities of the majority in our society. Torture might deter even more, but it is not considered humane. I will say more about the significance of humaneness with regard to the death penalty below.

Common sense informs us that most people would prefer to remain out of jail, that the threat of public humiliation is enough to deter some people, that a sentence of twenty years will deter most people more than a sentence of two years, that a life sentence will deter most would-be crimi-

---

53. After I had written this section, Michael Davis sent me his article, "Death, Deterrence, and the Method of Common Sense," *Social Theory and Practice* 7, no. 2 (Summer 1981). He offers a similar commonsense argument for the deterrent effect of the death penalty. His article is especially useful in that it shows just how little the statistics of social science demonstrate and why we should take the commonsense data as weightier.

nals more than a sentence of twenty years. I think that we have common-sense evidence that the death penalty is a better deterrent than prison sentences. For one thing, as Richard Herrnstein and James Q. Wilson have argued in *Crime and Human Nature*, a great deal of crime is committed on a cost-benefit schema, wherein the criminal engages in some form of risk assessment as to his or her chances of getting caught and punished in some manner. If he or she estimates the punishment mild, the crime becomes inversely attractive, and vice versa. The fact that those who are condemned to death do everything in their power to get their sentences postponed or reduced to long-term prison sentences, in a way lifers do not, shows that they fear death more than life in prison.

The point is this: Imprisonment constitutes one evil, the loss of freedom, but the death penalty imposes a more severe loss, that of life itself. If you lock me up, I may work for a parole or pardon, I may learn to live stoically with diminished freedom, and I can plan for the day when my freedom has been restored. But if I believe that my crime may lead to death, or loss of freedom followed by death, then I have more to fear than mere imprisonment. I am faced with a great evil plus an even greater evil. I fear death more than imprisonment because it alone takes from me all future possibility.

I am not claiming that the fear of legal punishment is all that keeps us from criminal behavior. Moral character, habit, fear of being shamed, peer pressure, fear of authority, or the fear of divine retribution may have a greater influence on some people. However, many people will be deterred from crime, including murder, by the threat of severe punishment. The abolitionist points out that many would-be murderers simply do not believe they will be caught. Perhaps this is true for some. While the fantastic egoist has delusions of getting away with his crime, many would-be criminals are not so bold or delusionary.

Former Prosecuting Attorney for the State of Florida, Richard Gernstein has set forth the commonsense case for deterrence. First of all, he claims, the death penalty certainly deters the murderer from any further murders, including those he or she might commit within the prison where he is confined. Secondly, statistics cannot tell us how many potential criminals have refrained from taking another's life through fear of the death penalty. He quotes Judge Hyman Barshay of New York: "The death penalty is a warning, just like a lighthouse throwing its beams out to sea. We hear about shipwrecks, but we do not hear about the ships the lighthouse guides safely on their way. We do not have proof of the number of ships its saves, but we do not tear the lighthouse down."[54]

Some of the commonsense evidence is anecdotal as the following quotation shows. British member of Parliament Arthur Lewis explains how he was converted from an abolitionist to a supporter of the death penalty:

> One reason that has stuck in my mind, and which has proved [deterrence] to me beyond question, is that there was once a professional burglar in [my] constituency who consistently boasted of the fact that he had spent about one-third of his life in prison. . . . He said to me "I am a professional burglar. Before we go out on a job we plan it down to every detail. Before we go into the boozer to have a drink we say 'Don't forget, no shooters'—shooters being guns." He adds "We did our job and didn't have shooters because at that time there was capital punishment. Our wives, girlfriends and our mums said, 'Whatever you do, do not carry a shooter because if you are caught you might be topped [executed].' If you do away with capital punishment they will all be carrying shooters."[55]

It is difficult to know how widespread this reasoning is. My own experience corroborates this testimony. Growing up in the infamous Cicero, Illinois, home of Al Capone and the Mafia, I had friends who went into crime, mainly burglary and larceny. It was common knowledge that one stopped short of killing in the act of robbery. A prison sentence could be dealt with—especially with a good lawyer—but being convicted of murder, which at that time included a reasonable chance of being electrocuted, was an altogether different matter. No doubt exists in my mind that the threat of the electric chair saved the lives of some of those who were robbed in my town. No doubt some crimes are committed in the heat of passion or by the temporally (or permanently) insane, but some are committed through a process of risk assessment. Burglars, kidnappers, traitors and vindictive people will sometimes be restrained by the threat of death. We simply don't know how much capital punishment deters, but this sort of commonsense, anecdotal evidence must be taken into account in assessing the institution of capital punishment.

---

54. Richard E. Gernstein, "A Prosecutor Looks at Capital Punishment" *Journal of Criminal Law: Criminology and Police Science* 51, no. 2 (1960).

55. British *Parliamentary Debates* fifth series, vol. 23, issue 1243, House of Commons, 11 May 1982. Quoted in Tom Sorell, *Moral Theory and Capital Punishment* (Oxford: Blackwell, 1987), 36.

John Stuart Mill admitted that capital punishment does not inspire terror in hardened criminals, but it may well make an impression on prospective murderers. "As for what is called the failure of the death punishment, who is able to judge of that? We partly know who those are whom it has not deterred; but who is there who knows whom it has deterred, or how many human beings it has saved who would have lived to be murderers if that awful association had not been thrown round the idea of murder from their earliest infancy."[56] Mill's points are well taken: (1) Not everyone will be deterred by the death penalty, but some will; (2) The potential criminal need not consciously calculate a cost-benefit analysis regarding his crime to be deterred by the threat. The idea of the threat may have become a subconscious datum "from their earliest infancy." The repeated announcement and regular exercise of capital punishment may have deep causal influence.

Gernstein quotes the British Royal Commission on Capital Punishment (1949–53), which concluded that there was evidence that the death penalty has some deterrent effect on normal human beings. Some of its evidence in favor of the deterrence effect includes:

1. "Criminals who have committed an offense punishable by life imprisonment, when faced with capture, refrained from killing their captor though by killing, escape seemed probable. When asked why they refrained from the homicide, quick responses indicated a willingness to serve life sentence, but not risk the death penalty."
2. "Criminals about to commit certain offenses refrained from carrying deadly weapons. Upon apprehension, answers to questions concerning absence of such weapons indicated a desire to avoid more serious punishment by carrying a deadly weapon, and also to avoid use of the weapon which could result in imposition of the death penalty."
3. "Victims have been removed from a capital punishment state to a non-capital punishment state to allow the murderer opportunity for homicide without threat to his own life. This in itself demonstrates that the death penalty is considered by some would-be-killers."[57]

---

56. *Parliamentary Debates*, third series, April 21, 1868. Reprinted in Peter Singer, ed., *Applied Ethics* (Oxford University Press, 1986), 97–104.
57. Ibid.

Gernstein then quotes former District Attorney of New York, Frank S. Hogan, representing himself and his associates:

> We are satisfied from our experience that the deterrent effect is both real and substantial . . . for example, from time to time accomplices in felony murder state with apparent truthfulness that in the planning of the felony they strongly urged the killer not to resort to violence. From the context of these utterances, it is apparent that they were led to these warnings to the killer by fear of the death penalty which they realized might follow the taking of life. Moreover, victims of hold-ups have occasionally reported that one of the robbers expressed a desire to kill them and was dissuaded from so doing by a confederate. Once again, we think it not unreasonable to suggest that fear of the death penalty played a role in some of these intercessions.
>
> On a number of occasions, defendants being questioned in connection with homicide have shown a striking terror of the death penalty. While these persons have in fact perpetrated homicide, we think that their terror of the death penalty must be symptomatic of the attitude of many others of their type, as a result of which many lives have been spared.[58]

It seems likely that the death penalty does not deter as much as it could due to its inconsistent and rare use. For example, out of an estimated 23,370 cases of murder, nonnegligent manslaughter, and rape in 1949, there were only 119 executions carried out in the United States. In 1953, only 62 executions out of 7,000 cases for those crimes took place. Few executions were carried out in the 1960s and none at all from 1967 to 1977. Gernstein points out that at that rate a criminal's chances of escaping execution are better than 100 to 1. Actually, since Gernstein's report, the figures have become even more weighted against the chances of the death sentence. In 1993, there were 24,526 cases of murder and nonnegligent manslaughter and only 56 executions; and in 1994, there were 23,305 cases of murder and nonnegligent manslaughter and only 31 executions—for a ratio of better than 750 to 1 in favor of the criminal. The average length of stay for a prisoner executed in 1994 was ten years and two months. If potential murderers perceived the death penalty as a highly probable outcome of murder, would they not be more reluctant to kill? Gernstein notes:

> The commissioner of police of London, England, in his evidence before the Royal Commission on Capital Punishment, told of a gang of armed robbers

---

58. Quoted in Gernstein, "A Prosecutor Looks at Capital Punishment."

who continued operations after one of their members was sentenced to death and his sentence commuted to penal servitude, but the same gang disbanded and disappeared when, on a later occasion, two others were convicted of murder and hanged.[59]

Gernstein sums up his data: "Surely it is a commonsense argument, based on what is known of human nature, that the death penalty has a deterrent effect particularly for certain kinds of murderers. Furthermore, as the Royal Commission opined the death penalty helps to educate the conscience of the whole community, and it arouses among many people a quasi-religious sense of awe. In the mind of the public there remains a strong association between murder and the penalty of death. Certainly one of the factors which restrains some people from murder is fear of punishment and surely, since people fear death more than anything else, the death penalty is the most effective deterrent."[60]

I should also point out that, given the retributivist argument for the death penalty, based on desert, the retentionist does not have to prove that the death penalty deters *better* than long prison sentences, but if the death penalty is deemed at least as effective as its major alternative, it would be justified. If evidence existed that life imprisonment were a *more effective* deterrent, the retentionist might be hard pressed to defend it on retributivist lines alone. My view is that the desert argument plus the commonsense evidence—being bolstered by the Best Bet Argument—strongly supports retention of the death penalty.

It is noteworthy that prominent abolitionists, such as Charles Black, Hugo Adam Bedau, Ramsey Clark, and Henry Schwartzchild, have admitted to Ernest van den Haag that even if every execution were to deter a hundred murders, they would oppose it, from which van den Haag concludes "to these abolitionist leaders, the life of every murderer is more valuable than the lives of a hundred prospective victims, for these abolitionists would spare the murderer, even if doing so will cost a hundred future victims their lives." Black and Bedau said they would favor abolishing the death penalty even if they knew that doing so would increase the homicide rate 1,000 percent.[61] This response of abolitionists is puzzling,

---

59. Ibid.
60. Ibid.
61. Cited in Ernest van den Haag, "The Death Penalty Once More, Unpublished manuscript: 18 available from van den Haag. In "A Response to Bedau"

since one of Bedau's arguments against the death penalty is that it doesn't bring back the dead. "We cannot do anything for the dead victims of crime. (How many of those who oppose the death penalty would continue to do so if, *mirabile dictu*, executing the murderer might bring the victim back to life?)"[62] Apparently, he would support the death penalty if it brought a dead victim back to life, but not if it prevented a hundred innocent victims from being murdered.

If the Best Bet Argument is sound, or if the death penalty does deter would-be murderers, as common sense suggests, then we should support some uses of the death penalty. It should be used for those who commit first-degree murder, for whom no mitigating factors are present, and especially for those who murder police officers, prison guards, and political leaders. Many states rightly favor it for those who murder while committing another crime, e.g., burglary or rape. It should also be used for treason and terrorist bombings.

The Golden Rule Argument

One more argument should be set forth, the Golden Rule Argument for the death penalty. The Golden Rule states that we should do unto others as we would have them do unto us. Reflect on the evil deeds perpetrated by those who blew up the Murrah Federal Building on Oklahoma City April 19, 1995, killing 168 people or reread the descriptions of heinous murders discussed by Mike Royko at the beginning of this part of this essay. If you had yielded to temptation and blown up the Murrah Federal Building or if you, like Steven Judy, had raped and murdered a helpless woman and then drowned her three small children,—or if you had kidnapped a young girl, placed her in your trunk, and then killed her, what punishment do you think would be fitting for *you*? What would you deserve? Would you want to live? Would not the *moral* guilt that you

---

(*Arizona State Law Journal* 4 [1977]) van den Haag states that both Black and Bedau said that they would be in favor of abolishing the death penalty even if "they knew that its abolition (and replacement by life imprisonment) would increase the homicide rate by 10%, 20%, 50%, 100%, or 1000%. Both gentlemen continued to answer affirmatively." Bedau confirmed this in a letter to me (July 28, 1996).

62. Hugo Adam Bedau, "How to Argue about the Death Penalty," in *Facing the Death Penalty*, ed. Michael Radelet (Temple University Press, 1989), 190.

would doubtless feel demand the death penalty? And would you not judge that such moral guilt was appropriate, so that anyone who did not feel it was morally defective? Would you not agree that you forfeited your right to life, that you had brought upon yourself the hangman's noose? Would you not agree that you *deserved* nothing less than death? Should we not apply these sentiments to murderers? Should we not apply the Golden Rule to those who do heinous evil? Are not some crimes so evil that the very stones cry out for retribution?

Objections to Capital Punishment

Let us examine six of the major objections to capital punishment, as well as the retentionist's responses to those objections.

1. *Objection*: Capital punishment is a morally unacceptable thirst for revenge. As former British Prime Minister Edward Heath put it,

> The real point which is emphasized to me by many constituents is that even if the death penalty is not a deterrent, murderers deserve to die. This is the question of revenge. Again, this will be a matter of moral judgment for each of us. I do not believe in revenge. If I were to become the victim of terrorists, I would not wish them to be hanged or killed in any other way for revenge. All that would do is deepen the bitterness which already tragically exists in the conflicts we experience in society, particularly in Northern Ireland.[63]

Response: Retributivism, as we argued in Part I, is not the same thing as revenge, although the two attitudes are often intermixed in practice. Revenge is a personal response to a perpetrator for an injury. Retribution is an impartial and impersonal response to an offender for an offense done against someone. You cannot desire revenge for the harm of someone to whom you are indifferent. Revenge always involves personal concern for the victim. Retribution is not personal but based on objective factors: the criminal has deliberately harmed an innocent party and so *deserves* to be punished, whether I wish it or not. I would agree that I or my son or daughter *deserves* to be punished for our crimes, but I don't wish any vengeance on myself or my son or daughter.

Furthermore, while revenge often leads us to exact more suffering from

---

63. British *Parliamentary Debates*, 1982, quoted in Sorrell, *Moral Theory*, 43.

the offender than the offense warrants, retribution stipulates that the offender be punished in proportion to the gravity of the offense. In this sense, the *lex talionis* which we find in the Old Testament is actually a progressive rule, where retribution replaces revenge as the mode of punishment. It says that there are limits to what one may do to the offender. Revenge demands a life for an eye or a tooth, but Moses provides a rule that exacts a penalty equal to the harm done by the offender.

2. *Objection*: Perhaps the murderer does deserve to die, but by what authority does the state execute him or her? Both the Old and New Testament says, " 'Vengeance is mine, I will repay,' says the Lord" (Prov. 25:21 and Romans 12:19). You need special authority to justify taking the life of a human being.[64]

Response: The objector fails to note that the New Testament passage continues with a support of the right of the state to execute criminals in the name of God: "Let every person be subjected to the governing authorities. For there is no authority except from God, and those that exist have been instituted by God. Therefore he who resists what God has appointed, and those who resist will incur judgment. . . . If you do wrong, be afraid, for [the authority] does not bear the sword in vain; he is the servant of God to execute his wrath on the wrongdoer" (Romans 13:1–4). So, according to the Bible, the authority to punish, which presumably includes the death penalty, comes from God.

But we need not appeal to a religious justification for capital punishment. We can site the state's role in dispensing justice. Just as the state has the authority (and duty) to act justly in allocating scarce resources, in meeting minimal needs of its (deserving) citizens, in defending its citizens from violence and crime, and in not waging unjust wars; so too does it have the authority, flowing from its mission to promote justice and the good of its people, to punish the criminal. If the criminal, as one who has forfeited a right to life, deserves to be executed, especially if it will likely deter would-be murderers, the state has a duty to execute those convicted of first-degree murder.

3. *Objection:* Miscarriages of justice occur. Capital punishment is to be rejected because of human fallibility in convicting innocent parties and sentencing them to death. In a survey done in 1985 Hugo Adam Bedau

---

64. Both Stephen Nathanson (in a letter of November 1996) and John Kleinig (in conversation) have raised this objection.

and Michael Radelet found that of the 7,000 persons executed in the United States between 1900 and 1985, 25 were innocent of capital crimes.[65] While some compensation is available to those unjustly imprisoned, the death sentence is irrevocable. We can't compensate the dead. As John Maxton, a member of the British Parliament puts it, "If we allow one innocent person to be executed, morally we are committing the same, or, in some ways, a worse crime than the person who committed the murder."[66]

Response: Mr. Maxton is incorrect in saying that mistaken judicial execution is morally the same or worse than murder, for a deliberate intention to kill the innocent occurs in a murder, whereas no such intention occurs in wrongful capital punishment.

Sometimes this objection is framed this way: It is better to let ten criminals go free than to execute one innocent person. If this dictum is a call for safeguards, then it is well taken; but somewhere there seems to be a limit on the tolerance of society towards capital offenses. Would these abolitionists argue that it is better that 50 or 100 or 1,000 murderers go free than that one guilty person be executed? Society has a right to protect itself from capital offenses even if this means taking a finite chance of executing an innocent person. If the basic activity or process is justified, then it is regrettable, but morally acceptable, that some mistakes are made. Fire trucks occasionally kill innocent pedestrians while racing to fires, but we accept these losses as justified by the greater good of the activity of using fire trucks. We judge the use of automobiles to be acceptable even though such use causes an average of 50,000 traffic fatalities each year. We accept the morality of a defensive war even though it will result in our troops accidentally or mistakenly killing innocent people.

The fact that we can err in applying the death penalty should give us pause and cause us to build an appeals process into the judicial system. Such a process is already in the American and British legal systems. That occasional error may be made, regrettable though this is, is not a sufficient reason for us to refuse to use the death penalty, if on balance it serves a just and useful function.

---

65. Hugo Adam Bedau and Michael Radelet, *Miscarriages of Justice in Potential Capital Cases* (1st draft Oct. 1985, on file at Harvard Law School Library), quoted in E. van den Haag "The Ultimate Punishment: A Defense," *Harvard Law Review* 99, no. 7 (May 1986): 1664.

66. Ibid., 47.

Furthermore, abolitionists are simply misguided in thinking that prison sentences are a satisfactory alternative here. It's not clear that we can always or typically compensate innocent parties who waste away in prison. Jacques Barzun has argued that a prison sentence can be worse than death and carries all the problems that the death penalty does regarding the impossibility of compensation:

> In the preface of his useful volume of cases, *Hanged in Error*, Mr. Leslie Hale refers to the tardy recognition of a minor miscarriage of justice—one year in jail: "The prisoner emerged to find that his wife had died and that his children and his aged parents had been removed to the workhouse. By the time a small payment had been assessed as 'compensation' the victim was incurably insane." So far we are as indignant with the law as Mr. Hale. But what comes next? He cites the famous Evans case, in which it is very probable that the wrong man was hanged, and he exclaims: "While such mistakes are possible, should society impose an irrevocable sentence?" Does Mr. Hale really ask us to believe that the sentence passed on the first man, whose wife died and who went insane, was in any sense *revocable?* Would not any man rather be Evans dead than that other wretch "emerging" with his small compensation and his reason for living gone?[67]

The abolitionist is incorrect in arguing that death is different than long-term prison sentences because it is irrevocable. Imprisonment also take good things away from us that may never be returned. We cannot restore to the inmate the freedom or opportunities he or she lost. Suppose an innocent 25-year-old man is given a life sentence for murder. Thirty years later the mistake is discovered and he is set free. Suppose he values three years of freedom to every one year of prison life. That is, he would rather live ten years as a free man than thirty as a prisoner. Given this man's values, the criminal justice system has taken the equivalent of ten years of life from him. If he lives until he is 65, he has, as far as his estimation is concerned, lost ten years, so that he may be said to have lived only 55 years.[68]

The numbers in this example are arbitrary, but the basic point is sound.

---

67. Jacques Barzun, "In Favor of Capital Punishment," *The American Scholar* 31, no. 2 (Spring 1962)

68. I have been influenced by similar arguments by Michael Levin (unpublished manuscript) and Michael Davis, "Is the Death Penalty Irrevocable?" *Social Theory and Practice* 10, no. 2 (Summer 1984).

Most of us would prefer a shorter life of higher quality to a longer one of low quality. Death prevents all subsequent quality, but imprisonment also irrevocably harms one in diminishing the quality of life of the prisoner.

4. *Objection*: The death penalty is unjust because it discriminates against the poor and minorities, particularly, African Americans, over rich people and whites. Former Supreme Court Justice William Douglas wrote that "a law which reaches that [discriminatory] result in practice has no more sanctity than a law which in terms provides the same."[69] Nathanson argues that "in many cases, whether one is treated justly or not depends not only on what one deserves but on how other people are treated."[70] He offers the example of unequal justice in a plagiarism case. "I tell the students in my class that anyone who plagiarizes will fail the course. Three students plagiarize papers, but I give only one a failing grade. The other two, in describing their motivation, win my sympathy, and I give them passing grades." Arguing that this is patently unjust, he likens this case to the imposition of the death penalty and concludes that it too is unjust.

Response: First of all, it is not true that a law that is applied in a discriminatory manner is unjust. Unequal justice is no less justice, however uneven its application. The discriminatory application, not the law itself, is unjust. A just law is still just even if it is not applied consistently. For example, a friend of mine once got two speeding tickets during a 100-mile trip (having borrowed my car). He complained to the police officer who gave him his second ticket that many drivers were driving faster than he was at the time. They had escaped detection, he argued, so it wasn't fair for him to get two tickets on one trip. The officer acknowledged the imperfections of the system but, justifiably, had no qualms about giving him the second ticket. Unequal justice is still justice, however regrettable. So Justice Douglas is wrong in asserting that discriminatory results invalidate the law itself. The discriminatory practice should be reformed, and in many cases it can be. But imperfect practices in themselves do not entail that the laws engendering these practices are themselves are unjust.

With regard to Nathanson's analogy with the plagiarism case, two things should be said against it. First, if the teacher is convinced that the motivational factors are mitigating factors, then he or she may be justified

---

69. Justice William Douglas in *Furman v Georgia* 408 U.S. 238 (1972).
70. Nathanson, *An Eye for an Eye?*, 62.

in passing two of the plagiarizing students. Suppose that the one student did no work whatsoever, showed no interest (Nathanson's motivation factor) in learning, and exhibited no remorse in cheating, whereas the other two spent long hours seriously studying the material and, upon apprehension, showed genuine remorse for their misdeeds. To be sure, they yielded to temptation at certain—though limited—sections of their long papers, but the vast majority of their papers represented their own diligent work. Suppose, as well, that all three had C averages at this point. The teacher gives the unremorseful, gross plagiarizer an F but relents and gives the other two D's. Her actions parallel the judge's use of mitigating circumstances and cannot be construed as arbitrary, let alone unjust.

The second problem with Nathanson's analogy is that it would have disastrous consequences for all law and benevolent practices alike. If we concluded that we should abolish a rule or practice, unless we treated everyone exactly by the same rules all the time, we would have to abolish, for example, traffic laws and laws against imprisonment for rape, theft, and even murder. Carried to its logical limits, we would also have to refrain from saving drowning victims if a number of people were drowning but we could only save a few of them. Imperfect justice is the best that we humans can attain. We should reform our practices as much as possible to eradicate unjust discrimination wherever we can, but if we are not allowed to have a law without perfect application, we will be forced to have no laws at all.

Nathanson acknowledges this latter response but argues that the case of death is different. "Because of its finality and extreme severity of the death penalty, we need to be more scrupulous in applying it as punishment than is necessary with any other punishment."[71] The retentionist agrees that the death penalty is a severe punishment and that we need to be scrupulous in applying it. The difference between the abolitionist and the retentionist seems to lie in whether we are wise and committed enough as a nation to reform our institutions so that they approximate fairness. Apparently, Nathanson is pessimistic here, whereas I have faith in our ability to learn from our mistakes and reform our systems. If we can't reform our legal system, what hope is there for us?

More specifically, the charge that a higher percentage of blacks than whites are executed was once true but is no longer so. Many states have

---

71. Ibid., 67.

made significant changes in sentencing procedures, with the result that currently whites convicted of first-degree murder are sentenced to death at a higher rate than blacks.[72]

One must be careful in reading too much into these statistics. While great disparities in statistics should cause us to examine our judicial procedures, they do not in themselves prove injustice. For example, more males than females are convicted of violent crimes (almost 90% of those convicted of violent crimes are males—a virtually universal statistic), but this is not strong evidence that the law is unfair, for there are psychological explanations for the disparity in convictions. Males are on average and by nature more aggressive (usually tied to testosterone) than females. Likewise, there may be good explanations why people of one ethnic group commit more crimes than those of other groups, explanations which do not impugn the processes of the judicial system.[73]

5. *Objection:* The Minimal Harm Argument against the death penalty. As I was preparing this essay, Hugo Adam Bedau sent me a paper attacking the death penalty on the grounds that "[S]ociety (acting through the authority of its government) must not use laws that impose more restrictive—violent, harmful, invasive—interference with human liberty than is necessary as a means to achieve legitimate social objectives."[74] Bedau ar-

---

72. The Department of Justice's *Bureau of Justice Statistics Bulletin* for 1994 reports that between 1977 and 1994, 2,336 (51%) of those arrested for murder were white, 1,838 (40%) were black, 316 (7%) were Hispanic. Of the 257 who were executed, 140 (54%) were white, 98 (38%) were black, 17 (7%) were Hispanic and 2 (1%) were other races. In 1994, 31 prisoners, 20 white men and 11 black men, were executed although whites made up only 7,532 (41%) and blacks 9,906 (56%) of those arrested for murder. Of those sentenced to death in 1994, 158 were white men, 133 were black men, 25 were Hispanic men, 2 were Native American men, 2 were white women, and 3 were black women. Of those sentenced, relatively more blacks (72%) than whites (65%) or Hispanics (60%) had prior felony records. Overall the criminal justice system does not seem to favor white criminals over black, though it does seem to favor rich defendants over poor ones.

73. For instance, according to FBI figures for 1992, the U.S. murder rate was 9.3, far higher than that of France (4.5), Germany (3.9) or Austria (3.9). Of the 23,760 murders committed in the United States that year, 55% of the offenders whose race was known were black and 43% white. Since blacks compose 12.1% of the U.S. population, the murder rate for blacks in 1992 was 45 per 100,000, while that for whites was 4.78—a figure much closer to that for European whites.

74. From Hugo Adam Bedau, "Moral Arguments and the Death Penalty: Is Absolute Abolition a Tenable Policy?" delivered at the Annual Meeting of the American Philosophical Association, 28 December 1996.

gues that the death penalty is never necessary to achieve valid social objectives, because "some other form of legitimate deprivation, such as the deprivation of liberty by means of long-term imprisonment, is sufficient." He cites as evidence that abolitionist jurisdictions such as Michigan, Wisconsin, Minnesota and Rhode Island have no worse crime records than states with the death penalty, such as Illinois. So, it seems to follow, the minimal harm argument urges us to abolish the death penalty in all states.

Response: First, Bedau seems to have neglected some vital statistics. Although the murder rates for Illinois and Michigan are similar, one should take into consideration urban areas where crime is rampant. For example, Detroit, Michigan has one of the highest crime rates in the nation, far higher than the much larger city of Chicago, Illinois. Detroit's homicide rate among juveniles grew from 8 per 100,000 to 30 per 100,000 during the course of the 1980s. Regarding the lower-than-average rates in Wisconsin and Minnesota, other factors besides the presence or absence of the death penalty could explain differences in homicide rates in these states. Bedau needs to take into account the general arguments for deterrence, as well as the fact that the death penalty is seldom carried out (31 executions in 1994). If the arguments Ehrlich, van den Haag, and others have set forth for the deterrent effect of the death penalty are correct, we could accept Bedau's general (do minimal harm) thesis and still advocate the death penalty.

Second, there is a retributive consideration to be brought into the argument. We—the state, using due process—should execute the murderer because he deserves it. The state has a prima facie obligation to give people what they deserve. Even as it has a duty to meet the needs of the deserving poor—by helping to create jobs, providing unemployment insurance and welfare—so it has a prima facie duty to punish those who do evil things to fellow citizens. In other words, one of the purposes of the state is retributive—both positive and negative. And of course the duty is prima facie. If the state doesn't have the means to do these things, or if mitigating circumstances exist, including the appropriateness of mercy to first offenders, then the duty may be overridden.

Note that an ancient tradition going as far back as the Book of Genesis holds that even in the state of nature murderers deserve death, so that anyone who finds a murderer has a duty to execute him. Recall that the first murderer, Cain, who slew his brother, complained, "Behold, thou hast driven me this day from the ground and whoever finds me will slay me" (Genesis 4:14). In forming the state we give up our right to carry out the moral law, entrusting this prerogative to the state.

6. *Objection:* The death penalty is a "cruel and unusual punishment." The death penalty constitutes a denial of the wrongdoer's essential dignity as a human being. No matter how bad a person becomes, no matter how terrible one's deed, we must never cease to regard a person as an end in himself or herself, as someone with inherent dignity. Capital punishment violates that dignity. As such it violates the Constitution of the United States of America, which forbids "cruel and unusual" punishments. Here is how Justice Thurgood Marshall stated it in *Gregg v Georgia:*

> To be sustained under the Eighth Amendment, the death penalty must [comport] with the basic concept of human dignity at the core of the Amendment; the objective in imposing it must be [consistent] with our respect for the dignity of [other] men. Under these standards, the taking of life "because the wrongdoer deserves it" surely must fail, for such a punishment has as its very basis the total denial of the wrongdoer's dignity and worth. The death penalty, unnecessary to promote the goal of deterrence or to further any legitimate notion of retribution, is an excessive penalty forbidden by the Eighth and Fourteenth Amendments.[75]

Similarly, in *Furman v Georgia* (1972) Justice William Brennan condemned capital punishment because it treats "members of the human race as nonhumans, as objects to be toyed with and discarded," adding that it is "inconsistent with the fundamental premise of the Clause that even the vilest criminal remains a human being possessed of common human dignity."[76]

Response: First of all, Justice Marshall differs with the framers of the Constitution about the meaning of "cruel and unusual" in declaring that the death penalty violates the Eighth Amendment's prohibition against "cruel and unusual" punishments—unless one would accuse the framers of the Constitution of contradicting themselves; for the Fifth and Fourteenth Amendments clearly authorize the death penalty.[77] The phrase

---

75. Justice Thurgood Marshall, *Gregg v Georgia* (1976).

76. Justice William Brennan, *Furman v Georgia* (1972).

77. The Fifth Amendment permits depriving people of "life, liberty or property," if the deprivation occurs with "due process of law," and the Fourteenth Amendment applies this provision to the states, "no State shall . . . deprive any person of life, liberty, or property, without due process of law."

"cruel and unusual" in the Eighth Amendment seems to mean cruel and *uncustomary or new* punishments, for, as van den Haag notes, "the framers did not want judges to invent *new* cruel punishments, but did not abolish customary ones."[78] But even if the framers did intend to prohibit the death penalty, I would argue that it is morally justified. The law is not always identical to what is morally correct.

Rather than being a violation of the wrongdoer's dignity, capital punishment may constitute a recognition of human dignity. As we noted in discussing Kant's view of retribution, the use of capital punishment respects the worth of the victim in calling for an equal punishment to be exacted from the offender, and it respects the dignity of the offender in treating him or her as a free agent who must be respected for his or her decisions and who must bear the cost of his or her acts as a responsible agent.

Let's look at these two points a bit more closely. The first—that capital punishment respects the worth of the victim—is bluntly articulated by the newspaper columnist, Mike Royko:

> When I think of the thousands of inhabitants of Death Rows in the hundreds of prisons in this country, I don't react the way the kindly souls do—with revulsion that the state would take these lives. My reaction is: What's taking us so long? Let's get that electrical current flowing. Drop the pellets now!
>
> Whenever I argue this with friends who have opposite views, they say that I don't have enough regard for that most marvelous of miracles—human life.
>
> Just the opposite: It's because I have so much regard for human life that I favor capital punishment. Murder is the most terrible crime there is. Anything less than the death penalty is an insult to the victim and society. It says, in effect, that we don't value the victim's life enough to punish the killer fully.[79]

It is precisely because the victim's life is sacred that the death penalty is sometimes the only fitting punishment for first-degree murder. I am accepting here the idea that there is something "sacred" or "dignified" about human life, though earlier I gave reasons which should cause secularists to doubt this.

Secondly, it's precisely because the murderer is an autonomous, free

---

78. Ernest van den Haag, "Why Capital Punishment?" *Albany Law Review* 54 (1990).

79. Mike Royko, *Chicago Sun-Times* (September 1983).

agent that we regard his or her act of murder as his own and hold him responsible for it. Not to hold the murderer responsible for his crime is to treat him as less than autonomous. Just as we praise and reward people in proportion to the merit of their good deeds, so we blame and punish them in proportion to the evil of their bad deeds. If there is evidence that the offender did not act freely, we would mitigate his sentence. But if the offender did act of his own free will, he bears the responsibility for those actions and deserves to be punished accordingly.

Of course, there are counter-responses to all of the retentionist's responses. Consider the utilitarian matter of cost. The appeals process, which is necessary to our system of justice, is so prolonged and expensive that it might not be worth the costs simply to satisfy our sense of retribution. Furthermore, most moderate retributivists do not argue that there is an *absolute* duty to execute first-degree murderers. Even the principle that the guilty should suffer in proportion to the harm they caused is not absolute. It can be overridden by mercy. But such mercy must be judicious, serving the public good.

In the same vein many argue that life imprisonment without parole will accomplish just as much as the death penalty. The retentionist would respond that death is a more fitting punishment for one who kills in cold blood, and utilitarians (deterrentists) would be concerned about the possibility of escape, murders committed by the murderer while incarcerated, and the enormous costs of keeping a prisoner incarcerated for life. Imprisonment without parole, advocated by many abolitionists as an alternative to the death penalty, should be given serious consideration in special cases, as when there is evidence that the murderer has suitably repented. But even in these cases the desert argument and the Best Bet argument would lean towards the death penalty.

No doubt we should work toward the day when capital punishment is no longer necessary, when the murder rate becomes a tiny fraction of what it is today, when a civilized society can safely incarcerate the few violent criminals in its midst, and where moral reform of the criminal is a reality. Perhaps this is why several European nations have abolished it (e.g., the murder rate in Detroit alone is 732 times that of the nation of Austria). I for one regret the use of the death penalty. I would vote for its abolition in an instant if only one condition were met: that those contemplating murder would set an example for me. Otherwise, it is better that the murderer perish than that innocent victims be cut down by the murderer's knife or bullet.

Is the Abolitionist Consistent?

Finally, I want to challenge the consistency of abolitionists who oppose capital punishment but support abortion. Former Supreme Court Justice William Brennan opposed the death penalty as "uniquely degrading to human dignity," but he had no trouble supporting abortion. I find this puzzling, in some cases entirely hypocritical. For abolitionists so stridently to oppose the death penalty for vicious murderers, who deserve death, and to support abortion of human fetuses, who are completely innocent of any wrong-doing, seems a glaring contradiction. Such is the Humpty Dumpty moral madness of our day that we condone the murder each year of two million human beings (from a biological classification at any rate), too helpless to defend themselves, and become apoplectic over the execution of an average of 65 cold-blooded murderers. "Protection for the Murderer—Death to the Innocent!" seems the implicit motto of the abolitionist who supports abortion.

I can understand how one can regretfully support abortion, as I do, since the fetus is not a full person and since utilitarian arguments may lead us to conclude that it is better for society not to produce unwanted and/ or deformed children. But if we accept these arguments, then it would seem we should, even regretfully, accept the desert and deterrent arguments for the death penalty. If it is not unjust to kill, even to cause great suffering, in an innocent fetus on the way to full personhood in the third trimester, is it unjust to execute someone who has with malice aforethought murdered another human being, especially when there is evidence that this execution will deter others from murdering?

I recognize that those who hold a pro-choice position will object that I am missing the point: that fetuses are not *persons*, so they have no right not to be killed. Given the secularist's assumption that persons are made by socialization, I can understand the conclusion that fetuses are not persons (and of course neither are infants persons, but we inconsistently try people for murder in cases of infanticide), but I don't think the personhood argument can bear the weight alone. The fetus progressively nears personhood, has all the physiological organization necessary to activate self-consciousness, and has a high probability of doing so. Women opt to kill their fetuses because of the threat or likelihood of personal suffering or inconvenience. They do so for valid self-interested or utilitarian reasons. Yet the fetuses are innocent of any crime. Should the state not be allowed to do to murderers what mothers are allowed to do to innocent fetuses? And for the same reasons (utility) and better reasons (desert)? The murderers, at least, deserve to be executed.

Conclusion

Both abolitionists and retributivists agree that punishment for crime is meant to deter (1) the criminal and (2) potential criminals from future crimes. In this way it is *future* oriented. But we could deter people from crimes by framing and punishing the innocent. That would violate justice. The innocent deserve better. So we must recognize the retributive core in punishment. It is a necessary condition that the person punished be guilty of the crime in question. He or she *deserves* the punishment. We also hold that the guilty *ought* to be punished (and punished to the degree of the gravity of the offense). That is, guilt is a *sufficient* condition for punishment (and punishment to the degree of the gravity of the offense). Of course, we are free to be merciful, to take mitigating circumstances into account, to punish the criminal less than he deserves. For example, we ought not rape the rapist or torture the torturer (though he deserves equivalent treatment), for desert is not an absolute value—only a strong prima facie one. Suppose that Charley, our murderer, tortures 35 people, rapes 17 of them and then burns all of his victims in boiling oil. Must we do all that to Charley? We can't kill him more than once (though I suppose we can resuscitate him every time his heart stops and begin the ghoulish process again). There are limits to the evil we should inflict on people— even though they may deserve more. The question is just where those limits lie. Here retributivists may reasonably differ among themselves, and some, the "mild retributivists," will argue that we should stop short of the death penalty.

I regard that as a mistake, for death is not necessarily a "cruel or unusual" punishment, but a fitting limit. The death penalty can be economically sound, cause minimal pain (not that we should complain about the criminal suffering some pain), express our condemnation of capital offenses, be deserved, and yet serve as an adequate deterrent—which long-term imprisonment does not do to the same degree. My argument is that it best meets the criteria of the two main theories of punishment: retribution and deterrence. True, it does not satisfy the mandates of the third theory of punishment, rehabilitation, as well as abolitionism does, but as we saw, rehabilitationism is intrinsically weak, so the fact that it is incompatible with capital punishment is not a good reason to reject capital punishment.

Here is the structure of the argument as I have presented it in this part of my essay :

1. There is no sound argument that prohibits all uses of capital punishment; that is, there are no good reasons to view capital punishment as necessarily wrong.
2. The best grounds for abolitionism is the idea of essential human positive worth, which entails that we treat humans with special dignity. But a religious interpretation of this doctrine also prescribes a duty to punish those who with free will destroy the life of another human, and a secular interpretation of human dignity can only be based on moral status and function, so that when criminals fail these tests they forfeit their dignity, their right to life.
3. There is a sound retributive argument from desert for the thesis that capital punishment is a prima facie duty for capital offenses. This is confirmed via the Golden Rule Argument.
4. There is no sound argument that enjoins capital punishment for all cases of first degree murder.
5. There is also a secondary argument based on deterrence—in the form both of anecdotal, commonsense evidence and the Best-Bet Argument—that urges the use of capital punishment.
6. Therefore, since no abolitionist objection to capital punishment succeeds, and since two strong prima facie arguments for capital punishment exist, the burden of proof shifts to the abolitionist to provide grounds for why a duty to execute cold-blooded murderers should be overridden by other penalties.

Conclusion: Until the positive arguments for capital punishment are defeated, reason urges us to accept its legitimacy and work for fairness in its application.

Contrary to hard retributivists like Kant, I hold that there is no absolute necessity to resort to the death penalty. My argument is that, absent mitigating circumstances, the person who murders in cold blood (that is, with mens rea) deserves the death penalty. Sometimes mercy or a lesser penalty should be applied because of the difficulty in realizing equal justice, or because juries will not convict people if they think they will be sending them to their death, or because of the likelihood of executing an innocent person. These problems must be taken into account, but they do not off-set the inherent justice of the death penalty for those who murder in cold blood. Eventually, we may find a better way to deal with criminals than we now have, which will produce a better—more moral—society. But even then, the murderer will deserve the death penalty.

2

Why the Death Penalty Should Be Abolished in America

Jeffrey Reiman

> *It is a fault to punish a fault in full.*
>
> Seneca, *On Clemency*

Death penalty advocates commonly press two claims in favor of executing murderers. The first is that the death penalty is a just punishment for murder, a murderer's just deserts. On this line of thought, we do injustice to the victims of murder if we do not execute their murderers. The second claim is that the death penalty is necessary to deter potential murderers. Here, the suggestion is that we do injustice to potential victims of murder if we do not execute actual ones. I accept that the death penalty is a just punishment for some murders—some murderers' just deserts—and that, if the death penalty were needed to deter future murders, it would be unjust to future victims not to impose it.[1] Notice, then, that I accept two of the strongest points urged in favor of the death penalty. If, granting these strong points, I can show that it would still be wrong to impose the death penalty, that should be a strong argument indeed. I shall argue for the following propositions:

---

1. It might be thought that we cannot *do* injustice by our *inaction*, and thus that this should rather say that we *allow* injustice by failing to punish murderers. However, the "we" in this phrase refers to us acting through the state, and I take the state to have (in part because it claims a monopoly on the right to punish criminals) a positive obligation to prevent grave injustice to its citizens. Then, when the state *allows* injustice to its citizens, it *does* them injustice.

67

1. that, though the death penalty is a just punishment for some murders, it is not unjust to punish murderers less harshly (down to a certain limit);
2. that, though the death penalty would be justified if needed to deter future murders, we have no good reason to believe that it is needed to deter future murders; and
3. that, in refraining from imposing the death penalty, the state, by its vivid and impressive example, contributes to reducing our tolerance for cruelty and thereby fosters the advance of human civilization as we understand it.

Taken together, these three propositions imply that we do no injustice to actual or potential murder victims, and we do some considerable good, in refraining from executing murderers. This conclusion will be reinforced by another argument, this one for the proposition

4. that, though the death penalty is *in principle* a just penalty for murder, it is unjust *in practice* in America because it is applied in arbitrary and discriminatory ways, and this is likely to continue into the foreseeable future.

This fourth proposition conjoined with the prior three imply the overall conclusion *that it is good in principle to avoid the death penalty and bad in practice to impose it.*

I shall proceed as follows. In section I, "Justifying Punishing," I consider the three main ways—retribution, fairness, and deterrence—in which punishment is thought morally justified, and I shall show how they can all be boiled down to one: *just desert*. In section II, "Death and Desert," I argue that the death penalty is just punishment for some murders, justly deserved by some murderers, but that it is not unjust to punish less harshly (down to a certain limit). In section III, "Death and Deterrence," I argue that the death penalty is not needed to deter future murderers, and thus we do no injustice by refraining from executing current murderers. In section IV, "Pain and Civilization," I defend the notion that punishing less harshly contributes to advancing human civilization as we understand it. In section V, "Just in Principle, Unjust in Practice," I indicate four ways in which the death penalty is administered unjustly in current-day

America and why it is likely to continue to be so.[2] The upshot of the first four sections is that it is *good in principle* to refrain from executing murderers, and the fifth section complements this conclusion by showing that executing murderers in America for the foreseeable future is likely to be *bad in practice*.

I. Justifying Punishing

Philosophers have tended to think that punishment can be justified in three distinct ways: *retribution*, that punishment is the offender's justly deserved payback for the harm he or she has caused; *fairness*, that punishment is a way of maintaining a fair distribution of civic burdens by imposing a burden on one who has shirked the burden of complying with the law; and *deterrence*, that punishment is an evil necessary to prevent greater future evils by giving potential criminals a disincentive to commit offenses.[3]

---

2. Sections II, III, and IV are based upon and substantially revise my "Justice, Civilization, and the Death Penalty: Answering van den Haag," *Philosophy and Public Affairs* 14, no. 2 (Spring 1985): 115–48. And section V is based upon and substantially revises my "The Justice of the Death Penalty in an Unjust World," in *Challenging Capital Punishment: Legal and Social Science Approaches*, ed. K. Haas & J. Inciardi (Beverly Hills, CA: Sage, 1988), 29–48.

3. Two other justifications for punishment are sometimes considered, namely, *incapacitation* (locking criminals up to protect us from their future crimes) and *moral education* (punishing to teach criminals the wrongness of what they did). Since incapacitation is aimed at preventing future crimes, I think it will be subject to the same considerations that pertain to the use of punishment for deterrence. The moral education approach stems from the laudable Platonic counsel that we should do no harm to anyone, and thus even punishment should be aimed at improving the offender. This approach suffers, I think, from three fatal flaws. First, there isn't evidence that many offenders don't know the wrongness of what they did. Second, if offenders really didn't know the wrongness of what they did, then they would not meet the requirements for moral responsibility and would better be treated as insufficiently rational or too immature to be held culpable. Third, if moral education is the justifying aim of punishment then it is doubtful that we are justified in punishing criminals who truly recognize the wrongness of their crimes before their sentences begin. Likewise, it would seem justified (perhaps even required) that we extend the sentences of those who have not learned the wrongness of what they did within the terms of their original sentences. Thus the moral education approach will tend in the direction of indeterminate sentencing, which

Each of these ways of justifying punishment will normally indicate different amounts of justified punishment. This may not seem troubling at first sight, since we might, as philosophers often do, opt for one rationale for punishment as the only really defensible one. But this is sure to result in counterintuitive outcomes for the same reasons that make the other two rationales plausible. I think that most people normally expect punishments to satisfy all three of the rationales for punishment. Thus, if the philosophical justification of punishment is to stay anywhere near the real world, we will have to show that all three rationales have a role to play in the determination of just punishment. And this does pose a problem, because philosophers have also argued that these punishment rationales are not compatible. For example, Immanuel Kant, the strictest of philosophical defenders of retribution, held that to punish someone for the purpose of deterrence is to use the person punished as a tool, a mere means, and thus to do him injustice.[4] However, if we punish only enough to give the offender his just retribution and not enough to deter future offenders, we seem to do injustice to potential victims.

Consequently, if the philosophical justification of punishment is to stay close to people's intuitions, we will have to show that such assertions of incompatibility are false, that the three rationales are not only compatible, but that their different prescriptions can be combined into a unitary mea-

---

shows, I think, the totalitarian tendency of any punishment regime that claims to do good for the criminal. Having said this much, I should add that my own view of the point of retributive punishment includes the idea that such punishment makes a statement to the criminal about his equality with his victim, and in this sense my view includes a certain amount of pedagogical content in punishment. Jean Hampton has striven to show that the moral education theory is "promising," though she admits that "[m]uch more work needs to be done before anyone is in a position to embrace the view wholeheartedly" (Jean Hampton, "The Moral Education Theory of Punishment," in *Punishment: A Philosophy and Public Affairs Reader*, ed. A. J. Simmons et al. [Princeton, NJ: Princeton University Press, 1995], 112–42; the quote is on 113).

4. Kant wrote that "[j]udicial punishment can never be used merely as a means to promote some other good for . . . civil society . . . ; for a human being can never be manipulated merely as a means to the purposes of someone else. . . . His innate personality protects him against such treatment." And further: "Only the Law of retribution (*jus talionis*) can determine exactly the kind and degree of punishment" (Immanuel Kant, "The Metaphysical Elements of Justice," pt. 1 of *The Metaphysics of Morals*, trans. J. Ladd [Indianapolis, IN: Bobbs-Merrill, 1965; originally published 1797], 100, 101).

sure of punishment capable of accomplishing the goal of each of the three without running afoul of either of the other two. I think that this can be done, but before turning to it, let us look at some arguments for the incompatibility of the three. This will give us a way to introduce the three rationales for punishment.

1. The Three Rationales for Punishment and Their Supposed Incompatibility

I shall speak at length about the retribution rationale and its various forms later. For the present, note that the retribution rationale normally takes its cue from the *lex talionis* ("an eye for an eye," and so on), which holds that the offender deserves harm equivalent to the harm he intentionally imposed (or attempted to impose)[5] on his victim. This doesn't mean that the punishment should duplicate the harm the criminal imposed, since that is often impossible. How, for example, could we duplicate the harm caused by a check forger or a spy? Rather, we are to find some penalty that (as near as we can judge) is equivalent to the harm caused, and (in our time) this will normally be some amount of time in prison (and sometimes death).[6]

Following Kant, I understand the *lex talionis* to take into account not only the harm caused by the criminal, but also the evil intention (called in the law *mens rea*) with which it is caused. Thus the punishment is to match criminals' evil, "in proportion to their inner viciousness" (to use Kant's phrase)[7] and in light of the harm viciously caused. It is because retributive

---

5. I shall not always repeat this qualification, but it should be taken as implied throughout.

6. Kant recognized that some crimes cannot be matched, either because it is impossible to do so, or because they are acts so evil that even when done to criminals who deserve them they "would themselves be punishable crimes against humanity in general" (Kant, "Metaphysical Elements of Justice," 132). Kant gives rape, pederasty, and bestiality as examples of such acts. Consequently, Kant allows—even goes on to suggest examples of—punishments that are equivalent to crimes without duplicating them. I do not, of course, mean to endorse Kant's specific proposals here.

7. Kant, "Metaphysical Elements of Justice," 103. Michael Davis agrees that "*lex talionis* includes both harm and fault in its calculation of deserved punishment" (Michael Davis, "Harm and Retribution," in *Punishment*, ed. Simmons et al., 198, see also 206).

punishment is for criminals' evil intention as well as for harm imposed that the *lex talionis* applies not only to completed crimes, but to attempts as well. In attempts, the evil intention is present and acted upon. Harm fails to occur only for reasons outside of the attempter's control.

Let us be clear about the relationship between *lex talionis* and retributivism. They are not the same. Retributivism—as the word itself suggests—is the doctrine that the offender should be *paid back* with suffering he deserves because of the evil he has intentionally done, and the *lex talionis* asserts that injury equivalent to what he intentionally imposed is what the offender deserves. In short, retribution refers to a class of punishment regimens that share the idea that punishment is justified as paying back the criminal with suffering that he deserves for the suffering he has caused. *Lex talionis* is a standard for measuring how much suffering is deserved. Thus we can speak of *lex talionis* as a version of retributivism, the version in which equivalence is the measure of deserved suffering.

Lex talionis is not the only version of retributivism. Another, which I shall call *proportional retributivism*, holds that what retribution requires is, not equivalence of harm between crimes and punishments, but "fit" or proportionality.[8] Our table of punishments should be organized ordinally so that it parallels the table of crimes. The worst crime will be punished by our worst punishment (even if less in harm than the crime), the second worst crime will be punished by our second worst punishment, and so on.[9] Note, here, that both this proportional form of retribution and the *lex talionis* form share the view that punishment is not to exceed the harm caused by the criminal. Either way, the *lex talionis* is the upper limit of punishment justified retributively. When I use the term "retribution," then, I mean a rationale for punishment that takes punishment to be justified as suffering deserved by the offender in light of the suffering he

---

8. Hugo Bedau writes: "[R]etributive justice need not be thought to consist of *lex talionis*. One may reject that principle as too crude and still embrace the retributive principle that the severity of punishments should be graded according to the gravity of the offense" (Hugo A. Bedau, "Capital Punishment," in *Matters of Life and Death,* ed. Tom Regan [New York: Random House, 1980], 177). See also Andrew von Hirsch, "Doing Justice: The Principle of Commensurate Deserts," and Hyman Gross, "Proportional Punishment and Justifiable Sentences," both in *Sentencing,* ed. Hyman Gross and Andrew von Hirsch (New York: Oxford University Press, 1981), 243–56 and 272–83, respectively.

9. For a clear formulation of this notion, see Michael Davis, "How to Make the Punishment Fit the Crime," *Ethics* 93, no. 4 (July 1983): 736–41.

caused, where the measure of the suffering deserved is either equivalence or proportionality, but not more than equivalence.

Alan Goldman maintains that this feature of the retributivist approach to punishment is based on the idea that a criminal forfeits rights equivalent to the rights of her victim that she violates. Consequently, legitimate retributive punishment cannot be more than the harm caused by the crime. Goldman adds that, on this retributivist rationale, punishment that exceeds the harm caused by the criminal is undeserved in the same way as punishment of the innocent is undeserved. Since punishment of the innocent is a grave injustice, it follows that excessive punishment of the guilty is also a grave injustice—even if our anger for the criminal or our sympathy for her victim obscures this fact.

Goldman goes on to point out that the punishments we mete out, particularly for property crimes, seem clearly to be far harsher than the harms caused by the crimes themselves. Indeed, he contends that, if punishment is also to deter potential criminals, then it *must* be harsher than the harms that crimes normally cause. The reason for this is that, in our society, the chance of apprehension for most crimes is considerably below 50 percent. "Given these odds," Goldman writes, "a person pursuing what he considers his maximum prospective benefit may not be deterred by the threat of an imposition of punishment equivalent to the violation of the rights of the potential victim."[10] If criminals can anticipate being punished only half the time they commit crimes, then, to make it irrational for criminals to commit a crime, a penalty must represent a loss at least twice the gain that criminals expect from their crimes. Consequently, at least with property crimes (where the loss to the victim and the gain to the criminal are roughly the same), and possibly others, we will have to impose penalties greater than the harms that criminals have caused. Then, if we would punish justly according to the retributive rationale, we cannot deter future criminals, and if we would deter future criminals, we must punish unjustly. Observes Goldman,

> Caught in this dilemma, our society does not limit punishment to deprivation of [the criminal's] rights [equivalent to the] rights of others which have been violated by the criminal. Especially in regard to crimes against property, punishments by imprisonment are far more severe, on the average, than the

---

10. Alan H. Goldman, "The Paradox of Punishment," in *Punishment*, ed. Simmons et al., 36.

harm caused to victims of these crimes. Probably because such punishment is administered by officials of the state, cloaked in appropriate ritual and vested with authority, most of us systematically ignore its relative severity. If, however, we imagine an apolitical context, in which there is money and property, but no penal institution, would theft of several thousand dollars justify the victim's taking the perpetrator and locking him away in some small room for five to ten years?[11]

The justification of punishment by *fairness* was put forth by Herbert Morris in a now-classic article titled "Persons and Punishment." Morris writes:

> A person who violates the rules [that is, the laws of a just legal system] has something that others have—the benefits of the system—but by renouncing what others have assumed, the burdens of self-restraint, he has acquired an unfair advantage. Matters are not even until this advantage is in some way erased. Another way of putting it is that he owes something to others, for he has something that does not rightfully belong to him. Justice—that is, punishing such individuals—restores the equilibrium of benefits and burdens by taking from the individual what he owes, that is, exacting the debt.[12]

A just legal system creates a mutually beneficial system of cooperation. Because members of society bear the burden of restraining themselves to abide by the law (even when lawbreaking might be tempting or in their interest), a benefit is created for everyone, namely, security of persons and possessions, not to mention regularity and predictability and the like. The lawbreaker is one who takes this benefit but refuses to bear the burden of self-restraint. He thus violates the principle of fairness, of which John Rawls writes, "[t]he main idea is that when a number of persons engage in a mutually advantageous cooperative venture according to rules, and thus restrict their liberty in ways necessary to yield advantages for all, those who have submitted to these restrictions have a right to a similar acquiescence on the part of those who have benefited from their submission."[13]

---

11. Ibid., 37.

12. Herbert Morris, "Persons and Punishment," in *Punishment and the Death Penalty: The Current Debate*, ed. R. M. Baird and S. E. Rosenbaum (Amherst, NY: Prometheus Books, 1995), 63.

13. John Rawls, *A Theory of Justice* (Cambridge, MA: Harvard University Press, 1971), 112; Rawls expresses indebtedness for this statement of the principle to H. L. A. Hart, "Are There Any Natural Rights?" *Philosophical Review* 64 (1955): 185f.

Michael Davis has tried to formulate a version of the fairness justification of punishment; he calls it the *unfair-advantage principle*. Continuing in the same vein as Morris, Davis writes: "Anyone who breaks a law does not bear the same burden the [law-abiding] rest do. Unless he is punished, he will, in effect, have gotten away with doing less than others. He will have an advantage they do not. According to the unfair-advantage principle, it is this advantage that the criminal law is supposed to take back by punishing the criminal for his crime."[14] Note, as it will be important later, that Davis understands this principle as a form of retributivism—an alternative, within retributivism, to the *lex talionis*. Because the unfair-advantage principle and the *lex talionis* measure punishment in different ways—the former by the value of the advantage unfairly taken from the law-abiding and the latter by the gravity of the harm imposed—the two rationales are likely to yield incompatible prescriptions for punishment:

> The advantage [that the criminal law is supposed to take back by punishing the criminal for his crime] bears no necessary relation to the harm the criminal actually did. . . . According to the unfair-advantage principle, the damage a criminal actually does is between him and his victim, a private matter to be settled by civil suit (or the moral equivalent). His *crime* consists only in the unfair advantage he necessarily took over the law-abiding by breaking the law in question. The measure of punishment due is the relative value of *that* advantage. The greater the advantage, the greater the punishment should be. The focus of the unfair-advantage principle is on what the *criminal* gained; the focus of *lex talionis*, on what *others* lost.[15]

Davis goes on to point to cases in which the *lex talionis* cannot, but the unfair-advantage principle can, account for the amount of punishment that appears justified. For example, Davis notes that Illinois, like many American and foreign jurisdictions, distinguishes the crimes of involuntary manslaughter and vehicular homicide, punishing the former with two to five years of imprisonment and the latter with one to three years of imprisonment. Both have the same mental requirement for guilt, recklessness, and the same harm, death. Accordingly, Davis maintains that *lex talionis* cannot account for the distinction between the penalties, nor may we dismiss it as an anomaly in view of how many legal systems recognize a similar distinction. Davis contends that the unfair-advantage principle can ac-

---

14. Michael Davis, "Harm and Retribution," 192.
15. Ibid.

count for the difference. He proposes that, to compare the unfair advantage in the two crimes, we should imagine that licenses to commit the two crimes with impunity were up for auction. Then, since "a license to commit involuntary manslaughter in any way whatever is more useful than a license to commit it in only one way, by use of a vehicle," the unfair advantage taken by the criminal who commits involuntary manslaughter is more valuable than that taken by the one who commits vehicular homicide. And this accounts for the greater punishment attached to involuntary manslaughter.[16]

Likewise, Davis thinks that *lex talionis* cannot explain recidivist statutes—such as the infamous "three strikes and you're out" laws that have recently been passed in a number of states—which impose extremely harsh punishment on people convicted of a third serious crime (punishment that may be more than the sum of the punishments for each of the three crimes). Even if a defender of *lex talionis* were to maintain that a repeat offender shows a deeper and more profound commitment to evil (greater "inner viciousness"), this will surely not account for the enormous difference in punishment for a third offense compared to the punishment that would be meted out for the same crime (and thus for the same harm) by a first offender. Davis contends that, by contrast, no such problem faces the unfair-advantage principle. As long as there is a rule against repeat offenses, a repeat offender takes a separate and additional advantage that a first offender does not take, though they commit the same offenses, and thus the recidivist deserves a punishment beyond that deserved by the first offender.[17]

Whether or not one is persuaded by Davis's analyses of these cases, I

---

16. Ibid., 207–12. This explanation of Davis's is not very satisfactory. Imagine two similar states with identical criminal justice systems, except that in one there is a single law against all involuntary manslaughter no matter what the implement used (vehicle, gun, hammer, etc.), and in the other there are separate laws against involuntary manslaughter for each implement with which one might commit that crime. If a person in each society commits involuntary manslaughter with the same implement (in the same way, etc.), the person in the first society will be charged under the general law and the person in the second will be charged under the law that specifies the implement used. According to Davis's suggestion, we would have to say that the person in the first society took greater advantage of the law-abiding than the person in the second society even though both performed the very same antisocial act. This doesn't seem plausible.

17. Ibid., 200.

think they do serve to show that his basic point is correct: There is a divergence between the punishments that *lex talionis* justifies and those justified by the fairness rationale. The former measures punishment by the harm imposed on the victim, while the latter measures punishment by the advantage taken by the criminal—and there is no reason to think these will coincide: "The advantage bears no necessary relation to the harm the criminal actually did."[18] In fact, there is considerable reason to think they will diverge, as Davis's examples suggest.

Since punishments based on the fairness rationale are likely to diverge from those justified by *lex talionis*, the former may turn out to be more or less than the latter. But then, recalling Goldman's argument, punishments based on fairness will either be more than *lex talionis* allows (and thus unjust according to traditional retributivism, for which *lex talionis* is the upper limit of just punishment) or less than deterrence needs. Consequently, there is no way to combine these different rationales for punishment into a single internally consistent standard. Or so it seems.

2. Combining the Three Rationales into One Measure of Justly Deserved Punishment

I want to suggest that this problem can be overcome. All of the rationales for punishment can be seen as forms of just desert, and thus they can be combined into a single internally consistent standard for determining how much punishment is justified. To show this, let me start by assuming a point that I will actually defend in the following section, namely, that the traditional (*lex talionis*) retributivist justification is already a theory of just desert: A criminal justly deserves the equivalent to the harm he has intentionally imposed on his victim. Let us look, then, at the other two rationales: fairness and deterrence.

We noted earlier that Davis takes the fairness rationale to be a form of retributivist justification of punishment. I don't think this is quite correct. Insofar as Davis holds that punishment is meant to "take back" the advantage that the criminal unfairly took, this seems more like *restitution* (to society) than *retribution* (to the offender). Normally, we would think that punishment is added on top of taking back the advantage a criminal took. (If you stole $100 from someone, you would certainly owe that money to

---

18. Ibid., 192.

your victim, and it would certainly be right to make you pay it back. And *then* you would be punished.) The point here is that taking back the advantage that the criminal took restores things to the way they were before the crime. And that is restitution, not retribution: Restitution involves restoring the *status quo ante,* the condition prior to the offense. However, since it was in this condition that the criminal's offense was committed, this condition constitutes the baseline from which retribution is exacted. Thus retribution involves imposing a loss on the offender measured from the status quo ante. It inherently requires making the criminal worse off than he was before the crime, and thus must do more than take back the criminal's unfairly taken advantage. Returning a thief's loot to his victim so that thief and victim now own what they did before the offense is restitution. Taking enough from the thief so that what he is left with is less than what he had before the offense is retribution, since that is just what the thief did to his victim, namely, make him worse off than he was before the offense.

Put otherwise, taking back the unfair advantage rectifies the fact that the criminal *has* an unfair advantage, and thus taking back the advantage would be appropriate even if the criminal had ended up with it without foul play. But that very fact shows that taking back the unfair advantage does nothing about the criminal's crime, which was the *taking* (not just the *having*) of that advantage. Consequently, a retributivist may punish *for* taking unfair advantage, but the punishment must be something other than taking back that advantage.

If the fairness rationale justifies punishment *for* taking unfair advantage, then, rather than pointing to a separate justification for punishment, the fairness view points to a separate harm caused by the offender—other than the harm caused to his immediate victim. This separate harm is a distinctly *social* harm. Unlike the harm of broken bones, this harm is possible only because a rule-governed cooperative arrangement exists, and the recipients of this harm are all the people who play by the rules on the expectation that others will play by the rules as well.

If the fairness rationale points to a distinct harm for which offenders are to be punished, we will need a justification for that punishment that fairness itself cannot provide. Fairness may—à la Morris and Davis—require taking back the unfair advantage, but fairness does not require this (or anything else) *as* punishment. The fairness view, then, is not really a justification for punishment at all; it is an elucidation of the nature of criminal harm. Having recognized that the criminal harms society by taking advantage of law-abiders, we will still need to know why it is justified to punish criminals for this after the advantage has been taken back. And to answer this we will have to appeal to one or both of the other two rationales: It is justified to punish criminals for taking unfair advantage (via retributivism) as payback for this particular harm or (via deterrence) to discourage potential criminals from so harming their fellows. (Note that, though these considerations will effectively assimilate the fairness account to that of retribution and deterrence, I shall continue to speak of fairness as a distinct rationale for punishment because it refers to a distinct harm that ought to be punished.) Punishment on the fairness rationale will be the offender's just deserts if, in the following section, I can redeem the assumption made in this section that retributive punishment is justly deserved, and more so if I can show that deterrent punishment is justly deserved, to which I turn now.

It may seem impossible to show that the punishment justified by deterrence is also a matter of just desert. Traditionally, deterrence has been given as a utilitarian rationale for punishment, in which suffering imposed on actual criminals is justified by its tendency to dissuade others from committing crimes, thereby reducing suffering overall. Far from being deserved by the criminal because of the evil she has done, punishment can work as deterrence even if the one punished is innocent and only publicly believed to be guilty. For the utilitarian, the relationship between guilt and punishment is a pragmatic one. We get a deterrent effect only if we punish individuals who are believed to be guilty. If individuals believed innocent were also punished, then citizens would not be able to avoid punishment by avoiding crime, and thus there would be no incentive to do so. As a practical matter, the safest way to punish people who are believed guilty is to punish those who are guilty. But then they are not punished because they deserve it; they are punished because, as a matter of practical fact, doing so is the best way to get other people to refrain from committing crimes.

However, the deterrence justification of punishment need not be based on utilitarianism. It can be arrived at in a different way, namely, as an expression of people's right to self-protection. I say "self-protection" rather than "self-defense" because the latter has a familiar legal meaning that appears to exclude deterrence. Legally, self-defense permits only as much physical resistance (including violence) as is needed to stop an ongoing attack. The idea of stopping attacks by threatening a harm that will be imposed only *after* the attack is over is not thought of as part of self-defense, as this is used in courts of law to justify violent acts that would normally be illegal. Nonetheless, Warren Quinn has made a convincing case that threats of post-attack harms are morally indistinguishable from what normally comes under self-defense, and therefore such threats can be thought of as permissible exercises of our right to protect ourselves from unjustified attacks.

Quinn takes it as uncontroversial that, to protect ourselves against un-justified violations of our rights, "we may arrange that an automatic cost *precede* or *accompany* the violation of some right, a cost not designed to frustrate the violation but rather to provide a strong reason not to attempt it. The one-way tire spikes placed at the exits of private parking areas [to dissuade drivers from entering through the exits] provide a commonplace example."[19] Given that we seem to have a right to protect ourselves in this way, Quinn contends that there is no moral reason that we cannot extend this right into a right to threaten harms that would occur subsequent to violations. He writes,

> Suppose the best fence that someone in the state of nature can erect to block an attack on his life cannot stop some vigorous and agile enemies. He would then, under this right [to protect oneself by arranging harms that accompany violations], be permitted to place dangerous spikes at the top of the fence in order to discourage those who could otherwise scale it. These spikes, like the more familiar ones in parking lots, would . . . provide most would-be offend-ers with excellent reasons to hold back. But suppose, to take the story one step further, our defender cannot arrange the spikes so that they offer a threat of injury to someone entering his territory but can arrange them so that they clearly offer a threat of injury to an enemy leaving his territory after an attack. And suppose that the latter arrangement would discourage attacks just as effectively as the former. It would, I submit, be very odd to think that he could have the right to build the first kind of fence but not the second.[20]

I think that Quinn is correct here. The narrow legal definition of "self-defense" is premised on the existence of a functioning legal system that will punish offenders and that aims thereby to replace socially dangerous

---

19. Warren Quinn, "The Right to Threaten and the Right to Punish," in *Pun-ishment,* ed. Simmons et al., 61.

20. Ibid., 63.

retaliation by citizens. Quinn ultimately wants to determine what such a legal system may rightly do, and for that he wants to identify our full right to self-protection by looking at what it seems we may rightly do in the absence of a functioning legal system. This is why he imagines his fence-builder in a state of nature. The right to self-protection we identify there will form the basis for what the legal system may rightly do once it exists. Consequently, we should not imagine ourselves having from the outset only the limited right to self-defense as defined in law. And then it seems that we have the right to protect ourselves by making it costly to attack us, and, if we have that right, it would "be very odd" (as Quinn says) to think we don't have the right to protect ourselves by threatening costs that will be imposed after an attack is completed. Quinn asks,

> What morally relevant difference could it make to a would-be wrongdoer that the injury whose prospect is designed to discourage him will come earlier or later? In either case, the injury is not there to stop him if he tries to attack but rather to motivate him not to attack. But building the second kind of fence is nothing more than creating an automatic cost to *follow* an offense.[21]

But this means that our right to self-protection includes the right to threaten harm that will occur after an attack as a means to motivate a would-be attacker to refrain. And then, when a just state exists with a valid claim to replace private self-protection with public protective mechanisms, the state will also have the right, as its citizens' agent, to threaten harm after offenses as a means to deter criminals from committing them.

What I want to add to this is the following. If we have the right to threaten harms that will follow offenses, and if we do so publicly so that all would-be offenders know it, then we can say that a person who freely chooses to offend voluntarily brings those harms upon himself. And what a person voluntarily brings upon himself that others have a right to impose, he deserves. Note that I am not saying that because a punishment is announced and known in advance therefore an offender deserves the punishment. Rather, my point is that, if we are morally entitled to threaten and eventually to impose a given punishment, then an offender who knowingly does the act for which the punishment is threatened deserves to suffer that punishment. Such an offender chooses to make himself precisely the sort of risk that justifies the threat of punishment originally and

---

21. Ibid.

that suffices to make him deserve punishment when it falls upon him.[22] If this isn't obvious, recall Quinn's strategy of starting from the right to self-defense narrowly construed and expanding that to the self-protective right to threaten punishment. If someone unjustly attacks another person and gets hurt when that person fights back in self-defense, we would normally say that the attacker deserved what he got. But then the person who gets his tires slashed trying to sneak into a parking lot (knowing that the spikes are there) deserves what he gets. So, too, the person who tries to scale the fence with spikes on it. And then, the person who attacks knowing that a legitimately threatened harm will befall him afterward deserves that as well.

How much deterrent punishment is thereby deserved? I think that the answer is that amount needed to deter rational people generally from committing the crime in question. Punishment justified by deterrence must be limited to what will deter *rational people generally* since the law is addressed to rational people generally and, since punishment aimed at deterrence must be threatened in advance, penalties cannot be tailored to different individuals' susceptibilities. Moreover, establishing punishments significantly more severe than are needed to deter rational people generally will surely threaten, and eventually punish, some criminals more than they deserve, and it may end up making the criminal justice system a greater danger to the society than are the criminals it aims to control. Consequently, this view does not allow for extreme punishments simply because they may be needed to deter people who face unusual temptations or who are unusually susceptible to those temptations. It allows, rather, punishment that makes crime generally, to use John Locke's words, "an ill bargain to the offender."[23]

Be clear on what I am not saying. I am not saying that, by committing a crime with a known penalty, a criminal deserves to be used as an example

---

22. None of this should be taken to suggest that we have the right to use force or violence only to protect ourselves against those who choose to endanger us. Far from it. We also have the right to protect ourselves against those who endanger us inadvertently (the accident-prone), or because they could not control themselves (dangerous maniacs). In these cases, however, we would not say that the recipients of our self-protective force or violence *deserved* that force or violence, nor that they were being *punished*.

23. John Locke, *Second Treatise of Government* (Indianapolis, IN: Hackett Publishing, 1980; originally published 1690), 12.

to deter others. Following Quinn, deterrence is justified because our right to self-protection entitles us to make credible threats of punishment before any offense takes place. The carrying out of threatened punishment is simply part of making the threats credible. When she chooses to offend, the offender brings upon herself, and thus deserves, the carrying out of the threat. Unlike retributive punishment, which is justified because the criminal deserves it, deterrent punishment is deserved because it is justified to threaten it.

So far, then, I have assumed (until the next section, when it will be argued) that retributive punishment is deserved, I have argued that deterrent punishment is deserved, and I have argued that punishment for taking unfair advantage is justified by retribution or deterrence or both, and thus it, too, is deserved. If I am correct here, it follows that offenders deserve suffering equivalent to the harms they have intentionally caused, they deserve to be punished for unfairly taking advantage by breaking the rules, and they deserve the protective measures that were rightly threatened as a means to deter them from committing their crimes. Most important, since all are cases of desert, they are all compatible.

What we need, however, is a way of combining the three rationales into a single measure of punishment. Should we, for example, determine the amount of punishment needed to satisfy each rationale and then simply add them up and impose the total amount on the offender?

Not quite, but this proposal suggests a possibility not considered by Davis. He assumes that, if there is a gap between *lex talionis* and some acceptable punishments that can be justified by the unfair-advantage principle, then *lex talionis* must be replaced by the fairness account. He doesn't consider the possibility that that gap might better be narrowed by supplementing *lex talionis* with fairness. Since the taking of unfair advantage *and* the harming of a victim are parts of the wrong done by the criminal, the natural conclusion is that the two are separate grounds of the criminal's rightful punishment. When Davis says that "the damage a criminal actually does is between him and his victim, a private matter to be settled by civil suit (or the moral equivalent). His *crime* consists only in the unfair advantage he necessarily took over the law-abiding by breaking the law," he reveals the flaw in his theory. Would we not have the right to punish people who harm us in a state of nature, or if we met them on some island where there was no law or none that was a component of a cooperative system to which we and they both belonged?[24] The damage and the unfair taking are both parts of the crime, and thus both are rightly punished.

Lex talionis and fairness respond to different components of a crime that each add to the wrong that was done. *Lex talionis* responds to the harm imposed on the victim of a crime and fairness to the advantage taken by the criminal. Since the harm and the unfair advantage are two separate wrongs, they must be added together to give us the total wrong done by the criminal. Accordingly, punishment à la *lex talionis* must be added to punishment à la fairness to yield the punishment that will retribute the offender for the total wrong she did. Then we can say that a criminal deserves the equivalent of the harm she imposed on her victim *plus* the equivalent of the harm she imposed on society by unfairly taking advantage.

What of deterrence then? The danger that a criminal poses and that justifies our threatening punishment to deter him is just the danger that he will cause harm to his victim and take an unfair advantage from the law-abiding. That danger is, then, not a separate component of the wrong the criminal does. Accordingly, it will not do to add an amount of punishment able to deter a given crime on top of the punishment that already satisfies *lex talionis* and fairness. Rather, if the punishment that satisfies those two rationales will also suffice to deter rational people generally from committing the crime, then that punishment will serve all three rationales and give the offender all that he deserves. However, if it takes more punishment to deter rational individuals generally than the amount needed to satisfy the first two rationales, then the least amount of punishment

---

24. "Imagine that, for whatever reason, your society 'dissolved' into disorder and chaos. Once again in your natural state, unprotected by the rule of law, you witness a man brutally robbing and murdering a defenseless victim. If it were within your power to do so, would you not feel justified in seeing to it that the murderer suffered for his crime? Would there be anything morally objectionable in your inflicting on him some harm, either to save others from his atrocities or . . . simply as a response to *what he did*? Would not anyone in the state of nature have a right to *punish* him for his moral crime?" (A. John Simmons, "Locke and the Right to Punish," in *Punishment*, ed. Simmons et al., 223–24; emphasis in original). If you are inclined to answer these three questions yes, no, yes—as I am— then you disagree with Davis that the punishable part of a crime is only its unfairness to the law-abiding. The harm caused is not merely a damage to be recouped privately. It is also rightly subject to punishment.

needed to deter rational individuals generally will satisfy all three rationales and be what the offender deserves.

To shore up this conclusion, I want to show how it enables us to deal with the problems of *lex talionis* versus deterrence pointed to by Goldman, as well as with the problems of *lex talionis* versus fairness that led Davis to think the latter must replace the former. Regarding Goldman's point, we can say that, if a punishment that will satisfy *lex talionis* is still not enough to deter criminals given the low likelihood of apprehension, then, on my view, the punishment can be increased beyond *lex talionis* to the level needed to deter rational people generally. And, contrary to Goldman, no injustice will thereby be done, because the offender deserves that much punishment.

Davis, we saw, pointed to some features of criminal punishment (lesser punishment for vehicular homicide than for involuntary manslaughter, greater punishment for repeat offenders) that could not be accounted for by *lex talionis*. He took this as a reason for replacing *lex talionis* with fairness. But that creates a problem for Davis, the mirror image of the problem he unearthed regarding *lex talionis*. Much as punishing only according to the harm done to the immediate victim can give counterintuitive results when the unfair advantage is not considered, so, too, punishing according to unfair advantage yields counterintuitive results because the harm caused to the victim is not considered. For example, it would seem that the value of the unfair advantage taken of the law-abiding by one who robs a great deal of money is greater than the value of the unfair advantage taken by a murderer, since the latter gets only the advantage of ridding his world of someone he dislikes while the former will be able to make a new life without the one he dislikes and have money left over for other things. Then the unfair-advantage principle leads to the counterintuitive conclusion that such robbers should be punished more severely (and regarded as more wicked) than murderers.[25]

Davis has responded to this type of objection, over several years, by refining his crime-license auction to get it to track the seriousness of the harms caused by crimes. So he has stipulated that the licenses will always

---

25. The fairness rationale for punishment has "counterintuitive implications regarding amounts of punishment for particular crimes, since crimes against property often bring more benefits to their perpetrators than do more serious crimes against persons" (Goldman, "Paradox of Punishment," 32).

be worth at least what others, fearing a particular crime, would pay those who hold licenses for it not to use their licenses; or that the society will, in light of the undesirability of a particular crime, limit the number of available licenses, thereby driving the price up because of scarcity of supply; or that the value of a crime will be a function of the risk of committing it and thus of the degree to which victims are likely to put up a fight; and other equally ingenious provisions.[26]

The need for all these complicated provisions disappears if we think of punishment as being justified by *lex talionis* and fairness and deterrence together. First of all, we will not have to make the advantage taken by the criminal track the seriousness of the harm he caused, because the *lex talionis* component of his punishment will be proportioned to that harm. With the degree of harm left to the side, we can view the unfairness aspect of a crime as constant across crimes. It is simply the unfairness of taking advantage of others' self-restraint, and this is the same harm—and thus deserves the same punishment—no matter what the particular crime is. Then we can say that criminals deserve punishment equivalent to the harm they caused their immediate victim, plus a small punishment premium for the fact that they caused that harm by breaking a law and thus unfairly taking advantage of the law-abiding. If this is not enough to deter rational people generally from committing this crime in the future, then the punishment could be raised until it is enough for that, without doing any injustice to the criminal.

Consider the resources this provides for dealing with the main problem cases that Davis has identified for *lex talionis*. The greater punishment for involuntary manslaughter than vehicular homicide might be due to the fact that vehicular homicide is a crime that virtually any citizen, no matter how otherwise "normal" and law-abiding, stands a fair chance of committing. As a result, the carelessness involved in it may appear to be within the range of normal inadvertence rather than callous or mean-spirited thoughtlessness, and thus the crime would reflect a less evil intention than other forms of recklessness. Its lesser punishment could be accounted for by the distinction that *lex talionis* makes between crimes that reflect

---

26. For the various provisions of his crime-license auction see Davis, "Harm and Retribution," 217–18; as well as Michael Davis, "How to Make the Punishment Fit the Crime," 744; and Michael Davis, *Justice in the Shadow of Death* (Lanham, MD: Rowman & Littlefield, 1996), 244–47, 262–73.

greater or lesser "inner viciousness." Or, it might be the case that, since vehicular homicide is the result of driving recklessly, and since drivers have independent self-interested reasons to drive carefully, vehicular homicide might be judged more easily deterrable than other forms of involuntary manslaughter. And that, too, could account for the former's lesser punishment. Similar resources are available to account for the greater penalties handed out to repeat offenders. Special measures may be needed to deter hardened and experienced criminals, and that, combined with the idea that repeat offenders show a greater "inner viciousness" (their repeated offending being a sign of their profound and abiding commitment to anti-social activities), will justify attaching a recidivist premium to third offenders.

I conclude this section, then, by saying that offenders deserve the least amount of punishment that imposes on them harm equivalent to the harm they caused their victims *and* the harm they caused to society by taking unfair advantage of the law-abiding *and* that will effectively deter rational people generally from committing such crimes in the future.

II. Death and Desert

In this section, I aim to show that execution is justly deserved punishment for some murders, *as a step toward arguing that it is not unjust to punish murder less harshly*. Note, then, that the fact that a punishment is justly deserved does not, in my view, entail that someone has a duty to impose that punishment. Rather, I shall argue in this section that desert creates *a right to punish*, not a duty to do so. To prepare the ground for this argument, I present here three commonplace observations that support the view that desert does not entail a duty to give what is deserved: First, the victim of an offense has the moral right to forgive the offending party rather than punish him though he deserves to be punished; second, we have no duty (not even a prima facie duty) to torture torturers even if they deserve to be tortured; and third, though great benefactors of humanity deserve to be rewarded, no one necessarily has a duty to provide that reward. At most, there is a very weak and easily overridden duty to provide the reward. On the other hand, I will claim that, when the state punishes a criminal, the state has a duty to punish in a way that does not trivialize the harm suffered by the criminal's victim. However, we shall see that this duty is compatible with administering punishment that is less that the full amount deserved.

In my view, the death penalty is a just punishment for murder because the *lex talionis* is just, although, it can be rightly applied only when its implied preconditions are satisfied. In section V, "Just in Principle, Unjust in Practice," I shall spell out those preconditions and argue that the current administration of the death penalty in America fails to satisfy them and is likely to continue so to fail for the foreseeable future.

1. Retributivism, *Lex Talionis,* and Just Desert

There is nothing self-evident about the justice of the *lex talionis* or, for that matter, of retributivism.[27] The standard problem confronting those who would justify retributivism is that of overcoming the suspicion that it does no more than sanctify the victim's desire to hurt the offender back. Since serving that desire amounts to hurting the offender simply for the satisfaction that the victim derives from seeing the offender suffer, and since deriving satisfaction from the suffering of others seems primitive, the policy of imposing suffering on the offender for no other purpose than giving satisfaction to his victim seems primitive as well. Consequently, defending retributivism requires showing that the suffering imposed on the wrongdoer has some worthy point beyond the satisfaction of victims. In what follows, I shall try to identify a proposition—which I call the *retributivist principle*—that I take to be the nerve of retributivism. I think this principle accounts for the justice of the *lex talionis* and indicates the point of the suffering demanded by retributivism. Not to do too much of the work of the death penalty advocate, I shall make no extended argument for this principle beyond suggesting the considerations that make it plausible. I shall identify these considerations by drawing, with some license, on G. W. F. Hegel and Kant.

I think that we can see the justice of the *lex talionis* by focusing on the striking affinity between it and the Golden Rule. The Golden Rule mandates, "Do unto others as you would have others do unto you," while the

---

27. "[T]o say 'it is fitting' or 'justice demands' that the guilty should suffer is only to affirm that punishment is right, not to give grounds for thinking so" (Stanley I. Benn, "Punishment," *The Encyclopedia of Philosophy*, ed. Paul Edwards [New York: Macmillan, 1967], vol. 7, p. 30).

lex talionis counsels, "Do unto others as they have done unto you." It would not be too far-fetched to say that the *lex talionis* is the law enforcement arm of the Golden Rule, at least in the sense that if people were actually treated as they treated others, then everyone would necessarily follow the Golden Rule, because then people could only willingly act toward others as they were willing to have others act toward them. This is not to suggest that the *lex talionis* follows from the Golden Rule, but rather that the two share a common moral inspiration: the equality of persons. Treating others as you *would* have them treat you means treating others as equal to you, because it implies that you count their suffering to be as great a calamity as your own suffering, that you count your right to impose suffering on them as no greater than their right to impose suffering on you, and so on. The notion of the equality of persons leads to the *lex talionis* by two approaches that start from different points and converge.

I call the first approach "Hegelian" because Hegel held (roughly) that crime upsets the equality among persons and that retributive punishment restores that equality by "annulling" the crime.[28] As we have seen, acting according to the Golden Rule implies treating others as your equals. Conversely, violating the Golden Rule implies the reverse: Doing to another what you would *not* have that other do to you violates the equality of persons by asserting a right toward the other that the other does not possess toward you. Doing back to you what you did "annuls" your violation by reasserting that the other has the same right toward you that you assert toward him. Punishment according to the *lex talionis* cannot heal the in-

---

28. "The sole positive existence which the injury [i.e., the crime] possesses is that it is the particular will of the criminal [i.e., it is the criminal's intention that distinguishes criminal injury from, say, injury due to an accident]. Hence to injure (or penalize) this particular will as a will determinately existent is to annul the crime, which otherwise would have been held valid, and to restore the right" (G. W. F. Hegel, *The Philosophy of Right*, trans. T. M. Knox [Oxford: Clarendon Press, 1962; originally published 1821], 69, see also 331n). I take this to mean that the right is a certain equality of sovereignty among the wills of individuals, that crime disrupts that equality by placing one will above others, and that punishment restores the equality by annulling the illegitimate ascendance. On these grounds, as I shall suggest below, the desire for revenge (strictly limited to the desire "to even the score") is more respectable than philosophers have generally allowed. And so Hegel wrote: "The annulling of crime in this sphere where right is immediate [i.e., the condition prior to conscious morality] is principally revenge, which is just in its content in so far as it is retributive" (ibid., 73).

jury that the other has suffered at your hands; rather, it rectifies the indignity he has suffered, by restoring him to equality with you.

This Hegelian account of retributivism provides us with a nonutilitarian conception of crime and punishment. This is so because "equality of persons" here does not mean equality of concern for their happiness, as it might for a utilitarian. On a utilitarian understanding of equality, imposing suffering on a wrongdoer equivalent to the suffering she has imposed would have little point (unless such suffering were exactly what was needed to deter future would-be offenders). Rather, equality of concern for people's happiness would lead us to impose as little suffering on the wrongdoer as is compatible with promoting the happiness of others. Instead of seeing morality as administering doses of happiness to individual recipients, the Hegelian retributivist envisions morality as maintaining the relations appropriate to equally sovereign individuals.[29] A crime, rather than representing a unit of suffering added to the already considerable suffering in the world, is an assault on the sovereignty of an individual that temporarily places one person (the criminal) in a position of illegitimate sovereignty over another (the victim). The victim (or his representative, the state) then has the right to rectify this loss of standing relative to the criminal by meting out a punishment that reduces the criminal's sovereignty to the degree to which she vaunted it above her victim's. It might be thought that this is a duty, not just a right, but that is surely too much. The victim has the right to forgive the violator without imposing punishment. This suggests that it is by virtue of having the right to punish the violator—having authority over the violator's fate equivalent to the authority over the victim's fate that the violator wrongly took—rather than having the duty to punish the violator, that the victim's equality with the violator is restored.

I call the second approach "Kantian" because Kant held (roughly) that, since reason (like justice) is no respecter of the sheer difference among individuals, when a rational being decides to act in a certain way toward his fellows, he implicitly authorizes similar action by his fellows toward

---

29. For this reason, I think this account of crime and punishment is especially appropriate to a liberal moral theory, and I have defended it as such. See my *Justice and Modern Moral Philosophy* (New Haven, CT: Yale University Press, 1990), 187–99, 306–07; and my *Critical Moral Liberalism: Theory and Practice* (Lanham, MD: Rowman & Littlefield, 1997), 235–70, esp. 240.

him.[30] A version of the Golden Rule, then, is a requirement of reason: Acting rationally, one always acts as he would have others act toward him.[31] Consequently, to act toward a person as he has acted toward others is to treat him as a rational being, that is, as if his act were the product of

---

30. According to Kant, "any undeserved evil that you inflict on someone else among the people is one that you do to yourself. If you vilify him, you vilify yourself; if you steal from him, you steal from yourself; if you kill him, you kill yourself." Since Kant held that "[i]f what happens to someone is also willed by him, it cannot be a punishment," he took pains to distance himself from the view that the offender *wills* his punishment. "The chief error contained in this sophistry," Kant wrote, "consists in the confusion of the criminal's [i.e., the murderer's] own judgment (which one must necessarily attribute to his reason) that he must forfeit his life with a resolution of the will to take his own life" (Kant, "Metaphysical Elements of Justice," 101, 105–106). I have tried to capture this notion of attributing a judgment to the offender, rather than a resolution of his will, with the term "authorizes." This is important, further, because, if we are to stay faithful to Kant, then we must avoid the suggestion that the criminal has willed the universalized version of the maxim on which he acted, since, for Kant, it is precisely the impossibility of willing the universalized version of a maxim that shows the wrongness of acting on that maxim. Thus, for example, R. A. Duff objects to a theory of punishment that might be confused with the theory I develop here, by asking: "How can we say that the criminal has, as a rational being, willed the universalized maxim which justifies his punishment (how can a rational being will what cannot be consistently willed)?" (R. A. Duff, *Trials and Punishments* [New York: Cambridge University Press, 1986], 202). This objection can be sidestepped by insisting that, though the criminal has not willed the universal version of his maxim, he has implicitly affirmed it. This may require moving some distance from Kant, but not a great distance. Kant held that there are two ways in which universalization may fail: some maxims are logically impossible to universalize, and some (though possible to universalize) are impossible to *will* in the universalized form (Immanuel Kant, *Grounding for the Metaphysics of Morals*, trans. J. W. Ellington [Indianapolis, IN: Hackett Publishing, 1981; originally published 1785], 32). If all crimes are of this latter sort, then criminals could be held to affirm their universalization but fail to will it; and, since it is doubtful that Kant ever succeeded in showing that any maxim was logically impossible to universalize, this may be a useful modification of Kant's theory. In any event, since my argument in this essay does not depend on taking a Kantian view of what makes crimes wrong, it is not vulnerable to Duff's criticism.

31. Cf. Kant, *Grounding for the Metaphysics of Morals*, 37n. Kant thinks that the Golden Rule, as commonly stated, places too much emphasis on what an agent *wants*, rather than on what he rationally endorses. Nonetheless, Kant affirms that the Golden Rule is derived from his own central moral principle, the categorical imperative.

a rational decision. From this, it may be concluded that we have a duty to do to offenders what they have done, since this amounts to according them the respect due rational beings. And Kant asserts as much.[32] Here, too, however, the assertion of a duty to punish seems excessive, since, if this duty arose because doing to people what they have done to others is necessary to accord them the respect due rational beings, then we would have a duty to do to all rational persons *everything*—good, bad, or indifferent—that they do to others. The point, rather, is that, by his acts, a rational being *authorizes* others to do the same to him; he doesn't *compel* them to. Here, again, the argument leads to a right, rather than a duty, to exact the *lex talionis*. It should be clear that the Kantian argument, like the Hegelian one, rests on the equality of persons. A rational agent implicitly authorizes having done to him action similar to what he has done to another only if he and the other are similar in the relevant ways.

The Hegelian and Kantian approaches arrive at the same destination from opposite sides. The Hegelian approach starts explicitly from the victim's equality with the criminal and infers from it the victim's right to do to the criminal what the criminal has done to the victim. The Kantian approach starts explicitly from the criminal's rationality and implicitly from his equality with his victim and infers from these the criminal's authorization of the victim's right to do to the criminal what the criminal has done to the victim. Taken together, these approaches support the following proposition: *The equality and rationality of persons imply that an offender deserves, and his victim has the right to impose on him, suffering equal to that which he imposed on the victim.* This is the proposition I call the *retributivist principle*. This principle provides that the *lex talionis* is the criminal's just desert and the victim's—or, as her representative, the state's—right. Remember that this refers both to what the criminal deserves for harming a particular individual and to what he deserves for unfairly taking advantage of all those who have obeyed the law. Moreover, this principle also indicates the point of retributive punishment, namely, to affirm the equality and rationality of persons, victims and offenders alike. And the point of this affirmation is, like any moral affirmation, to make a statement.

---

32. "Even if a civil society were to dissolve itself by common agreement of all its members . . . , the last murderer remaining in prison must first be executed, so that everyone will duly receive what his actions are worth" (Kant, "Metaphysical Elements of Justice," 102).

It impresses upon the criminal his equality with his victim (which earns him a like fate) and his rationality (by which his actions are held to authorize his fate), and it makes a statement to the society, so that recognition of the equality and rationality of persons becomes a visible part of our shared moral environment that none can ignore in justifying their actions to one another.

I do not contend that it is easy or even always possible to figure out what penalties are equivalent to the harms imposed by offenders. Hugo Bedau, for example, has observed that, apart from murder and possibly some other crimes against the person, "we have no clear intuitions at all about what such equivalences consist in."[33] Even if this is so, however, it is still worth knowing what the criterion of deserved punishment is. At very least, it gives us a way of critiquing penalties that strike us as way out of line with the crimes they retribute. Moreover, if there are some crimes—murder and other crimes against the person—for which we do have clear intuitions about the equivalences, we might be able to fill in much of the rest of a scheme of retributive penalties by using our less-than-clear intuitions about other crimes to make ordinal judgments of relative severity. In any event, knowing what criminals deserve according to *lex talionis* gives us something at which to aim, a target in light of which we might eventually sharpen our intuitions.

When I say that, with respect to the criminal, the point of retributive punishment is to impress upon him his equality with his victim, I mean to be understood quite literally. If the sentence is just and the criminal rational, then the punishment should normally *force* upon him recognition of his equality with his victim, recognition of their shared vulnerability to suffering and their shared desire to avoid it, as well as recognition of the fact that he counts for no more than his victim in the eyes of their fellows. For this reason, the retributivist requires that the offender be sane not only at the moment of his crime, but also at the moment of his punishment—while this latter requirement would be largely pointless (if not downright malevolent) to a utilitarian. Incidentally, it is, I believe, the desire that the offender be forced by suffering punishment to recognize his equality with his victim, rather than the desire for that suffering itself, that constitutes what is rational in the desire for revenge.[34]

---

33. Hugo Bedau, personal correspondence to author.
34. See note 28 above.

The retributivist principle represents a conception of moral desert the complete elaboration of which would take us beyond the scope of the present essay. In its defense, however, it is worth noting that our common notion of moral desert includes (at least) two elements: (1) a conception of individual responsibility for actions that is "contagious," that is, one that confers moral justification on the punishing (or rewarding) reactions of others; and (2) a measure of the relevant cost of actions that determines the legitimate magnitude of justified reactions. Broadly speaking, the Kantian notion of authorization implicit in rational action supplies the first element, and the Hegelian notion of upsetting and restoring equality of persons supplies the second. It seems, then, reasonable to take the equality and rationality of persons as implying moral desert in the way asserted in the retributivist principle. I shall assume henceforth that the retributivist principle is true.

2. The Top and the Bottom End of the Range of Just Punishments

The truth of the retributivist principle establishes that *lex talionis* is the offender's just desert; but, since it establishes this as a right of the victim rather than the victim's duty, it does not settle the question of whether or to what extent the victim or the state ought to exercise this right and exact the *lex talionis*. This is a separate moral question because strict adherence to the *lex talionis* amounts to allowing criminals, even the most barbaric of them, to dictate our punishing behavior. As Bedau points out, "Where criminals set the limits of just methods of punishment, as they will do if we attempt to give exact and literal implementation to *lex talionis*, society will find itself descending to the cruelties and savagery that criminals employ."[35] It seems certain that there are at least some crimes, such as rape or torture, that we ought not to try to match. And this is not merely a matter of imposing an alternative punishment that produces an equivalent amount of suffering, as, say, some number of years in prison that might "add up" to the harm caused by a rapist or a torturer. Even if no amount of time in prison would add up to the harm caused by a torturer, it still seems that we ought not to torture him even if this were the only way of making him suffer as much as he has made his victim suffer. Or consider someone who has committed several murders in cold blood. On the *lex*

---

35. Bedau, "Capital Punishment," 176.

talionis, it would seem that such a criminal might justly be brought to within an inch of death and then revived (or to within a moment of execution and then reprieved) as many times as he has killed (minus one), and then finally executed. But surely this is a degree of cruelty that would be monstrous.

Since the retributivist principle establishes the *lex talionis* as the victim's right, it might seem that the question of how far this right should be exercised is "up to the victim." Indeed, this would be the case in the state of nature. But once, for all the good reasons familiar to readers of Locke, the state comes into existence, public punishment replaces private, and the victim's right to punish reposes in the state. With this, the decision as to how far to exercise this right goes to the state as well. To be sure, since (at least with respect to retributive punishment) the victim's right is the source of the state's right to punish, the state must exercise its right in ways that are faithful to the victim's right. When I try to spell out the upper and lower limits of just punishment, these limits may be taken as indicating the range within which the state can punish and remain faithful to the victim's right.

I suspect that it will be widely agreed that the state ought not to administer punishments of the sort described above even if required by the letter of the *lex talionis* and that, thus, even granting the justice of *lex talionis,* there are occasions on which it is morally appropriate to diverge from its requirements. We must distinguish such morally based divergence from divergence based on practicality. Like any moral principle, the *lex talionis* is subject to "ought implies can," that morality cannot ask more of us than is practically possible. It will usually be impossible to do to an offender exactly what she has done—for example, her offense will normally have had an element of surprise that is not possible for a judicially imposed punishment—but this fact can hardly free her from having to bear the suffering she has imposed on another. Thus, for reasons of practicality, the *lex talionis* must necessarily be qualified to call for doing to the offender *as nearly as possible* what she has done to her victim. When, however, we refrain from raping rapists or torturing torturers, we do so for reasons of morality, not of practicality. And, given the justice of the *lex talionis,* these moral reasons cannot amount to claiming that it would be unjust to rape rapists or torture torturers. Rather, the claim must be that, even though it would be just to rape rapists and torture torturers, other moral considerations weigh against doing so.

On the other hand, when, for moral reasons, we refrain from exacting the *lex talionis* and impose a less harsh alterative punishment, it cannot automatically be the case that we are doing an injustice to the victim. Otherwise, we would have to say it was unjust to imprison our torturer rather than torturing him or to simply execute our multiple murderer rather than "multiply executing" him. Surely it is counterintuitive (and irrational to boot) to set the demands of justice so high that a society would have to choose between being barbaric and being unjust. That would effectively price justice out of the moral market.

The implication of the notion that justice permits us to avoid extremely cruel punishments is that there is a range of just punishments that includes some that are just though they exact less than the full measure of the *lex talionis*. What are the top and bottom ends of this range? In considering this question, remember that I argued that punishment sufficient to deter rational people generally is part of what a criminal deserves, and that punishment insufficient to deter does injustice to potential criminals. It follows that all punishments within the range of just punishments must be sufficient to deter rational people generally from the crime in question. Assume, then, for purposes of simplicity, that we are trying to identify the range of just punishments from within a series of punishments of increasing harshness all of which suffice to provide adequate deterrence.

Within this series of punishments, the top end of the range of just punishments is given by *lex talionis*, and the bottom end is, in a way, as well. Based on the argument of the previous section, the top end, the point after which more or harsher punishment is undeserved and thus unjust, is reached when we impose a punishment that is equivalent to the harm caused by the criminal (including both the harm done to his immediate victim and the harm done to the law-abiding by his unfair taking of advantage). As for the bottom end, recall that, if the retributivist principle is true, then denying that the offender deserves suffering equal to that which she imposed amounts to denying the equality and rationality of persons. From this, it follows that we fall below the bottom end of the range of just punishments when we act in ways that are incompatible with the *lex talionis* at the top end. We do injustice to the victim when we treat the offender in a way that is no longer compatible with sincerely believing that she deserves to have done to her what she has done to her victim. In this way, the range of just punishments remains faithful to the victim's right.

This way of understanding just punishment enables us to formulate proportional retributivism so that it is compatible with acknowledging the justice of the *lex talionis*. If we take the *lex talionis* to spell out the offender's just desert, and if other moral considerations require us to refrain from matching the injury caused by the offender while still allowing us to punish justly, then surely we impose just punishment if we impose the closest morally acceptable approximation to the *lex talionis*. Proportional retributivism, then, in requiring that the worst crime be punished by the society's worst punishment and so on, could be understood as translating the offender's just desert into its nearest equivalent in the society's table of morally acceptable punishments. Then, the two versions of retributivism *(lex talionis* and proportional) are related in that the first states what just punishment would be if nothing but the offender's just desert mattered and the second locates just punishment at the meeting point of the offender's just desert and the society's moral scruples.

Inasmuch as proportional retributivism modifies the requirements of the *lex talionis* only in light of other moral considerations, it is compatible with believing that the *lex talionis* spells out the offender's just desert, much in the way that modifying the obligations of promisers in light of other moral considerations is compatible with believing in the binding nature of promises. That a person is justified in failing to keep a promised appointment because she acted to save a life is compatible with still believing that promises are binding. So, too, justifiably doing less than *lex talionis* requires in order to avoid cruelty is compatible with believing that offenders still deserve what *lex talionis* would impose.

Proportional retributivism so formulated preserves the point of retributivism and remains faithful to the victim's right that is its source. Since it punishes with the closest morally acceptable approximation to the *lex talionis,* it effectively says to the offender: You deserve the equivalent of what you did to your victim, and you are getting less only to the degree that our moral scruples limit us from duplicating what you have done. Such punishment, then, affirms the equality of persons by respecting, *as far as seems morally permissible*, the victim's right to impose suffering on the offender equal to what she received, and it affirms the rationality of the offender by treating him as authorizing others to do to him what he has done, though they take him up on it only *as far as it seems to them morally permissible*. Needless to say, the alternative punishments must in some convincing way be comparable in gravity to the crimes that they punish, or else they will trivialize the harms those crimes caused and be no longer compatible with sincerely believing that the offender deserves to have done to him what he has done to his victim and no longer capable of impressing upon the criminal his equality with the victim. If we punish rapists with a small fine, for instance, we do an injustice to their victims because this trivializes the suffering rapists have caused and thus is incompatible with believing that they deserve to have done to them something comparable to what they have done to their victims. If, on the other hand, instead of raping rapists, we impose on them some serious penalty—say, a substantial term of imprisonment—then we do no injustice even though we refrain from exacting the *lex talionis*.[36]

To sum up: When, because we are simply unable to duplicate the criminal's offense, we modify the *lex talionis* to call for imposing on the offender as nearly as possible what he has done, we are still at the top end of punishment justified via *lex talionis*, modifying the *lex talionis* only for reasons of practical possibility. When, because of our own moral scruples, we do less than this, we still act justly as long as we punish in a way that is compatible with sincerely believing that the offender deserves the full measure of the *lex talionis*. If this is true, then it is not unjust to spare murderers as long as they can be punished in some other suitably grave way. For example, a natural life sentence with no chance of parole might be a civilized equivalent of the death penalty—after all, people sentenced to life imprisonment have traditionally been regarded as "civilly dead."[37]

It might be objected that no punishment short of death will serve the point of retributivism with respect to murderers because no punishment short of death is commensurate with the crime of murder. For, while some number of years of imprisonment may add up to the amount of harm done by rapists or assaulters or torturers, no number of years will add up to the harm done to the victim of murder. But justified divergence from the *lex*

---

36. For a very thoughtful and provocative discussion of the punishment deserved for rape, see Davis, *Justice in the Shadow of Death*, 183–229.

37. I am indebted to my colleague Robert Johnson for this suggestion. Prisoners condemned to spend their entire lives in prison, Johnson writes, "experience a permanent civil death, the death of freedom. The prison is their cemetery, a 6' by 9' cell their tomb. Interred in the name of justice, they are consigned to mark the passage of their lives in the prison's peculiar dead time, which serves no larger human purpose and yields few rewards. In effect, they give their civil lives in return for the natural lives they have taken" (Robert Johnson, *Death Work: A Study of the Modern Execution Process* [Belmont, CA: Wadsworth Publishing, 1990], 158).

talionis is not limited only to changing the form of punishment while maintaining equivalent severity. Otherwise, we would have to torture torturers rather than imprison them, if they tortured more than could be made up for by years in prison (or by the years available to them to spend in prison, which might be few for elderly torturers), and we would have to subject multiple murderers to "multiple executions." If justice allows us to refrain from these penalties, then justice allows punishments that are not equal in suffering to their crimes. It seems to me that if the objector grants this much, then she must show that a punishment less than death is not merely incommensurate to the harm caused by murder, but so far out of proportion to that harm that it trivializes the harm and thus effectively denies the equality and rationality of persons.

Now, I am vulnerable to the claim that a sentence of life in prison that allows parole after six or eight years does indeed trivialize the harm of (premeditated, cold-blooded) murder. But I cannot see how a sentence that would require a murderer to spend his full natural life in prison, or even the lion's share of his adult life (say, the twenty years between age thirty and age fifty), can be regarded as anything less than extremely severe and thus no trivialization of the harm he has caused. At least with respect to life sentences without parole, there appears to be widespread agreement on this. For example, surveys of Americans in recent years have consistently shown a majority approving of the death penalty for murderers. However, where surveys have offered the choice between the death penalty and life in prison without parole, respondents preferred the latter "*if* imprisonment included financial restitution to the families of victims."[38] And when juries have the possibility of sentencing murderers to life imprisonment without parole, the number of people given death sentences declines dramatically.[39]

---

38. Mark Costanzo and Lawrence T. White, "An Overview of the Death Penalty and Capital Trials: History, Current Status, Legal Procedures, and Cost," *Journal of Social Issues* 50, no. 2 (1994): 9–10. Of surveys that show a majority in favor of the death penalty, a 1995 Gallup Poll is typical. Asked: "Are you in favor of the death penalty for persons convicted of murder?," 77 percent of respondents were in favor, 13 percent were opposed, and 10 percent had no opinion (U.S. Department of Justice, Bureau of Justice Statistics, *Sourcebook of Criminal Justice Statistics, 1994*, ed. Kathleen Maguire and Ann L. Pastore [Washington, DC: U.S. Government Printing Office, 1995], 181).

39. "The number of people given the death sentence in Virginia has plummeted since the state began allowing jurors to sentence murderers to life without

I take it, then, that the justice of the *lex talionis* implies that it is just to execute murderers, but not that it is unjust to spare them as long as they are systematically punished in some other suitably grave way—and as long as the deterrence requirement can be satisfied, to which we now turn.

III. Death and Deterrence

I have maintained that any penalty that is insufficient to deter rational people from committing the crime to which it is attached falls below the bottom end of the range of just punishment because it is unjust to potential victims. Thus, were the death penalty proven a better deterrent to the murder of innocent people than life in prison, we might have to grant the necessity of instituting the death penalty. But it is far from proven that the death penalty is a superior deterrent to murder than life in prison, or than even less harsh but still substantial prison sentences, such as twenty years without parole.

1. Social Science and the Deterrent Effect of the Death Penalty

Prior to the 1970s, the most important work on the comparative deterrent impact of the death penalty versus life imprisonment was that of Thorsten Sellin, whose research indicated no increase in the incidence of homicide in states that abolished the death penalty and no greater incidence of homicide in states without the death penalty compared to similar states with the death penalty.[40] In 1970, based on a review of the findings of empirical research on the impact of the death penalty on homicide rates (including Sellin's study), Hugo Bedau concluded that the claim that the death penalty is superior to life imprisonment as a deterrent to crimes

---

parole two years ago. . . . Similar declines also have occurred in Georgia and Indiana, two other states that have introduced life without parole in recent years" (Peter Finn, "Given Choice, Va. Juries Vote for Life," *Washington Post*, February 3, 1997, A1).

40. Thorsten Sellin, *The Death Penalty* (Philadelphia: American Law Institute, 1959). For a summary of pre-1970 deterrence research and additional references, see William C. Bailey and Ruth D. Peterson, "Murder, Capital Punishment, and Deterrence: A Review of the Evidence and an Examination of Police Killings," *Journal of Social Issues* 50, no. 2 (1994), esp. 55.

generally, and to the crime of murder particularly, "has been discon-firmed," because the evidence shows uniformly the nonoccurrence of the results that one would expect were the death penalty a superior deter-rent.[41] In 1975, Isaac Ehrlich, a University of Chicago econometrician, published the results of a statistical study purporting to prove that, in the period from 1933 to 1969, each execution may have deterred as many as eight murders.[42] This finding was, however, widely challenged.[43] Criticism of Ehrlich's work focuses mainly on the fact that he found a deterrent impact of executions in the period from 1933 to 1969, which includes the period of 1963 to 1969, a time when hardly any executions were carried out and crime rates rose for reasons that are arguably independent of the existence or nonexistence of capital punishment. When the 1963–1969 period is excluded, no significant deterrent effect shows.[44]

In 1978, after Ehrlich's study, the editors of a National Academy of Sciences' study of the impact of punishment wrote: "In summary, the flaws in the earlier analyses (i.e., Sellin's and others) and the sensitivity of the more recent analyses to minor variation in model specification and the serious temporal instability of the results lead the panel to conclude that the available studies provide no useful evidence on the deterrent effect of capital punishment."[45] The authors of a 1996 review of "the vast literature on the question of general deterrence" conclude "that, despite a wide

41. Hugo A. Bedau, "Deterrence and the Death Penalty: A Reconsideration," *Journal of Criminal Law, Criminology, and Police Science* 61, no. 4 (1970): 539–48.

42. Isaac Ehrlich, "The Deterrent Effect of Capital Punishment: A Question of Life and Death," *American Economic Review* 65 (June 1975): 397–417.

43. For reactions to Ehrlich's work, see Alfred Blumstein, Jacqueline Cohen, and Daniel Nagin, eds., *Deterrence and Incapacitation: Estimating the Effects of Criminal Sanctions on Crime Rates* (Washington, DC: National Academy of Sciences, 1978), esp. 59–63 and 336–60; Brian E. Forst, "The Deterrent Effect of Capital Punishment: A Cross-State Analysis," *Minnesota Law Review* 61 (May 1977): 743–67; and Deryck Beyleveld, "Ehrlich's Analysis of Deterrence," *British Journal of Criminology* 22 (April 1982): 101–23. For Ehrlich's response to his critics, see Isaac Ehrlich, "On Positive Methodology, Ethics, and Polemics in De-terrence Research," *British Journal of Criminology* 22 (April 1982): 124–39.

44. For a summary of the criticisms of Ehrlich's study, see Victor Kappeler, Merle Blumberg, and Gary Potter, *The Mythology of Crime and Criminal Justice*, 2nd ed. (Prospect Heights, IL: Waveland, 1996), 314–15. See also Bailey and Peterson, "Murder, Capital Punishment, and Deterrence," 55–56.

45. Blumstein et al., eds., *Deterrence and Incapacitation*, 9.

range of methodologies that have been employed to address this issue, there is no evidence that capital punishment is more effective as a deterrent to murder than incarceration."[46]

Note that, while the deterrence research commented upon here generally compares the deterrent impact of capital punishment with that of life imprisonment, the conclusion as to capital punishment's failure to deter murder more than does incarceration goes beyond life in prison. The fact is that, "[i]n the United States, a substantial proportion of inmates serving a life sentence are eventually released on parole."[47] Since this is public knowledge, we should conclude from these studies that capital punishment does not deter murder more effectively than prison sentences that are less than life, though still substantial, such as twenty years.

2. Common Sense and the Deterrent Effect of the Death Penalty

Conceding that it has not been proven that the death penalty deters more murders than life imprisonment, Ernest van den Haag has argued that neither has it been proven that the death penalty does not deter more murders.[48] Thus, his argument goes, we must follow common sense, which teaches that the higher the cost of something, the fewer the people who will choose it. Therefore, at least some potential murderers who would not be deterred by life imprisonment will be deterred by the death penalty. Van den Haag continues:

> [O]ur experience shows that the greater the threatened penalty, the more it deters. . . .
> Life in prison is still life, however unpleasant. In contrast, the death penalty does not just threaten to make life unpleasant—it threatens to take life alto-

---

46. Kappeler et al., *The Mythology of Crime and Criminal Justice*, 325.

47. Ibid., 313.

48. "Other studies published since Ehrlich's contend that his results are due to the techniques and periods he selected, and that different techniques and periods yield different results. Despite a great deal of research on all sides, one cannot say that the statistical evidence is conclusive. Nobody has claimed to have disproved that the death penalty may deter more than life imprisonment. But one cannot claim, either, that it has been proved statistically in a conclusive manner that the death penalty does deter more than alternative penalties. This lack of proof does not amount to disproof" (Ernest van den Haag and John P. Conrad, *The Death Penalty: A Debate* [New York: Plenum, 1983], 65).

gether. This difference is perceived by those affected. We find that when they have the choice between life in prison and execution, 99% of all prisoners under sentence of death prefer life in prison. . . .

From this unquestioned fact a reasonable conclusion can be drawn in favor of the superior deterrent effect of the death penalty. Those who have the choice in practice . . . fear death more than they fear life in prison. . . . If they do, it follows that the threat of the death penalty, all other things equal, is likely to deter more than the threat of life in prison. One is most deterred by what one fears most. From which it follows that whatever statistics fail, or do not fail, to show, the death penalty is likely to be more deterrent than any other.[49]

Those of us who recognize how commonsensical it was, and still is, to believe that the sun moves around the earth will be less willing than van

---

49. Van den Haag and Conrad, *The Death Penalty*, 68–69. An alterative formulation of this "commonsense argument" is put forth and defended by Michael Davis in "Death, Deterrence, and the Method of Common Sense," *Social Theory and Practice* 7, no. 2 (Summer 1981): 145–77. Davis's argument is like van den Haag's except that, where van den Haag claims that people *do* fear the death penalty more than lesser penalties and *are* deterred by what they fear most, Davis claims that it is *rational* to fear the death penalty more than lesser penalties and thus *rational* to be more deterred by it. Thus, he concludes that the death penalty is the most effective deterrent *for rational people*. He admits that this argument is "about rational agents, not actual people" ("Death, Deterrence, and the Method of Common Sense," 157). To bring it back to the actual criminal justice system that deals with actual people, Davis claims that the criminal law makes no sense unless we suppose the potential criminal to be (more or less) "rational" (ibid., 153). In short, the death penalty is the most effective deterrent because it would be rational to be most effectively deterred by it, and we are committed by belief in the criminal law to supposing that people will do what is rational. The problem with this strategy is that a deterrence justification of a punishment is valid only if it proves that the punishment actually deters actual people from committing crimes. If it doesn't prove that, it misses its mark, no matter what we are committed to supposing. Unless Davis's argument is a way of proving that the actual people governed by the criminal law will be more effectively deterred by the death penalty than by lesser penalties, it is irrelevant to the task at hand. And if it is a way of proving that actual people will be better deterred, then it is indistinguishable from van den Haag's version of the argument and vulnerable to the criticisms of it that follow. In his latest version of the commonsense argument, Davis seems to waffle on whether it is about actual people or not. Davis asserts that the commonsense finding that "[t]he death penalty is the most effective deterrent (among those humanely available)" is a *conceptual truth*. And, "[t]he discoveries of social science cannot affect the findings of common sense concerning what would deter

den Haag to follow common sense here, especially when it comes to doing something awful to our fellows. Moreover, there are good reasons for doubting common sense on this matter. Here are three.

1. From the fact that one penalty is more feared than another, it does not follow that the more feared penalty will deter more than the less feared, unless we know that the less feared penalty is not fearful enough to deter everyone who can be deterred—and this is just what we don't know with regard to the death penalty.[50] This point is crucial because it shows that *the commonsense argument includes a premise that cannot be based on common sense*, namely, that the deterrence impact of a penalty rises without limit in proportion to the fearfulness of the penalty. All that common sense could possibly indicate is that deterrence impact increases with fearfulness of penalty *within a certain normally experienced range.* Since few of us ever face a choice between risking death and risking life-time confinement, common sense has no resources for determining whether this difference in fearfulness is still within the range that increases deterrence. To figure that out, we will have to turn to social science—as a matter of common sense! And when we do, we find that most of the research we have on the comparative deterrent impact of execution versus life imprisonment suggests that there is no difference in deterrent impact between the death penalty and life imprisonment.[51]

Since it seems to me that whoever would be deterred by a given likelihood of death would be deterred by an *equal* likelihood of life behind bars, I suspect that the commonsense argument only seems plausible because we evaluate it while unconsciously assuming that potential criminals

---

rational agents." Two chapters later, however, Davis writes: "My argument purports to show that, absent proof (or at least strong evidence) that the deterrent tendency of the death penalty is swamped in some way or other, common sense requires us to suppose some deterrent effect" (*Justice in the Shadow of Death*, 21 and 50).

50. "[G]iven the choice, I would strongly prefer one thousand years in hell to eternity there. Nonetheless, if one thousand years in hell were the penalty for some action, it would be quite sufficient to deter me from performing that action. The additional years would do nothing to discourage me further. Similarly, the prospect of the death penalty, while worse, may not have any greater deterrent effect than does that of life imprisonment" (David A. Conway, "Capital Punishment and Deterrence: Some Considerations in Dialogue Form," *Philosophy and Public Affairs* 3, no. 4 [Summer 1974]: 433).

51. See notes 40 through 46 above and accompanying text.

will face larger likelihoods of death sentences than of life sentences. If the likelihoods were equal, it seems to me that where life imprisonment were improbable enough to make it too distant a possibility to worry much about, a similar low probability of death would have the same effect. After all, we are undeterred by small likelihoods of death every time we walk the streets. And if life imprisonment were sufficiently probable to pose a real deterrent threat, it would pose as much of a deterrent threat as death. And then it seems that any lengthy prison sentence—say, twenty years— dependably imposed and not softened by parole, would do the same.

2. In light of the fact that the number of privately owned guns in America is substantially larger than the number of households in America, as well as the fact that about twelve hundred suspected felons are killed or wounded by the police in the line of duty every year, it must be granted that anyone contemplating committing a crime already faces a substantial risk of ending up dead as a result.[52] It's hard to see why anyone *who is not already deterred by this* would be deterred by the addition of the more distant risk of death after apprehension, conviction, and appeal.

3. Van den Haag has maintained that deterrence works not only by means of cost-benefit calculations made by potential criminals, but also by the lesson about the wrongfulness of murder that is slowly learned in a society that subjects murderers to the ultimate punishment.[53] If, however, I am correct in claiming that the refusal to execute even those who deserve

---

52. The U.S. Bureau of Alcohol, Tobacco, and Firearms estimated the number of privately owned guns in 1990 at 200,000,000. See Albert Reiss and Jeffrey Roth, eds., *Understanding and Preventing Violence* (Washington, DC: National Academy Press, 1993), 256. For a similar estimate, see Gary Kleck, *Point Blank: Guns and Violence in America* (New York: Aldine de Gruyter, 1991), 17. There are approximately 95,000,000 households in the United States. In a 1979 study, Sherman and Langworthy estimated that between 500 and 700 felons were killed annually by the police in the line of duty (Lawrence W. Sherman and Robert H. Langworthy, "Measuring Homicide by Police Officers," *Journal of Criminal Law and Criminology* 70, no. 4 [Winter 1979]: 546–60). Public outcry and better training seem to have lowered this number to around 400. The FBI reports 462 such killings in 1994 and 383 in 1995 (Federal Bureau of Investigation, *Uniform Crime Reports for the United States: 1995* [Washington, D.C.: U.S. Government Printing Office, 1996], 22). A survey of studies of police shootings by Binder and Fridell concludes that "approximately 30 percent of persons shot by the police will actually die" (in Kappeler et al., *The Mythology of Crime and Criminal Justice*, 214).

53. Van den Haag and Conrad, *The Death Penalty*, 63.

it has a civilizing effect, then the refusal to execute also teaches a lesson about the wrongfulness of murder. My claim here is admittedly speculative, but no more so than van den Haag's to the contrary. And my view has the added virtue of accounting for the failure of research to show an increased deterrent effect from executions, *without having to deny the plausibility of van den Haag's commonsense argument that at least some additional potential murderers will be deterred by the prospect of the death penalty.* If there is a deterrent effect from *not executing,* then it is understandable that while executions will deter some murderers, this effect will be balanced out by the weakening of the deterrent effect of not executing, such that no net reduction in murders will result.[54] This, by the way, also disposes of van den Haag's argument that, in the absence of knowledge one way or the other on the deterrent effect of executions, we should execute murderers rather than risk the lives of innocent people whose murders might have been deterred if we had executed. If there is a deterrent effect of not executing, it follows that we risk innocent lives either way. And if this is so, it seems that the only reasonable course of action is to refrain from imposing what we know is a horrible fate.[55]

---

54. A related claim has been made by those who defend the so-called brutalization hypothesis by presenting evidence to show that murders increase following an execution. See, for example, William J. Bowers and Glenn L. Pierce, "Deterrence or Brutalization: What Is the Effect of Executions?" *Crime and Delinquency* 26, no. 4 (October 1980): 453–84. Bowers and Pierce conclude that each execution gives rise to two additional homicides in the month following and that these are real additions, not just a change in timing of the homicides (481). My claim, it should be noted, is not identical to this, since, as I indicate in the text, what I call "the deterrent effect of not executing" is not something whose impact is to be seen immediately following executions, but an effect that occurs over the long haul; further, my claim is compatible with finding no net increase in murders due to executions. Nonetheless, should the brutalization hypothesis be borne out by further studies, it would certainly lend support to the notion that there is a deterrent effect of not executing.

55. Van den Haag writes: "If we were quite ignorant about the marginal deterrent effects of execution, we would have to choose—like it or not—between the certainty of the convicted murderer's death by execution and the likelihood of the survival of future victims of other murderers on the one hand, and on the other his certain survival and the likelihood of the death of new victims. I'd rather execute a man convicted of having murdered others than put the lives of innocents at risk. I find it hard to understand the opposite choice" (van den Haag and Conrad, *The Death Penalty,* 69). Conway was able to counter this argument earlier by pointing

I conclude then that we have no good reason to think that we need the death penalty to protect innocent people from murder. Life in prison (or, at least, a lengthy prison term without parole) dependably meted out, will do as well.

IV. Pain and Civilization

The arguments of the previous two sections prove that, though the death penalty is a just punishment for murder, no injustice is done to actual or potential victims if we refrain from imposing the death penalty. In this section, I shall show that, in addition, there are good moral reasons for refraining.

The argument that I gave for the justice of the death penalty for murderers proves the justice of beating assaulters, raping rapists, and torturing torturers. Nonetheless, I take it that it would not be right for us to beat assaulters, rape rapists, or torture torturers, *even though it were their just deserts*—and even if this were the only way to make them suffer as much as they made their victims suffer. Calling for the abolition of the death penalty, though it be just, then, amounts to urging that we as a society place execution in the same category of sanction as beating, raping, and torturing and treat it as something it would also not be right for us to do to offenders, *even if it were their just deserts*.

To argue for placing execution in this category, I must show what would be gained therefrom. To show that, I shall indicate what we gain from placing torture in this category and argue that a similar gain is to be had from doing the same with execution. I select torture because I think the

---

out that the research on the marginal deterrent effects of execution was *inconclusive*, not in the sense of *tending to point both ways*, but rather in the sense of *giving us no reason to believe that capital punishment saves more lives than life imprisonment*. He could then answer van den Haag by saying that the choice is, not between risking the lives of murderers and risking the lives of innocents, but between killing a murderer with no reason to believe lives will be saved and sparing a murderer with no reason to believe lives will be lost (Conway, "Capital Punishment and Deterrence," 442–43). This, of course, makes the choice to spare the murderer more understandable than van den Haag allows. While the great majority of studies still support Conway's argument here, that claim is weakened by the advent of Ehrlich's research, which, contested though it may be, is research that points the other way.

reasons for placing it in this category are, due to the extremity of torture, most easily seen—but what I say here applies with appropriate modification to other severe physical punishments, such as beating and raping. First, and most evident, placing torture in this category broadcasts the message that we as a society judge torturing so horrible a thing to do to a person that we refuse to do it even when it is deserved. Note that such a judgment does not commit us to an absolute prohibition on torturing. No matter how horrible we judge something to be, we may still be justified in doing it if it is necessary to prevent something even worse. Leaving this aside for the moment, what is gained by broadcasting the public judgment that torture is too horrible to inflict even if deserved?

1. The Advancement of Civilization and the Modern State

I think that the answer to the question just posed lies in what we understand as civilization. In *The Genealogy of Morals,* Friedrich Nietzsche says that in early times "pain did not hurt as much as it does today."[56] The truth in this intriguing remark is that progress in civilization is characterized by a lower tolerance for one's own pain and that suffered by others. And this is appropriate, since, via growth in knowledge, civilization brings increased power to prevent or reduce pain, and, via growth in the ability to communicate and interact with more and more people, civilization extends the circle of people with whom we empathize.[57] If civilization is characterized by lower tolerance for our own pain and that of others, then publicly refusing to do horrible things to our fellows both signals the level of our civilization *and, by our example, continues the work of civilizing.* This gesture is all the more powerful if we refuse to do horrible things to

56. Friedrich Nietzsche, *The Genealogy of Morals,* in *The Birth of Tragedy and the Genealogy of Morals,* trans. Francis Golffing (New York: Doubleday, 1956; originally published 1887), 199–200.

57. Van den Haag writes that our ancestors "were not as repulsed by physical pain as we are. The change has to do not with our greater smartness or moral superiority but with a new outlook pioneered by the French and American revolutions [namely, the assertion of human equality and with it 'universal identification'], and by such mundane things as the invention of anesthetics, which make pain much less of an everyday experience" (van den Haag and Conrad, *The Death Penalty,* 215); cf. van den Haag's *Punishing Criminals* (New York: Basic Books, 1975), 196–206.

those who deserve them. I contend, then, that the more horrible things we are able to include in the category of what we will not do, the more civilized we are and the more civilizing. Thus we gain from including torture in this category, and, if execution is especially horrible, we gain still more by including it.

But notice, it is not just any refraining from horrible punishments that is likely to produce this gain. It is important to keep in mind that I am talking about modern states, with their extreme visibility, their moral authority (tattered of late but not destroyed), and their capacity to represent millions, even hundreds of millions, of citizens. It is when modern states refrain from imposing grave harms on those who deserve them that a powerful message about the repugnant nature of such harms is broadcast. It is this message that I contend contributes to civilization by increasing people's repugnance for such harmful acts generally. And, I believe that, because of modern states' unique position—their size, visibility, and moral authority, modern states have a duty to act in ways that advance civilization.

Needless to say, the content, direction, and even the worth of civilization are hotly contested issues, and I shall not be able to win those contests in this brief space. At a minimum, however, I take it that civilization involves the taming of the natural environment and of the human animals in it, and that the overall trend in human history is toward increasing this taming, though the trend is by no means unbroken or without reverses. On these grounds, we can say that growth in civilization generally marks human history, that a reduction in the horrible things we tolerate doing to our fellows (even when they deserve them) is part of this growth, and that, once the work of civilization is taken on consciously, it includes carrying forward and expanding this reduction. It might be objected that this view of civilization is ethnocentric, distinct to citizens of modern Western states but not shared, say, by hardy nomadic tribes. My response is that, while I do not believe the view is limited in this way, if it is, then so be it. I am, after all, addressing the citizens of a modern Western state and urging that they advance civilization by refraining from imposing the death penalty. What other guide should these citizens use than their own understanding of what constitutes civilization?

Some evidence for the larger reach of my claim about civilization and punishment is found in what Émile Durkheim identified, nearly a century ago, as "two laws which seem . . . to prevail in the evolution of the apparatus of punishment." The first, the *law of quantitative change*, Durkheim formulates thusly:

> The intensity of punishment is the greater the more closely societies approximate to a less developed type—and the more the central power assumes an absolute character.

And the second, which Durkheim refers to as the *law of qualitative change*, is this:

> Deprivations of liberty, and of liberty alone, varying in time according to the seriousness of the crime, tend to become more and more the normal means of social control.[58]

Several things should be noted about these laws. First of all, they are not two separate laws. As Durkheim understands them, the second exemplifies the trend toward moderation of punishment referred to in the first.[59] Second, the first law really refers to two distinct trends, which usually coincide but do not always. Moderation of punishment accompanies both the movement from less to more advanced types of society and the movement from more to less absolute rule. Normally these go hand in hand, but where they do not, the effect of one trend may offset the effect of the other. Thus, a primitive society without absolute rule may have milder punishments than an equally primitive, but more absolutist, society.[60] This complication need not trouble us, since the claim I am making refers to the first trend, namely, that punishments tend to become milder as societies become more advanced; and that this is a trend in history is not refuted by the fact that it is accompanied by other trends and even occasionally offset by them. Finally, and most important for our purposes, Durkheim's

---

58. Émile Durkheim, "Two Laws of Penal Evolution," *Economy and Society* 2 (1973): 285, 294. This essay was originally published in French in *Année Sociologique* 4 (1899–1900).

59. Durkheim writes that "of the two laws which we have established, the first contributes to an explanation of the second" (ibid., 299).

60. The "two causes of the evolution of punishment—the nature of the social type and of the governmental organ—must be carefully distinguished" (ibid., 288). Durkheim cites the ancient Hebrews as an example of a society of the less-developed type that had milder punishments than societies of the same social type, due to the relative absence of absolutist government among the Hebrews (ibid., 290).

claim that punishment becomes less intense as societies become more advanced is a generalization that he supports with an impressive array of evidence from historical societies from pre-Christian times to the time in which he wrote—and this supports my claim that reduction in the horrible things we do to our fellows is in fact part of the advance of civilization.[61]

Against this it might be argued that there are many trends in history, some good, some bad, and some mixed, and thus that the mere existence of some historical trend is not a sufficient reason to continue it. Thus, for example, history is marked generally by growth in population, but we are not for that reason called upon to continue the work of civilization by continually increasing our population. What this suggests is that in order to identify something as part of the work of civilizing, we must show not only that it generally advances over the course of history, but that its advance is, on some independent grounds, clearly an advance for the human species—that is, either an unmitigated gain or at least consistently a net gain. And this implies that even trends we might generally regard as advances may in some cases bring losses with them, such that when they did, it would not be appropriate for us to lend our efforts to continuing them. Of such trends, we can say that they are advances in civilization except when their gains are outweighed by the losses they bring—and that we are called upon to further these trends only when their gains are not outweighed in this way. It is clear, in this light, that increasing population is a mixed blessing at best, bringing both gains and losses. Consequently, population increase is not always an advance in civilization that we should further, though at times it may be.

What can be said of reducing the horrible things that we do to our fellows even when deserved? First of all, given our attitude toward suffer-

---

61. Durkheim's own explanation of the progressive moderation of punishments is somewhat unclear. He rejects the notion that it is due to the growth in sympathy for one's fellows, since this, he maintains, would make us more sympathetic with victims and thus harsher in punishments. He argues instead that the trend is due to the shift from understanding crimes as offenses against God (and thus warranting the most terrible of punishments) to understanding them as offenses against men (thus warranting milder punishments). He then seems to come around nearly full circle by maintaining that this shift works to moderate punishments by weakening the religious sentiments that overwhelmed sympathy for the condemned: "The true reason is that the compassion of which the condemned man is the object is no longer overwhelmed by the contrary sentiments which would not let it make itself felt" (ibid., 303).

ing and pain, it seems clearly a gain. Is it, however, an unmitigated gain? Would such a reduction ever amount to a loss? It seems to me that there are two conditions under which it would be a loss, namely, if the reduction made our lives more dangerous, or if not doing what is justly deserved were a loss in itself. As for the former, as I have already indicated, I accept that if some horrible punishment is necessary to deter equally or more horrible acts, then we might have to impose the punishment. (After all, in self-defense, we accept the imposition by the defender of harms equal to those threatened by his attacker.) Thus my claim is that reduction in the horrible things we do to our fellows is an advance in civilization as *long as our lives are not thereby made more dangerous* and that it is only then that we are called upon to extend that reduction as part of the work of civilization. Assuming, then, that we suffer no increased danger by refraining from doing horrible things to our fellows when they justly deserve them, does such refraining to do what is justly deserved amount to a loss?

The answer to this must be that refraining to do what is justly deserved is a loss only where it amounts to doing an injustice. But such refraining to do what is just is not doing what is unjust, unless what we do instead falls below the bottom end of the range of just punishments. Otherwise, it would be unjust to refrain from torturing torturers, raping rapists, or beating assaulters. If there is no injustice in refraining from torturing torturers, then there is no injustice in refraining from doing horrible things to our fellows generally, when they deserve them, as long as what we do instead is compatible with believing that they do nonetheless deserve those horrible things. Thus, if such refraining does not make our lives more dangerous, then it is no loss, and, given our vulnerability to pain, it is a gain. Consequently, reduction in the horrible things we do to our fellows, when those things are not necessary to our protection, is an advance in civilization.

2. The Horribleness of the Death Penalty

To complete the argument, however, I must show that execution is horrible enough to warrant its inclusion alongside torture. Against this it will be said that execution is not especially horrible, since it only hastens a fate that is inevitable for all of us.[62] I think that this view overlooks important

---

62. Van den Haag seems to waffle on the question of the unique awfulness of

differences in the manner in which people reach their inevitable ends. I contend that execution is especially horrible, and it is so in a way similar to (though not identical with) the way in which torture is especially horrible. I believe we view torture as especially awful because of two of its features, which also characterize execution: intense pain and the spectacle of one person being completely subject to the power of another.[63] This latter is separate from the issue of pain, since it is something that offends us about unpainful things, such as slavery (even voluntarily entered) and prostitution (even voluntarily chosen as an occupation).[64] Execution

---

execution. For instance, he takes it not to be revolting in the way that ear cropping is, because "[w]e all must die. But we must not have our ears cropped" (van den Haag and Conrad, *The Death Penalty*, 190). Here, he cites John Stuart Mill's parliamentary defense of the death penalty, in which Mill maintained that execution only *hastens* death. Mill's point was to defend the claim that "[t]here is not . . . any human infliction which makes an impression on the imagination so entirely out of proportion to its real severity as the punishment of death" (John Stuart Mill, "Parliamentary Debate on Capital Punishment within Prisons Bill," in *Philosophical Perspectives on Punishment*, ed. Gertrude Ezorsky [Albany, NY: State University of New York Press, 1972; Mill made the speech in 1868], 273). Van den Haag seems to agree, since he maintains that, since "we cannot imagine our own nonexistence . . . [t]he fear of the death penalty is in part the fear of the unknown. It . . . rests on a confusion" (*The Death Penalty*, 258–59). On the other hand, he writes: "Execution sharpens our separation anxiety because death becomes clearly foreseen. . . . Further, and perhaps most important, when one is executed he does not just die, he is put to death, forcibly expelled from life. He is told that he is too depraved, unworthy of living with other humans" (ibid., 258). I think, incidentally, that it is an overstatement to say that we cannot imagine our own nonexistence. If we can imagine any counterfactual experience (e.g., how we might feel if we didn't know something that we do in fact know), then it doesn't seem impossible that we can imagine what it would "feel like" not to live. I think I can arrive at a pretty good approximation of this by trying to imagine how things "felt" to me in the eighteenth century. The sense of the awful difference between being and not being alive that enters my experience when I do this makes the fear of death—not as a state, but as the absence of life—seem hardly to rest on a confusion.

63. Hugo Bedau has developed this latter consideration at length with respect to the death penalty. See Hugo A. Bedau, "Thinking about the Death Penalty as a Cruel and Unusual Punishment," *U.C. Davis Law Review* 18 (Summer 1985): 917ff. This article is reprinted in Hugo A. Bedau, *Death Is Different: Studies in the Morality, Law, and Politics of Capital Punishment* (Boston: Northeastern University Press, 1987); and Hugo A. Bedau, ed., *The Death Penalty in America: Current Controversies* (New York: Oxford University Press, 1997).

64. I am not here endorsing this view of voluntarily entered slavery or prostitu-

shares this separate feature, since killing a bound and defenseless human being enacts the total subjugation of that person to his fellows.

Execution, even by physically painless means, is characterized not only by the spectacle of subjugation, but also by a special and intense psychological pain that distinguishes it from the loss of life that awaits us all. Interesting in this regard is the fact that, although we are not terribly squeamish about the loss of life itself, allowing it in war, in self-defense, as a necessary cost of progress, and so on, we are, as the extraordinary hesitance of our courts testifies, quite reluctant to execute.[65] I think this is because execution involves the most psychologically painful features of death. We normally regard death from human causes as worse than death from natural causes, since a humanly caused shortening of life lacks the consolation of unavoidability. And we normally regard death whose coming is foreseen by its victim as worse than sudden death because a foreseen death adds to the loss of life the terrible consciousness of that impending loss.[66] As a humanly caused death whose advent is foreseen by its victim, an execution combines the worst of both. Indeed, it was on just such grounds that Albert Camus regarded the death penalty as itself a kind of torture: "As a general rule, a man is undone by waiting for capital punishment well before he dies. Two deaths are inflicted on him, the first being

---

tion. I mean only to suggest that it is the belief that these relations involve the extreme subjugation of one person to the power of another that is at the basis of their offensiveness. What I am saying is quite compatible with finding that this belief is false with respect to voluntarily entered slavery or prostitution.

65. "[F]or whatever reasons . . . , prosecutors seek the death penalty only in a fraction of all the cases where they could. Again, for a variety of reasons—appropriate mitigating evidence, sympathy for the defendant, lingering doubts about the defendant's guilt—juries bring in a death sentence only in a fraction of all cases where a prosecutor seeks it. When one considers these facts in conjunction with the fact that each capital trial begins by eliminating on the voir dire every prospective juror who evidences opposition to the death penalty, the number of death sentences is surprisingly small" (Hugo A. Bedau, "Interpreting the Eighth Amendment: Principled vs. Populist Strategies," *Thomas M. Cooley Law Review* 13 [1996]: 806).

66. This is no doubt partly due to modern skepticism about an afterlife. Earlier peoples regarded a foreseen death as a blessing allowing time to make one's peace with God. Writing of the early Middle Ages, Philippe Ariès says, "In this world that was so familiar with death, sudden death was a vile and ugly death; it was frightening; it seemed a strange and monstrous thing that nobody dared talk about" (Philippe Ariès, *The Hour of Our Death* [New York: Vintage, 1982], 11).

worse than the second, whereas he killed but once. Compared to such torture, the penalty of retaliation seems like a civilized law."[67]

Thus far, by analogy with torture, I have argued that execution should be avoided because of how horrible it is to the one executed. But there are reasons of another sort that follow from the analogy with torture. Torture is to be avoided not only because of what it says about what we are willing to do to our fellows, but also because of what it says about us who are willing to do it. To torture someone is an awful spectacle not only because of the intensity of pain imposed, but also because of what is required to be able to impose such pain on one's fellows. The tortured body cringes, using its full exertion to escape the pain imposed upon it—it literally begs for relief with its muscles as it does with its cries. To torture someone is to demonstrate a capacity to resist this begging, and that, in turn, demonstrates a kind of hard-heartedness that a society ought not to parade.

This is true not only of torture, but of all severe corporal punishment. Indeed, I think this constitutes part of the answer to the puzzling question of why we refrain from punishments like whipping, even when the alternative (some months in jail versus some lashes) seems more costly to the offender. Imprisonment is painful to be sure, but it is a reflective pain, one that comes with comparing what is to what might have been and that can be temporarily ignored by thinking about other things. But physical pain has an urgency that holds body and mind in a fierce grip. Of physical pain, as Orwell's Winston Smith recognized, "you could only wish one thing: that it should stop."[68] By refraining from torture in particular and corporal punishment in general, we both refuse to put a fellow human being in this grip and refuse to show our ability to resist this wish. The death penalty is the last corporal punishment used officially in the Western world. It is corporal not only because it is administered via the body, but also because the pain of foreseen, humanly administered death strikes its victim with the urgency that characterizes intense physical pain, causing even hardened criminals to cry, faint, and lose control of their bodily functions. There is something to be gained by refusing to endorse the hardness of heart necessary to impose such a fate.

---

67. Albert Camus, "Reflections on the Guillotine," in Albert Camus, *Resistance, Rebellion, and Death* (New York: Knopf, 1961), 205.

68. George Orwell, *1984* (New York: New American Library, 1983; originally published 1949), 197.

By placing execution alongside torture in the category of things we will not do to our fellow human beings even when they deserve them, our state broadcasts the message that totally subjugating a person to the power of others and confronting him with the advent of his own humanly administered demise is too horrible to be done by civilized human beings to their fellows even when they have earned it: too horrible to do, and too horrible to be capable of doing. And I contend that the state's broadcasting this message loud and clear would, in the long run, contribute to the general detestation of murder and be, to the extent to which it worked itself into the hearts and minds of the populace, a deterrent. In short, refusing to execute murderers though they deserve it both reflects and continues the taming of the human species that we call civilization—and it should, over time, contribute to reducing the incidence of murder. Thus, I take it that the abolition of the death penalty, though that penalty is a just punishment for murder, is part of the civilizing mission of modern states.

Notice, before moving on, that I have not here argued that the death penalty is *inhumane*.[69] Inhumane punishments are normally thought to be incompatible with respecting the person of the offender and thus forbidden except perhaps under the most extreme circumstances. Speaking of the death penalty, Kant wrote that "the death of the criminal must be kept entirely free of any maltreatment that would make an abomination of the humanity residing in the person suffering it."[70] Torture almost surely and maybe even execution are inhumane, but I have argued only that they are horrible, that is, that they are punishments that cause their recipients extreme pain, physical and/or psychological. I have tried to show the ways in which the death penalty, even imposed without physical pain, is still a horrible punishment in that it causes extreme psychological suffering often to the point of loss of physical control. I then urged that it would be good for the state to avoid doing such things to people, not simply because it is always morally preferable to impose less pain rather than more, but also because the state—by virtue of its size, high visibility, and moral author-

---

69. Michael Davis takes me to be trying to prove that the death penalty is inhumane, and, since I don't try that, he is able, with predictable ease, to prove that I don't succeed. See Davis, "The Death Penalty, Civilization, and Inhumaneness," *Social Theory and Practice* 16 (Summer 1990): 245–59; and Davis, *Justice in the Shadow of Death*, 47–63.

70. Kant, "Metaphysical Elements of Justice," 102.

ity—is able to have impact on citizens beyond the immediate act it authorizes.

In particular, I have suggested that the state, by the vivid example of its unwillingness to execute even those—*especially those*—who deserve it, would contribute to the process of civilizing humankind, which I take in part to include reducing our tolerance for pain imposed on our fellows. I have called this an advance in civilization for two reasons: first, because history shows that the harshness of punishments seems generally to decline over time, and second, because it seems good to reduce our willingness to impose pain on our fellows. The first condition here is empirical, a matter of what history actually records. And while I think that the elimination of ear cropping, branding, drawing and quartering, and boiling in oil, as well as the practice of throwing members of unpopular religions to the lions for public entertainment, all suggest that the taming that I have in mind is the general trend of history, there are exceptions, of course. The Nazis, for example, tortured their enemies with awful ferocity. But most would recognize Nazism as a step backward in civilization. So, my claim is a broad empirical claim, much in the vein of Richard Rorty's recent suggestion that, in the West, there has been a tendency to want to reduce or eliminate cruelty.[71] But it is equally a moral claim. I have argued that even stable historical trends do not count as advances in civilization unless they are also, on independent grounds, good.[72]

In sum, my argument is that, though the death penalty is just punishment for some murders, execution is a horrible thing to do to our fellows, and, if the state can avoid execution without thereby doing injustice to actual or potential victims of murder, then, in addition to whatever is good about causing less pain, the state would also, by its example, contribute to a general reduction in people's tolerance for doing painful things to one another, a reduction that I think is an advance in civilization. And I think that modern states are morally bound to promote the advance of civilization because they are uniquely positioned to do so and because of the

---

71. Richard Rorty, *Contingency, Irony, and Solidarity* (Cambridge: Cambridge University Press, 1989), 184–85.

72. Michael Davis incorrectly treats my claim about civilization exclusively as an empirical claim about actual historical trends. See Davis, "The Death Penalty, Civilization, and Inhumaneness," 251; and Davis, *Justice in the Shadow of Death*, 53.

goodness that must characterize a trend if it is to count as an advance in civilization.

Recall that I argued, in section I, that offenders deserve the least amount of punishment that imposes on them harm equivalent to the harm they caused their victims *and* the harm they caused to society by taking unfair advantage of the law-abiding *and* that will effectively deter rational people from committing such crimes in the future. If we take these conjuncts separately, it should be clear from the previous section's argument that the deterrence component can be satisfied with life in prison or some lengthy prison term. Since I take the fairness component to be the same in any crime, it will not in itself add more than a small increment to any particular punishment. Consequently, it, too, should be satisfied if we impose a lengthy prison term on murderers. As for the first component, the *lex talionis* indicates that the murderer justly deserves to die, and nothing I have argued alters this conclusion. However, I have also argued that retribution can be satisfied without executing murderers, so long as they are punished in some other suitably severe way. It follows that, though the death penalty is justly deserved punishment for some murderers, all the rationales for punishment will be satisfied if murderers are sentenced to life in prison or at least to a substantial prison term, such as twenty years without parole. I have argued in the present section that refraining from executing murderers will contribute to the advance of civilization and may, in the long run, reduce the incidence of murder. In sum, there are no moral reasons against, and some very good ones for, abolishing the death penalty. All of this has been based on the idea that the death penalty is just punishment for murder in principle. Additional reasons for abolishing the death penalty appear when we look at it in practice.

V. Just in Principle, Unjust in Practice

On February 3, 1997, the "American Bar Association, the nation's largest and most influential organization of lawyers . . . , voted overwhelmingly to seek a halt to the use of the death penalty, asserting that it is administered through 'a haphazard maze of unfair practices.' "[73]

---

73. Saundra Torry, "ABA Endorses Moratorium on Capital Punishment," *Washington Post*, February 4, 1997, A4.

When it is pointed out to van den Haag that the death penalty has been and is still likely to be administered in an unfair and discriminatory fashion, he replies that the question of the justice of the death penalty and the justice of its administration are two separate questions: "Objections to unwarranted discrimination are relevant to the discriminatory distribution of penalties, not to the penalties distributed."[74] Having said this, van den Haag believes that he has disposed of the objection concerning discrimination, since he has shown that discriminatory application, though admittedly wrong, is not something wrong with the death penalty itself. He is correct in believing that these two questions are distinct and that distinguishing them shields the death penalty from the force of the objection. It does so, however, at a considerable price.

Van den Haag is correct that the justice of a penalty and the justice of a penalty's distribution are theoretically separate matters: We can consistently believe that fining double-parkers in a discriminatory fashion is unjust while believing that fines are a just penalty for double-parking. It is possible to admit that the discriminatory application of a penalty is unjust and still maintain that the penalty itself is in principle a just one. Thus van den Haag can agree with his critics that the discriminatory application of the death penalty is unjust, and still maintain that the penalty itself is in principle a just response to murder. But this way of disposing of the objection carries a high price tag because the very separation of the questions by means of which van den Haag evades the objection dramatically limits the scope of the conclusions he can reach from that point on. Moral assessment of the way a penalty is actually going to be carried out is a necessary ingredient in any determination of the justice of adopting that penalty as our policy. By separating the question of the justice of the death penalty itself from that of the justice of the way it is likely to be carried out, van den Haag separates as well his answer to the question of the justice of the death penalty itself from any answer to the question whether the death penalty is just as an actual policy. As a result, van den Haag may prove that the death penalty is in principle a just response to murder—but at the cost of losing the right to assert that it is just for us to adopt it in practice here and now in America.

If there is reason to believe that a policy will be administered unjustly, then that is reason for believing that it is *unjust* to adopt that policy here

---

74. Van den Haag, *Punishing Criminals*, 221.

and now in America, even though the policy is just in principle. This is not to say that injustice in the administration of a policy automatically makes it wrong to adopt the policy. It might still be that all the available alternatives are worse, such that, on balance, we do better by adopting this policy than by adopting any of the other possible candidates. However, in the absence of a showing that all alternatives are worse, I take it that it is wrong to adopt an unjust policy, and thus that the likelihood of substantially unjust administration of a policy has the effect of making it wrong to adopt that policy. I say "substantially" here in order to make clear that I do not claim that every, even the slightest, injustice has this effect. Given the inevitability of human error, some miscarriages of justice are inevitable in implementing any policy. Thus, I shall say that in situations in which we have reason to expect that a policy will be administered with *substantial* injustice, then that policy will likely be unjust *in practice,* and in situations in which there is not reason to believe that all alternative policies will be worse, it would be wrong to adopt a policy that is likely to be unjust *in practice* even if it was just *in principle.*

In section II, I argued that the death penalty was a just punishment for at least some murders. But that argument was made without reference to the actual way in which the death penalty is likely to be meted out in current-day America. Consequently, the argument proves that the death penalty is a just punishment for murder in principle. I shall now argue that when we apply the standard of justice implicit in that argument to the actual ways in which the death penalty is likely to be imposed in America today and into the foreseeable future, we find that instituting the death penalty in current-day America is unjust in practice.

When I argued that death is just punishment for murder according to the *lex talionis,* I indicated that this justification can be rightly applied only when its implied preconditions are satisfied. What are these preconditions? First, the retributive justification of the death penalty that I have defended depends on the penalty's capacity to affirm or act out the equal worth of persons. Hence a precondition of punishing justly as retribution is that the state punish in a way that treats persons as of equal worth. Second, the death penalty affirms the equal worth of persons only on the assumption that the murderer is wholly responsible for his or her crime. This is a necessary precondition of the moral legitimacy of asking him or her to pay the whole price of the harm he or she has caused, namely, a life for a life.[75] Hence a precondition of executing murderers justly as retribution is that neither the state nor the society it represents bears responsibility for what murderers have done. And third, the death penalty is a just punishment for murder according to the *lex talionis* only if the death penalty imposes a harm on the murderer roughly equivalent to the harm the murderer caused his victim. Consequently, a precondition of executing murderers justly as retribution for murder is that the death penalty be imposed without being accompanied by other harms to the murderer that make the penalty substantially worse than murder itself. Insofar as the state violates any of these preconditions of the retributive justice of the death penalty, it does injustice in practice (according to the very standard of justice by which the death penalty is justified) and, thereby, loses its right to justify its executions retributively. In this sense, a theory of the moral justification of punishment is also a theory of the moral conditions that the state must satisfy to have the right to punish.

In the remainder of this section, I shall present four ways in which the administration of the death penalty in America, currently and into the foreseeable future, violates one or more of the above-mentioned preconditions. All of these are reasons why the death penalty, justified in principle retributively, will be unjust in practice according to the very values underlying that retributive justification. I shall close the section with briefer arguments that reach the same conclusion about the death penalty justified in principle by fairness and deterrence. With that, my argument against the death penalty will be complete.

1. Discrimination in the Application of the Death Penalty among Convicted Murderers

A long line of researchers has found that, among equally guilty murderers, the death penalty is more likely to be given to blacks than to whites

---

75. Note that my claim here is a moral claim, not a legal one. The law often holds several people wholly responsible for the same act. On the other hand, the law calls for reducing responsibility under conditions of duress and, in entrapment, the law calls for eliminating culpability entirely where the state plays a role in making a crime more attractive.

and to poor defendants than to well-off ones. Though discrimination was one of the grounds upon which death penalty statutes were ruled unconstitutional in *Furman v Georgia* in 1972, there is strong evidence that it remains in the sentencing procedures ruled constitutional four years later in *Gregg v Georgia*: "Among killers of whites [in Florida], blacks are five times more likely than whites to be sentenced to death."[76] This pattern of discrimination was also evidenced, though in less pronounced form, in Texas, Ohio, and Georgia. More recently, studies have presented evidence for discrimination among convicted murderers on the basis of the race of their victims, with killers of whites standing a considerably larger chance of being sentenced to death than killers of blacks.[77] Since 1976, 82 percent of the murder victims in cases that resulted in executions were white, though whites are victims in less than half the murders committed in the United States. Of persons executed for interracial murders since 1976, four were whites who killed blacks, eighty-four were blacks who killed whites. Supreme Court Justice Harry Blackmun, who voted *for* the death penalty in 1972 and 1976, said in a 1994 dissent: "Even under the most sophisticated death penalty statutes, race continues to play a major role in determining who shall live and who shall die."[78]

---

76. W. J. Bowers and G. L. Pierce, "Racial Discrimination and Criminal Homicide under Post-*Furman* Capital Statutes," in *The Death Penalty in America*, 3rd ed., ed. Hugo A. Bedau (New York: Oxford University Press, 1982), 210, 211.

77. See D. Baldus, C. Pulaski, and G. Woodworth, *Equal Justice and the Death Penalty* (Boston: Northeastern University Press, 1990). Their study was the basis of the most recent (and unsuccessful) major constitutional challenge to the death penalty based on racial discrimination, namely, *McCleskey v Kemp*, 753 F2d 877 (1987). For other studies that reveal discrimination in capital sentencing based on race of victim, see R. Paternoster, "Race of Victim and Location of Crime: The Decision to Seek the Death Penalty in South Carolina," *Journal of Criminal Law and Criminology* 74, no. 3 (1983): 754–88; R. Paternoster, "Prosecutorial Discretion in Requesting the Death Penalty: A Case of Victim-Based Racial Discrimination," *Law and Society Review* 18 (1984): 437–78; S. Gross and R. Mauro, "Patterns of Death: An Analysis of Racial Disparities in Capital Sentencing and Homicide Victimization," *Stanford Law Review* 37 (1984): 27–120; Michael L. Radelet and Glenn L. Pierce, "Race and Prosecutorial Discretion in Homicide Cases," *Law and Society Review* 19 (1985): 587, 615–19.

78. Justice Harry Blackmun, dissenting from denial of certiorari, *Callins v Collins*, 114 US 1127, 1135 (1994). See also Richard C. Dieter, *Twenty Years of Capital Punishment: A Re-evaluation*, report by the Death Penalty Information Center [Washington, DC: June 1996], 4. Michael Radelet reviewed records of

It should be clear that a society that adopts the death penalty when it is likely to be applied in this way chooses to bring about injustice. Any society that punishes in such a discriminatory fashion loses the right to appeal to the retributive justification of the death penalty defended earlier. That justification depends on the penalty's affirmation of the equal worth of persons, and a society that reserves the death penalty for murderers coming from certain racial and socioeconomic groups clearly treats these people as of less worth than others. Likewise, a society that reserves the death penalty for the killers of whites but not of blacks treats blacks as of less worth than whites.

2. Discrimination in the Definition of Murder

Those acts that the law calls "murder" are by no means the only ways that people kill their fellow citizens in America. There is, for example, considerable evidence that many more Americans die as a result of diseases caused by preventable conditions in the workplace (toxic chemicals, coal and textile dust, etc.) than die at the hands of the murderers who show up in arrest and conviction records or on death row.[79] In 1985, three corporate executives were found guilty of murder and sentenced to twenty-five years in prison for the death of an employee that was caused by exposure to hydrogen cyanide in a film reprocessing plant.[80] The executives, it was held, knew fully the dangerousness of the situation and failed to warn their employees. Most interesting for our purposes is that this was recognized as *the first case of its kind.* The uniqueness of this case and its outcome testify that general practice is to ignore or treat lightly the subjection of workers to lethal hazards on the job.

15,978 American executions since 1739, and found thirty cases—two-tenths of 1 percent of executions!—in which a white was executed for a crime against a black. In ten of these cases, the victim was a black slave (a white man's property), and in five more, the occupational status of the black victim was higher than that of the white assailant (Michael L. Radelet, "Executions of Whites for Crimes against Blacks: Exceptions to the Rule?" *Sociological Quarterly* 30, no. 4 [1989]: 529–44).

79. Jeffrey Reiman, *The Rich Get Richer and the Poor Get Prison: Ideology, Class, and Criminal Justice,* 5th ed. (Needham Heights, MA: Allyn & Bacon, 1998), 71–78.

80. *Facts on File* (New York: Facts on File, 1985), 495.

It might be thought unfair to class such things as the failure to remove deadly occupational hazards as murder because this failure is not an act intentionally aimed at ending life. However, many state homicide statutes categorize unintended deaths caused by extreme recklessness as murder.[81] Thus, if loss of life is among the foreseeable likely consequences of failure to remove occupational hazards, as long as the victims have not freely and knowingly consented to put themselves at risk, the individual responsible for this failure ought to be held responsible for (at least) reckless homicide, and possibly murder, regardless of the particular outcome he hoped for when he acted.

It is reasonable to assume that there is some ordinary level of risk that is accepted by all members of society as an implicit condition of enjoying the benefits of progress, and of course there are some cases in which workers can be said to have freely and knowingly consented to risk the special occupational hazards that accompany their jobs; but there are as well a large number of cases in which individuals taking hazardous jobs had no realistic alternative and a large number of cases in which extraordinary hazards were known only to management—and concealed. Consider, for example, the Manville (formerly Johns Manville) asbestos case. It is predicted that 240,000 Americans who have worked with asbestos will die from asbestos-related cancer in the next thirty years. Documents made public during congressional hearings in 1979 show "that Manville and other companies within the asbestos industry covered up and failed to warn millions of Americans of the dangers associated with the fireproof, indestructible insulating fiber."[82] An article in the *American Journal of Public Health* attributes thousands of deaths to the cover-up.[83] In cases like these, employees can hardly be held to have freely put themselves at risk.

There is also evidence that the number of people who die from other practices not normally treated as murder, such as performance of unnecessary surgery and prescription of unneeded drugs, is higher than the num-

---

81. Nancy Frank, "Unintended Murder and Corporate Risk-Taking: Defining the Concept of Justifiability," *Journal of Criminal Justice* 16 (1988): 18.

82. Russell Mokhiber, *Corporate Crime and Violence: Big Business Power and the Abuse of Public Trust* (San Francisco: Sierra Club, 1988), 278, 285.

83. David E. Lilienfield, "The Silence: The Asbestos Industry and Early Occupational Cancer Research—A Case Study," *American Journal of Public Health* 81, no. 6 (June 1991): 791.

ber of reported murder victims. And these examples can be multiplied. Moreover, the difference between the kinds of killings that are treated as murder and the kinds that are not is not an arbitrary or haphazard difference; it is a systematic identification of the ways that poor people kill as "murder" and the ways that well-off people kill as something else: "disasters," "social costs of progress," or "regulatory violations" at worst.[84]

If in our society murder is not the intentional taking of life, but the intentional taking of life *by poor people,* this has quite the same moral effect as the first sort of discrimination. It treats well-off killers as of greater worth than poor killers, and it supports the presumption that in our society murderers are not punished because they are murderers, but because they are poor. Then, adoption of the death penalty in practice amounts to instituting unjust discriminatory treatment of the poor. And this disqualifies the society from claiming that it is executing murderers to pay them in kind for their crimes and to affirm the equal worth of human beings.

3. Discrimination in the Recruitment of Murderers

The first two sorts of discrimination just considered are built into the criminal justice system; the sort that I shall now take up is arguably built into the structure of the society that that criminal justice system protects. That the death rows of our nation are populated primarily by poor people is not only the result of discriminatory sentencing. In large measure, it is the result of the fact that murder, or at least what we call murder, is done primarily by people at the bottom of society. "In the case of homicide, the empirical evidence indicates that poverty and poor economic conditions are systematically related to higher levels of homicide."[85] One confirmation of the link between poverty and homicide is that "[a]bout ninety percent of those facing capital charges cannot afford their own lawyer."[86]

---

84. Reiman, *The Rich Get Richer*, 78–81; see also 51–53.

85. Richard M. McGahey, "Dr. Ehrlich's Magic Bullet: Economic Theory, Econometrics, and the Death Penalty," *Crime and Delinquency* 26, no. 4 (October 1980): 502. Some of that evidence can be found in Peter Passell, "The Deterrent Effect of the Death Penalty: A Statistical Test," *Stanford Law Review* (November 1975): 61–80.

86. R. Tabak and M. Lane, "The Execution of Injustice: A Cost and Lack-of-Benefit Analysis of the Death Penalty," *Loyola of Los Angeles Law Review* 23 (1989): 59, 70, cited in Dieter, *Twenty Years of Capital Punishment*, 5. The quality

If people are subjected to remediable unjust social circumstances beyond their control, and if harmful actions are a predictable response to those conditions, then those who benefit from the unjust conditions and refuse to remedy them share responsibility for the harmful acts—and thus neither the doing nor the cost of those acts can be assigned fully to the offenders alone. For example, if a slave kills an innocent person while making his escape, at least part of the blame for the killing must fall on those who have enslaved him. And this is because slavery is unjust, not merely because the desire to escape from slavery is understandable. The desire to escape from prison is understandable as well, but if the imprisonment were a just sentence, then we would hold the prisoner, and not his keepers, responsible if he killed someone while escaping. Consequently, if poverty in America is unjust, and if murder is a predictable result of this unjust poverty, then the society that refuses to remedy this poverty bears some responsibility for the murders that result.

The author of a study of the distribution of wealth in America from colonial times to the present concludes that "at no time has the majority of the U.S. adult population or households managed to gain title to any more than about ten percent of the nation's wealth."[87] This distribution of wealth is unjust in light of all of the currently popular theories of justice: *utilitarianism* (given the relative numbers of rich and poor in America, as well as the principle of declining marginal returns, redistribution could make the poor happier without an offsetting loss in happiness among the rich), or John Rawls's theory of *justice as fairness* (the worst-off shares in our society could still be increased, so the difference principle is not yet satisfied), or Robert Nozick's *libertarianism* (the original acquisition of property in America was marked by the use of force against Native Ameri-

---

of legal aid received by these indigent capital defendants is woefully bad and, due to cuts in funding, getting worse. A 1993 study by the American Bar Association "found the whole system of indigent defense to be in a state of crisis, citing a long history of warnings on this problem. In particular, it noted that death penalty defendants have been hardest hit by inadequate funding" (Richard Dieter, *With Justice for Few: The Growing Crisis in Death Penalty Representation*, report by the Death Penalty Information Center [Washington, DC: October 1995], 20 [reporting the findings of R. Klein and R. Spangenberg, *The Indigent Defense Crisis*, prepared for the ABA Section of Criminal Justice Ad Hoc Committee on the Indigent Defense Crisis, 1993]).

87. Carole Shammas, "A New Look at Long-Term Trends in Wealth Inequality in the United States," *American Historical Review* 98, no. 2 (April 1993): 421.

cans and blacks, from which both groups still suffer).[88] However, given the legacies of slavery and Jim Crow; the fact of widespread discrimination based on race, religion, and gender; and the vast differences in educational opportunity facing people of different economic statuses; it hardly takes sophisticated philosophical analysis to conclude that America's lopsided distribution of wealth is unjust.

Since there is reason to believe that the vast majority of murders in America are a predictable response to the frustrations and disabilities of impoverished social circumstances, and that that impoverishment is a remediable injustice from which others in America benefit, American society bears some of the responsibility for these murders and thus has no right to exact the full cost of murders from its murderers until America has done everything possible to rectify the conditions that produce their crimes.

Van den Haag notes the connection between crime and poverty, and he explains it and its implications as follows: "Poverty does not compel crime; it only makes it more tempting."[89] And it is not absolute poverty that makes crime more tempting, only relative deprivation, the fact that some have less than others.[90] In support of this, van den Haag marshals data showing that, over the years, crime has risen along with the standard of living at the bottom of society. Since, unlike absolute deprivation, relative deprivation will be with us no matter how rich we all become as long as some have more than others, he concludes that this condition that increases the temptation to crime is just an ineradicable fact of social life, best dealt with by giving people strong incentives to resist the temptation.

This argument is flawed in several ways. First, the claim that crime is connected with poverty ought not to be simplistically interpreted as meaning that a low absolute standard of living itself causes crime. Rather, what seems to be linked to crime is the general breakdown of stable communities, institutions, and families, such as has occurred in our cities in recent decades as a result of economic and demographic trends largely out of individuals' control. Of this breakdown, poverty is today a sign and a cause, in that poverty leaves people with few defenses against the breakdown and few avenues of escape from it. It is this general breakdown that

---

88. See John Rawls, *A Theory of Justice*; and Robert Nozick, *Anarchy, State, and Utopia* (New York: Basic Books, 1974). For an extended discussion of these theories of justice, see Reiman, *Justice and Modern Moral Philosophy*.

89. Van den Haag and Conrad, *The Death Penalty*, 207.

90. Ibid., 115.

spawns crime. And this claim is quite compatible with finding that people who have lower absolute standards of living, but who dwell in more stable social surroundings with traditional institutions still intact, have lower crime rates than contemporary poor people who have higher absolute standards of living. Second, the implication of the link between poverty and crime is not simply that it is relative deprivation that tempts people to commit crime, for if that were the case, the middle class would be stealing as much from the rich as the poor do from the middle class. That this is not the case suggests that there is some threshold after which crime is no longer so tempting, and while this threshold changes historically, it is in principle one all could reach. Thus, it is not merely the (supposedly ineradicable) fact of having less than others that makes crime so tempting. Finally, everything is altered if the temptation to crime is the result, not of an ineradicable social fact, but of an injustice that can be remedied or relieved.

Insofar as we as a society tolerate the existence of remediable unjust social conditions that make crime a more reasonable alternative for a specific segment of society than for other segments, we are accomplices in the crimes that quite predictably result. As such, we lose the right to extract the full price from the criminal, and this means we lose the right to take the murderer's life in return for the life he has taken. Since the vast majority of murderers will come from the bottom of society, adopting the death penalty as their punishment imposes more harm on them than they have earned—and that means that adopting the death penalty in practice amounts to bringing about injustice.

4. Life on Death Row as Torture

The argument that the person condemned to be executed lives a life of torture stems from Albert Camus.[91] Recently, this argument has been fleshed out in fuller psychological detail by Robert Johnson, who, in his book *Condemned to Die*, recounts the painful psychological deterioration suffered by a substantial majority of the death row prisoners he studied.[92] Since the death row inmate faces execution, he is viewed as having nothing

---

91. See note 67 above and accompanying text.
92. Robert Johnson, *Condemned to Die: Life under Sentence of Death* (New York: Elsevier, 1981), 129ff.

to lose and thus treated as the most dangerous of criminals. As a result, his confinement and isolation are nearly total. Since he has no future for which to be rehabilitated, he receives the least and the worst of the prison's facilities. Since his guards know they are essentially warehousing him until his death, they treat him as something less than human—and so he is brutalized, taunted, powerless and constantly reminded of it. The result of this confinement, as Johnson reports it, is quite literally the breaking down of the structures of the ego—a process not unlike that caused by brainwashing. Since we do not reserve the term "torture" only for processes resulting in physical pain, but recognize processes that result in extreme psychological suffering as torture as well (consider sleep deprivation or the so-called Chinese water torture), Johnson's application of this term to the conditions of death row confinement seems reasonable.

It might be objected that some of the responsibility for the torturous life of death row inmates must be attributed to the inmates themselves, since in pressing their legal appeals, they delay their executions and thus prolong their time on death row. However, the unusually high rate at which capital murder convictions and sentences are reversed on appeal (estimated at nearly ten times the rate of reversals in noncapital cases; roughly half of all capital cases in the 1980s were reversed on appeal) strongly supports the idea that such appeals are necessary to test the legality of murder convictions and death penalty sentences.[93] To hold the inmate somehow responsible for the delays that result from his appeals, and thus for the (increased) torment he suffers as a consequence, is effectively to confront him with the choice of accepting execution before its legality is fully tested or suffering torture until it is. Since no just society should expect (or even want) a person to accept a sentence until its legal validity has been established, it is unjust to torture him until it has and perverse to assert that he has brought the torture on himself by his insistence that the legality of his sentence be fully tested before it is carried out.

Although it is possible that the worst features of death row might be ameliorated, it is not at all clear that its torturous nature is ever likely to be eliminated, or even that it is possible to eliminate it. In order to protect themselves against natural, painful, and ambivalent feelings of sympathy for a person awaiting a humanly inflicted death, it may be psychologically

---

93. See Costanzo and White, "An Overview of the Death Penalty," 12–14; see also Bedau, ed., *Death Penalty in America*, 243.

necessary for the guards who oversee a condemned person to think of him as less than human and treat him as such. Johnson writes: "I think it can also be argued . . . that humane death rows will not be achieved in practice because the purpose of death row confinement is to facilitate executions by dehumanizing both the prisoners and (to a lesser degree) their executioners and thus make it easier for both to conform to the etiquette of ritual killing."[94]

If conditions on death row are and are likely to continue to be a real form of psychological torture, what are the implications for the justice of the death penalty in practice? One must admit that it is no longer merely a penalty of death—it is now a penalty of torture until death. And if this is so, then it can no longer be thought of as an amount of suffering equal to that imposed by the murderer, leaving aside those murderers who have tortured their victims. Thus, at least for ordinary murderers, the death penalty would exceed the suffering they had caused and could not be justified on the retributivist basis defended above. As to whether it would be justified retribution for murderers who had tortured their victims, perhaps it would, but probably not for many. The reason is that as we move away from common instrumental murders to the pointlessly cruel ones, we move at the same time toward offenders who are more likely to be sociopaths and less likely to be fully in control of their actions in the way that legitimates retributive punishment.

My primary concern in this section has been to demonstrate that the same moral considerations that show *lex talionis* to be a just standard of desert—in particular, the recognition and affirmation of the equal worth of all persons—show as well that it would be unjust to institute the death penalty in America, in light of how it is likely to be carried out. I shall only briefly suggest how similar arguments might be made about the other two punishment rationales discussed earlier, fairness and deterrence.

Jeffrie Murphy considers the applicability of the fairness rationale to the punishment of the typical criminals in present-day American society. Writes Murphy,

> The retributive theory really presupposes . . . a "gentlemen's club" picture of . . . society. . . . The rules benefit all concerned and, as a kind of debt for the benefits derived, each man owes obedience to the rules. In the absence

---

94. Robert Johnson, personal correspondence to author.

of such obedience, he deserves punishment in the sense that he owes payment for the benefits. . . . But to think that [this picture] applies to the typical criminal, from the poorer classes, is to live in a world of social and political fantasy. . . . [Such criminals] certainly would be hard-pressed to name the benefits for which they are supposed to owe obedience.[95]

Poor people are deprived of the material benefits of cooperation, and the frequent result of this is that they are deprived of the security benefits as well, inasmuch as they have little choice but to live in crime-ridden neighborhoods, where police are at best able to keep violence from getting out of hand and barely able to provide real protection for all citizens. Insofar as the benefits of obeying the law are not distributed equally to all, neither is the duty to obey, nor the debt incurred for disobeying, the same for all. Consequently, while punishment may be justified in principle for taking unfair advantage, instituting such punishment in an unjust society is unjust in practice according to the values underlying the fairness view: It punishes people for defaulting on payment for benefits they haven't received.

Since deterrence is an extension of the right of self-defense, it does not turn on notions of equal worth or personal responsibility. One is morally permitted to kill a homicidal maniac in self-defense, even though there is no assertion that he is responsible for his acts or that killing him affirms anything about his worth compared to anyone else's. Thus, even if the above-considered unjust conditions obtain, our society might still avail itself of the deterrence justification—even an unjust society has the right to defend its innocent members against harm.

But if we revert to the deterrence justification, two things must be borne in mind. First, as I argued above, we do not have reason to believe that capital punishment has a greater deterrent impact on murder than less harsh penalties. Thus, deterrence does not now justify the death penalty. Second, since the deterrence approach justifies a penalty as the least harsh means necessary to produce the obtainable level of deterrence, it can be invoked for any given punishment only if no less harsh means will produce the same deterrent effect. But there is no reason to limit the means under consideration to punishments. To use the deterrence approach to justify punishment, one must have exhausted all the ways of preventing crime

---

95. Jeffrie Murphy, "Marxism and Retribution," in *Punishment*, ed. Simmons et al., 26.

that are less harsh than punishment, in order to show that only some form of punishment is the least harsh means to deter crime. This implies that, in order to appeal to the deterrence justification for punishment, we must already have tried to eliminate crime by such nonpunitive means as eliminating the conditions like poverty that cause crime. Until we do this, our appeals to deterrence—even if valid in principle—will ring just as hollow in practice as do our appeals to retribution.

It may be objected that the various injustices catalogued in this section characterize the imposition of prison sentences as well as the death penalty, and, thus, if those injustices are grounds for abolishing the death penalty, then they are equally grounds for abolishing imprisonment. However, recall that I maintained that the injustice of a policy would not necessarily count against instituting that policy if all feasible alternatives were worse. Since I have already given arguments for preferring imprisonment to executions, and since injustice in the imposition of a milder penalty is a milder injustice than injustice in the imposition of a harsher penalty, eliminating the death penalty and limiting our punishments to imprisonment with its injustices is not worse, and is arguably better, than maintaining the death penalty with its injustices. Moreover, if, as we commonly suppose, some kind of imprisonment is needed for our criminal justice system to provide what protection and justice it can, then abolishing imprisonment is a worse alternative than maintaining it. Nothing in my argument, then, implies that we should abolish imprisonment.

I conclude that it is wrong to maintain the death penalty in practice in the United States as punishment for murder—although the penalty itself is in principle a just punishment for murder. And since I have earlier shown that it would be good to punish murder with less harsh penalties than death, I think I have shown that it is morally right in principle and in practice to abolish the death penalty in America.

3

Reply to Jeffrey Reiman

Louis P. Pojman

In his perspicacious and challenging essay "Why the Death Penalty Should be Abolished in America"[1] Jeffrey Reiman qualifiedly accepts the two claims in favor of executing murderers: retributivism and deterrence. Regarding retributivism, he says, some murderers deserve the death penalty. Regarding deterrence, he says, "if the death penalty were needed to deter future murders, it would be unjust to future victims not to impose it." Then he argues five points:

1. Although the death penalty is a just punishment for some murderers, "it is not unjust to punish murderers less harshly (down to a certain limit)."
2. We have "no good reason to believe that the death penalty is needed to deter future murders."
3. In "refraining from imposing the death penalty, the state, by its vivid and impressive example, contributes to reducing our tolerance for cruelty and thereby fosters the advance of human civilization as we understand it."
4. Conclusion: Theses 1 to 3, taken together, "imply that we do no injustice to actual or potential murder victims, and we do some considerable good, in refraining from executing murders."

1. Reiman's essay is one of the clearest, most cogent expressions for abolitionism that I have read, and I appreciate the careful judiciousness of his reasoning. Note that while we come to radically different conclusions, we agree on many essential points. We are both retributivist, holding to a strong notion of justice as desert. We both acknowledge that just desert would in principle permit torturing the torturer. I'm especially impressed by Reiman's ambitious attempt to bring several principles of punishment into a unity.

5. This conclusion (Thesis 4) is reinforced by the fact that, "though the death penalty is *in principle* a just penalty for murder, it is unjust *in practice* in America because it is applied in arbitrary and discriminatory ways and this is likely to continue into the foreseeable future."

Regarding thesis 1, unlike many abolitionists who argue that the death penalty is unjust in principle, Reiman is a retributivist as I am, holding that the guilty deserve to be punished. The difference between us is that I hold that we ought to punish the guilty with a penalty equivalent to the harm caused or the wrong done, which he denies. He writes, "the fact that a punishment is justly deserved does not, in my view, entail that someone has a duty to impose that punishment. Rather, ... desert creates *a right to punish*, not a duty to do so." I hold that justice consists in giving people what they deserve, so that there is a duty to impose the death penalty on some murderers, even if it is only a prima facie duty, which may be overridden by other moral concerns. Regarding thesis 2, Reiman accepts that if the death penalty were needed to deter future murders, he would favor it. But he and I disagree on whether it is needed to deter future murders. Regarding thesis 3, Reiman holds that turning away from the death penalty will help civilize our society. I am doubtful here and will argue against this point. Thesis 4, of course, follows from 1 to 3, so I will reject it, since I reject thesis 2 and 3. Regarding thesis 5, that the application of the death penalty is arbitrary and discriminatory, *so we should abandon its use*, I am skeptical. We should reform our system but not abandon the use of the death penalty. I will argue, contrary to Reiman: (1) That justice as desert creates duties to give people what they deserve; (2) that the death penalty is needed as a deterrence; (3) that abolishing the death penalty at this time does not promote civilization; and (4) that the "fact" that the application of the death penalty is sometimes arbitrary and discriminatory in America does not warrant our abolishing the institution in America.

Does Justice as Desert Create Duties?

Reiman holds that some murderers deserve the punishment of the death penalty but that we have no duty to punish them this way. If I understand him, he and I agree that the State has a *right* to punish the guilty in pro-

portion to the gravity of their crime, which may include executing the
murderer. Although granting the State this right is sufficient to establish
the permissibility of capital punishment in some cases, it will make the
retentionist's case stronger if one can defend the thesis that society has a
duty to execute those who kill with malice aforethought. I hold that desert
creates a *prima facie* duty to punish with a harm equivalent to the crime.
In Part I of my essay I developed an argument along the following lines:

1. Justice, as giving people what they deserve, consists in rewarding the good
   according to their virtue and the bad according to their vice.
2. We ought to be just, whenever we can. This includes having laws to promote justice.
3. Therefore, we ought to institute laws and legal procedures to punish the
   guilty according to their vice (i.e., according to the evil they have intentionally done).
   My principle (DD = "desert creates duties") of treating (rewarding or
   punishing) people according to their desert can be formulated this way:
   Let S = the subject, and x = the treatment (good or bad treatment):
   DD: If S deserves x, and you are in a position to give S x, and no moral
   reason overrides or neutralizes giving S x, then you have a duty to give
   S x.

Perhaps the formula needs to be qualified. If others are in an even better
position to give S x or if S specifically deserves to get x from someone else,
you may not have a duty to give S x. I will assume that the qualifications
will not affect the central point that someone's deserving treatment of
various kinds creates an obligation on others to give that person what he
or she deserves. A neutralizing reason may include the fact that we simply
don't know that someone deserves some reward and punishment, so that
we are not required to give him what he deserves.

As I noted, mitigating circumstances, overriding duties (including the
duty to err on the side of mercy), and practical considerations may offset
this prima facie duty. While we may have a general duty to benevolence,
to come to the aid of anyone who deserves to be helped, special obligations to our family, friends, and community may override that general duty
to benevolence. Similarly, our duty to punish the guilty according to their
deserts may be overridden by other obligations. Because we have judicial
procedures which have been instituted to carry out justice, we may not
take the "law into our own hands" as it were, but ought to follow due
process, even when it yields unjust results in individual cases. Similarly,

while the torturer may deserve to be tortured, our duty to give him what he strictly deserves may be offset by considerations of mercy, existing cultural practices, utility, or simply because the personal (e.g., psychological) costs in carrying out torture are unacceptable. Nonetheless, desert has normative force, creating an obligation to give people what they deserve. We intuitively sense this when we object that an employer is exploiting workers by paying them far less than they deserve. Cheating and stealing are kinds of undeserved acquisitions of goods. The person who is not grateful to his benefactor, who does not sense an obligation to reciprocate for services rendered, lacks a moral virtue. Desert claims are normative, as reflected in the Hindu and Buddhist doctrine of karma (people deserve the fruits of their deeds—whatsoever a man sows that shall he reap), in the Judeo-Christian idea of divine judgment (God rewards the good with life in heaven and the evil with life in hell), in Kant's idea that people ought to flourish or suffer equivalent to their virtue or vice, and in Marx's Labor Theory of Value (that the entrepreneur ought to give the worker what he deserves, so that not to do so is a kind of theft). I confess it is intuitively self-evident that the good deserve to prosper and the evil to suffer—until they repent—and that in an ideal universe the virtuous and vicious would get what they deserve. Those harmed through no fault of their own would be compensated. Even though we obviously cannot bring this state of justice about in our universe, isn't part of our duty to try to do so whenever feasible? Don't we have some basic duty to reward and punish according to deserts, when we have the ability to do so and have some idea of what people do deserve?

Note that Reiman objects to a version of theorem DD, but offers no argument against it except three alleged counter-examples.

> I present here three compelling claims that support the view that desert does not entail a duty to give what is deserved: First, the victim of an offense has the right to forgive the offending party rather than punish him though he deserves to be punished; second, we have no duty (not even a prima facie duty) to torture torturers even if they deserve to be tortured; and third, though great benefactors of humanity deserve to be rewarded, no one necessarily has a duty to provide that reward.

These counterexamples certainly should give us pause, but, we may ask, Do any of these counterexamples actually undermine DD? Let's examine them in order.

(1) The right to forgive the offender shows that we don't have a duty to give what is deserved. To evaluate this claim we need to understand what forgiveness is. I follow Bishop Joseph Butler in defining forgiveness as the "forswearing of resentment."[2] If this is so, then I can forgive someone without withdrawing the requirement of punishment. Suppose I am abused, raped and robbed by a close relative. I may forgive him his deeds but still believe he should accept the penalties enjoined by our legal system. Furthermore, it may be inappropriate or immoral to forgive him if he feels no remorse and has not repented of the evil he has done to me. My forgiving him may depict a vice in me, a lack of sufficient self-respect. The concept of forgiveness seems to work best where there is repentance on the part of the offender, though utilitarian reasons may also be operative. But suppose you want to go further than this and agree with Reiman that the offended person has a right to forgive the offender in a manner that enjoins removing the penalty which he deserves. This does not necessarily count against DD, for we could still say that the prima facie duty to give people what they deserve can be overridden by our right to forgive and show mercy. The point is that the offended person has no duty to forgive an unrepentant offender, so that the prima facie obligation persists until it is overridden.

(2) Reiman's second claim is that "we have no duty (not even a prima facie duty) to torture torturers even if they deserve to be tortured." But isn't the correct assessment that we do have a prima facie duty to bring it about that the torturer is punished in kind but that other moral considerations may override this duty? The social costs to torturing the torturer may be too high. I may be psychologically brutalized by torturing the offender. Here a certain benign cultural relativity may prevail, so that in some cultures a general revulsion will be directed at the practice of torture, whereas in others it will not. The practice cannot be viewed in isolation from the whole fabric of a culture. Furthermore, the torturer may not deserve to be tortured, but he may deserve some different (lesser or greater) punishment. If his deed was done under social pressure (say, a Nazi prison guard

---

2. Joseph Butler, *Fifteen Sermons* (London, 1726), Sermon 8 "Upon Resentment" and Sermon 9 "Upon Forgiveness and Injuries." My views have been influenced by the discussion of Jeffrie Murphy and Jean Hampton in their book, *Forgiveness and Mercy* (Cambridge University Press, 1988) and by Tziporah Kasachkoff.

who is following orders by torturing a prisoner), he may deserve severe punishment, but it may not require us to torture him.

Note that Reiman sometime writes as though he recognizes the prima facie duty to give the torturer what he deserves:

> When, however, we refrain from raping rapists or torturing torturers, we do so for reasons of morality, not of practicality. And, given the justice of the *lex talionis*, these moral reasons cannot amount to claiming that it would be unjust to rape rapists or torture torturers. Rather, the claim must be that, even though it would be just to rape rapists and torture torturers, other moral considerations weigh against doing so.

But isn't this exactly what DD asserts? We have a prima facie duty to do justice, justice might require us to torture the torturer. But other moral reasons override this prima facie duty. To continue to reject DD Reiman would have argue that justice imposes no obligations on us, which seems to remove justice from the sphere of morality as a definite principle. I don't think he wants to do this.

(3) Reiman's third counterexample is the claim that no one necessarily has a duty to provide a reward to a great benefactor of society. Once again, my principle would enjoin a prima facie duty for society to provide the benefactor with an appropriate reward, but there may be other moral grounds that override this, for "no one necessarily has a duty to provide that reward." My inclination is to say that we go astray when we think that financial rewards are the only way to give benefactors what they deserve. What they deserve is gratitude, admiration, respect, and perhaps special consideration in having their needs met before those of others. How should we reward Mother Teresa for the enormous good she has done for others? One might ask her. Actually, my wife and I did ask her, while visiting her in Calcutta in 1990. She said that the way we could honor her would be by carrying out the spirit of her programs, in helping orphans, the poor, and the unborn (supporting the right-to-life movement). Perhaps some would have moral reservations about the last item, but it gives us some clue as to how to reward great benefactors. Or consider a military hero, call him Sergent York, who has saved his battalion by risking his life against intense enemy fire with the result that the battalion was able to win a decisive victory in the war. Ten people, including Sgt. York are in need of an organ (say a liver transplant), and none of the other

candidates' service to society is as great as his. Might it not be the case that we have a prima facie duty to give the scarce organ to him?

I conclude this discussion in defense of DD. We do have a prima facie duty to give people what they deserve. Justice requires it.

2. Is the Death Penalty Needed in Order to Deter Future Murders?

I have already discussed this point in Part II of my essay defending the death penalty, so I will be brief here. Reiman, in arguing that the death penalty doesn't deter (any better than long-term prison sentences) commits a common abolitionist mistake of arguing that because the sum of the sociological evidence shows no significant deterrent effect of the death penalty, the evidence supports the thesis that there *is no significant deterrent effect*. The inference is invalid, for the sociological evidence doesn't *show that there is no deterrent effect*. It doesn't show either that there is or is not a deterrent effect. It is inconclusive on the matter. One can see why. There simply are too many variables to be controlled for, including social conditions, genetic make-up, such demographical factors as age and racial distribution, law enforcement factors, knowledge of the consequences of getting caught, and opportunity factors—just to name a few broad categories. Perhaps if we experimented by executing people who committed murder on the even months but gave long prison sentences to those who committed murders on the odd months, we could come close to providing reliable data on the likelihood of the deterrent effect of the death penalty. Until we have better ways of measuring the effects of social policy, we should take the sociological evidence with a grain of salt.

Reiman doesn't deal with van den Haag's Best Bet Argument, which strikes me as sound. If we don't have hard evidence that the death penalty deters, we should bet on it saving potential murder victims rather than bet on saving the lives of the murderers. No doubt he will comment on this in his response, but since I don't know what that response is, I can only ask you to remind yourself of the argument in Part II of my essay.

Reiman is correct in arguing that the fact that one penalty is feared more than another doesn't entail that it will deter more than a less feared one. He thinks that the lack of statistical correlation for deterrence places the burden of proof on the retentionist who argues that the death penalty does deter. I argued, following recognized work in criminology, that the criminal, in planning many crimes, engages in a cost-benefit form of analysis in which he takes into consideration (if only subconsciously) the overall value of his criminal act. If the crime's pay-off is likely to be high and the chances of getting caught are low, the attractiveness of the crime is heightened; but if the penalty for the crime is lowered, the crime increases in attractiveness. Conversely, if the penalty increases, the attractiveness decreases. Long-term imprisonment without parole is likely to be, on this account, a greater deterrent than short-term imprisonment or long-term imprisonment with parole. The possibility of long-term imprisonment *plus* the possibility of the death penalty is likely to be an even greater deterrent, even as the possibility of winning the division championship plus the Super Bowl championship would be a greater incentive for a professional football team than merely the chance of winning the division championship. All things being equal, the greater the evil, the greater the deterrence, and the greater the blessing, the greater the incentive.[3] Not all murderers reason in this way, but the overall consciousness of many criminals seems to follow this pattern. Criminals often act rationally (from their point of view) in committing crimes, including the crime of murder. Furthermore, the anecdotal evidence, which I cited in Part II, cannot be dismissed as insignificant. Some criminals have transported their potential victims across borders from retentionist states to abolitionist states before they commit murder, and others have testified that they were deterred by the threat of execution. I have personal knowledge of the deterrent effect of the death penalty. Both a friend and my brother became involved in criminal activity (robbery) for a time. My friend carried a gun but kept it unloaded, while my brother wouldn't even carry a gun though it would have made his work easier. They acted as they did for fear of using it, lest they end up in the electric chair. I rest my case.

---

3. To support this point Reiman quotes David Conway in note 67 "[G]iven the choice, I would strongly prefer one thousand years in hell to eternity. Nonetheless, if one thousand years in hell were the penalty for some action, it would be quite sufficient to deter me from performing that action." The point about the threshold effect of deterrence is well taken, but it doesn't settle anything. The threat of life imprisonment probably deters many would-be criminals, but, doubtless, others would only be deterred from some crimes by a penalty as severe as death. Perhaps only the possibility of a thousand years in hell would deter other criminals.

3. Will Abolishing the Death Penalty at This Time Promote Civilization in America?

Reiman argues that the death penalty is a just punishment for certain heinous crimes but that it should nevertheless be eliminated on the grounds
that we would thereby become more civilized because the death penalty
increases pain and *involves the total subjugation* of one person by others,
as does slavery and prostitution.[4] I question whether there is any necessary
connection between eliminating the death penalty and civilization. First, I
want to challenge Reiman's two criteria for increased civilization: the lessening of pain and the lessening of subjugation of people by others. I agree
that, all things being equal, these are good things and may enhance civilization, but, again, they may not. Suppose, for example, we find a way to
extend life, but that the unfortunate means to do so is painful surgery
(many cardiac patients report such excruciating pain while undergoing an-
gioplasty and stent treatment). Isn't it obvious that some pain is instru-
mentally good? For pain sensation may cause suitable limb and life-saving
behavior, it warns us of such dangers as fire or electrical shock, and it may
also enable us to empathize with others, thus making us kinder and gentler
people. But, of course, we could meet Reiman's requirement for less pain
while retaining the death penalty, for we can execute the criminal without

---

4. Ernest van den Haag has pointed out that these analogies fail since slavery,
unlike murder, is involuntary and prostitution may be voluntary but need not involve the total subjugation of one person by another. Yet Reiman thinks that there
is something evil about subjugation even if it is voluntary. He doesn't say what
that is.

Sometimes abolitionists point out that all the other Western civilizations have
abolished the death penalty, so that we are in the dubious company of South Africa
and Russia in retaining it. This kind of reasoning ignores the vastly different extent
of the problem of crime in the United States compared with that of Western Europe, where the murder rate is often a tiny fraction of what it is here. It also
assumes that the majority must be right, a position I find objectionable and in
need of argument. Abolitionists always cite Europe when claiming that civilized
nations must renounce capital punishment. However, one can read this trend another way: Perhaps they are nations dying, nations that no longer have the heart
to stand up for what is right and maintain a deep sense of justice based on desert.
When the good and the bad are treated equally well, when merit and individual
responsibility are sacrificed for a shortsighted utility, when sentimentality replaces
commitment to the good, even a good that calls on us to inflict punishment on
the evil, society is on the road—not to hell—but to oblivion.

any pain whatsoever—by a painless lethal injection. But is it really a good thing to eliminate pain in the punishment of murderers? Doesn't the murderer deserve some pain?

Regarding the subjugation of one person by another, Reiman writes:

> I contend that execution is especially horrible, and it is so in a way similar to (though not identical with) the way in which torture is especially horrible. I believe we view torture as especially awful because of two of its features, which also characterize execution: intense pain and the spectacle of one person being completely subject to the power of another. This latter is separate from the issue of pain, since it is something that offends us about unpainful things, such as slavery (even voluntarily entered) and prostitution (even voluntarily chosen as an occupation). Execution shares this separate feature, since killing a bound and defenseless human being enacts the total subjugation of that person to his fellows.

While we may agree that full autonomy is a good thing, there are many goods which may conflict with autonomy and override it. Here are a few: a good upbringing and education, entering a religious order, restraining violent people who either are not autonomous or use their autonomy to harm, and submitting to training which will result in higher expected personal utility. All these processes involve subjecting yourself to another. Children are in "total subjugation" to their parents. Patients undergoing surgery are in "total subjugation" to their surgeons. Education requires a great deal of subjugation to a regime and to teachers. The long-term prison sentences which Reiman advocates for murderers may involve every bit as much subjugation as slavery, perhaps more subjugation than slavery under a benign master who may have the slave's interests at heart. Parents have their children's interest at heart. Religious people wholly subjugate themselves to God or a religious authority. How is this different from voluntary slavery? Subjugation itself is not necessarily evil. It all depends on whether the limiting of freedom is morally justified, all things considered. The question is whether the prisoner, including the murderer on death row, deserves to be subjugated, deserves to have his freedom restricted. I would think Reiman believes that he does, and so I find him simply inconsistent here.

Civilville

Let me tell a story in order to illustrate my contention that although the death penalty may cause extra suffering and subjugation it may nevertheless be an ingredient of a civilized society. Civilville is a society like ours. Its laws are similar, and it has retained the death penalty. Where it is different than ours pertains to legal reform: It underwent moral and legal reform some time ago, eliminating arbitrariness in the application of the death penalty. This legal reform came about through appointing special nonpartisan panels of experts as the jurors in murder trials. The reforms eliminated much of the influence of race and wealth and encouraged the factual presentation of evidence, so that not only has the great majority of citizens come to believe in the fairness of the system but citizens have cooperated with the police and judicial system as never before in the history of Civilville. Whether or not the death penalty actually deters would-be murders is still a debatable issue, but the murder rate has gone down by virtue of citizen reporting. Because community morale is high, citizens are not hesitant to report suspicious activities, give testimony, and vote for judges and lawmakers of high integrity.

Civilville has also undergone moral reform. Its people have gradually become more sensitive to the needs of others and strive mightily to be fair. Most of the citizens are vegetarians, judging the killing of animals for food to be an unnecessary evil. They also have a low abortion rate, holding that whether or not fetuses are persons, they will, if allowed to develop in society, become persons and are, unlike criminals, innocent. The citizens are meritocrats, believing that the good should prosper and the evil should be punished, and that the most qualified people should get the best positions and the less able should be encouraged to improve themselves. Because the principle of just desert is deeply rooted in their souls, people of Civilville are retributivists who advocate that the good should be rewarded for their social contributions and criminals should be punished in proportion to the viciousness of their crimes. It's true that mercy mitigates strict justice, so they do not torture the torturer or rape the rapist (though they deserve that), but they do castrate the rapist and execute those convicted of first-degree murder.

I interviewed the people of Civilville and asked them whether they thought that substituting long prison sentences for the death penalty would make them more civilized. They admitted that while in some cases long sentences might be kinder, for the most part the death penalty for heinous crimes symbolized their meritocratic position that those who murder innocent people deserve to be executed by the State. They are perplexed by many liberals in our society who, without the slightest hesitation, advocate aborting innocent fetuses and eating innocent animals but become apoplectic about executing mass murderers. I would be proud to call myself a citizen of Civilville.

Pain, Suffering, and Progress

Reiman and I share a common concern for a just society. We are both committed to a more moral, civilized world, but we differ on the way to get there. He wants to eliminate or greatly lessen pain and physical suffering, reducing it to "reflective pain . . . that comes with comparing what is to what might have been and that can be temporarily ignored by thinking about other things." He quotes Nietzsche, that "pain did not hurt as much [in olden times] as it does today." He means that people used to tolerate pain better than they do now. My immediate questions are: How do we know this, and how is this relevant? I've heard the same argument used regarding depriving minorities and Native Americans of benefits ("they don't feel it as much as we do" or "they have a greater tolerance for pain and hardship than we do"). If people at different times can tolerate pain better than those at other times, can't people of different cultures tolerate pain better than those of others? Should we take this into consideration? If we found that some people tolerated being deprived of their rights better than other people, would our depriving them of those rights be less wrong? I doubt it, and I also doubt whether the criminal's inability to tolerate as much pain as his ancestors is a good reason for not inflicting on him the suffering he justly deserves.

Be this as it may, I too want to ameliorate *some* pain and suffering, gratuitous pain and suffering. I am against torturing people except when it will prevent a catastrophe (because of its stand against torture and for human rights, I am a member of Amnesty International), and I am a vegetarian because the wanton treatment and killing of animals, especially in animal factories, involves unnecessary cruelty. But I'm not against *all* pain and suffering. It is true that we live in an anesthetized culture where drugs are a multibillion-dollar industry. Corporal punishment is frowned upon, spanking is considered out of date, and our lives have become disembodied, centered on impersonal and abstract notions (often the products of technology, like the computer). But I'm not sure that this abstractification and anesthetization of existence is all for the good. I worry that we may be adopting a mindless Epicureanism at the expense of a Stoic ability to face hardship bravely, to resolutely endure the aches of existence for the sake of becoming stronger. Some suffering can be redemptive. Freud rejected painkillers for his pain, preferring mental lucidity with torment to a painless but dulled mind. Maybe we have become soft and flabby, fearful of the pain and suffering which are necessary or relevant to achieving civilization. If Plato is right, that nothing great was ever accomplished without great struggle and great suffering, then the elimination or inappropriate reduction of it may actually destroy civilization, bringing to pass T. S. Eliot's refrain that "the world ends not with a bang but a whimper."[5] On the contrary, being held accountable for one's deeds, may involve experiencing the suffering that accompanies our mistakes. We learn by the pain of our failures, as well as by the pleasures of our successes. They are valuable reinforcement mechanisms.

Reiman seems to advocate the abolition not only of capital punishment, but of virtually all corporal punishment. He is no doubt horrified at Singapore's practice of caning criminals, such as in the case of the caning of the American Michael Fay, who broke a Singapore law by vandalizing property with graffiti. Reiman wants to reduce all punishment to deprivation of freedom. He has quoted Nietzsche to the effect that pain hurts more in the present than it did in the past, but perhaps we should quote Nietzsche once more, this time as a commentator on Reiman's proposal to eliminate physical and mental suffering in punishment:

> There is a point in the history of society when it becomes so pathologically soft and tender that among other things it sides even with those who harm it, criminals, and does this quite seriously and honestly. Punishing somehow seems unfair to it, and it is certain that imagining "punishment" and "being supposed to punish" hurts it, arouses fear in it. "Is it not enough to render him *undangerous?* Why still punish? Punishing itself is terrible." With this question, herd morality, the morality of timidity, draws its ultimate conse-

---

5. T. S. Eliot "The Hollow Men" in *Collected Poems 1909–1962* (New York: Harcourt, Brace, Jovanovich, 1934). The poem ends:
This is the way the world ends
This is the way the world ends
This is the way the world ends
Not with a bang but a whimper.
A lot more needs to be said on the importance of suffering and struggle for civilization. I have noticed that corporal punishment has different effects on different children in the process of socialization.

quence. . . . The imperative of herd timidity: "We want that some day there should be *nothing anymore to be afraid of!*"[6]

Writing well over one hundred years ago, Nietzsche predicted that people would some day call this "progress."

4. Is the Application of the Death Penalty in America Arbitrary and Discriminatory, and If So, Does That Fact Entail That We Should Abolish It?

Reiman quotes approvingly the news report of February 3, 1997: "The American Bar Association, the nation's largest and most influential organization of lawyers . . . , voted overwhelmingly to seek a halt to the use of the death penalty, asserting that it is administered through 'a haphazard maze of unfair practices.'" I take it that this quotation is meant to lend authority to Reiman's case that the application of the death penalty in the United States is arbitrary and discriminatory. His main argument is that if the conditions for the application of a policy are unjust, the policy itself becomes unjust in practice, however just it may be in principle. I have already addressed this issue in Part II of my essay. Here I wish only to make three points.

1. There are many things wrong with our criminal justice system, and both Reiman and I and, presumably, you, the reader, deplore them and want to fix them. The American Bar Association (ABA) and Reiman have called for the suspension of all executions, arguing that the death penalty is applied arbitrarily and unfairly. This is a non sequitur.

If the ABA and Reiman wanted to make the death penalty less arbitrary and unfair, they would support measures to improve and streamline evidence gathering, trials, sentencing, appeals, and execution processes, so that punishment would be applied more fairly to all regardless of economic and educational status, gender and race. For one thing, they could provide more pro bono service for the poor than they now do. They could reform the jury system, so that more enlightened, impartial jurors were chosen instead of less capable ones. They could apply justice more consistently and swiftly. But I suspect that those ABA members who voted for a mora-

---

6. Friedrich Nietzsche, *Beyond Good and Evil*, trans. Walter Kaufmann (Random House, 1966), 114.

torium on the death penalty aren't as interested in judicial reform as they are in abolition of the death penalty. After all, whose fault is it that the criminal justice system contains "a haphazard maze of unfair practices"? Who is it that creates our laws? What group dominates Congress, whence national statutes derive? What group dominates state legislatures, whence state laws derive? What group makes up our judicial system, which carries out the laws and practices? That the American Bar Association, the official organization of lawyers, complains about a legal practice and calls on the nation to halt it is tantamount to the American Medical Association announcing that because of egregious medical malpractice in the nation doctors will refuse to treat AIDS or cancer patients.

Here is how I see the alleged arbitrary and discriminatory problem: The institution of capital punishment with regard to social functions is complex. The death penalty can be abused. It can operate in a manner that ignores mitigating circumstances, arbitrarily, and even prejudicially. The process can be corrupted so that innocent people are executed for crimes they did not commit. In this sense, the death penalty is like a fire engine. Fire engines serve a useful purpose. They are effective in putting out fires, saving property and lives. But occasionally they run over and even kill a pedestrian. This is tragic; but if only a few pedestrians are killed, we don't cease to use fire engines. But suppose that fire trucks begin to run over a lot of people, so that they become dangerous weapons, whose effectiveness is seriously compromised. In this case, we would probably decide not to use them, resorting to other means to put out fires. The same holds for capital punishment. If and when it becomes an institution producing more harm than good, we should cease to use it. But until that time, we should strive to train those who use this institution in a manner that ensures it will be used justly. It would seem that the institution is still viable and that we should do everything possible to improve and reform it.[7]

---

7. One point of contention between Reiman and myself is the issue of egalitarianism. Reiman holds that all people are of equal worth. I deny that. All people should be equal under the law and held to the same moral standards, but some people are worth more than others. For example, Mother Teresa, Mahatma Gandhi, Albert Schweitzer, Abraham Lincoln and Martin Luther King Jr. are worth more than Adolf Hitler, Joseph Stalin, Jeffrey Dahmer, Steven Judy, Ted Bundy, Timothy McVeigh and other parasites of society. Although egalitarian rhetoric pervades our culture, I suggest it is an unexamined falsehood.

Consider Smith, a man of low morals and lower intelligence, who abuses his

2. Reiman exaggerates the arbitrary and discriminatory aspect of the application of the death penalty. At least it is not clear that our system is as bad as he claims it is. As I showed in Part II the claim that blacks are penalized for crimes more than whites fails to note that blacks, especially young black males, commit proportionately far more violent crimes than whites. (Even Rev. Jesse Jackson admitted that when he was walking down city streets and heard footsteps behind him, his heart began to pound— until he looked behind him and with relief noticed that the young people were white.) Exactly who or what is ultimately responsible for this phenomenon of black violence is a difficult question, but if we are to treat black males as moral agents, we must hold them to the same standards as Asians, Hispanics, and whites. My own conviction is that by sending a message that blacks are merely victims of social oppression, we encourage irresponsible living and loss of self-respect.

3. If abolitionists like Reiman and the ABA who call for a moratorium on the death penalty in the whole of the United States really were concerned about legal reform, wouldn't they propose a policy of surveying each state's application of the death penalty? Suppose, for example, that we find that California's policy results in widespread abuse and sentencing of innocents to the death penalty, but Arizona's policy proceeds fairly. We

---

wife and children, who hates exercising or work, for whom novels are dull and art a waste of time, and whose joy it is to spend his days as a couch potato, drinking beer, while watching mud wrestling, violent sports, and soap operas on TV. He is an avid voyeur, devoted to child pornography. He is devoid of intellectual curiosity, eschews science, politics, and religion, and eats and drinks in a manner more befitting a pig than a person. Smith lacks wit, grace, humor, technical skill, ambition, courage, self-control, and wisdom. He is antisocial, morose, lazy, a freeloader who feels no guilt about living on welfare when he is perfectly able to work, has no social conscience and barely avoids getting caught for his petty thievery. He has no talents, makes no social contribution, lacks a moral sense, and from the perspective of the good of society, would be better off dead. But Smith is proud of one thing: that he is "sacred," of "infinite worth," equal in intrinsic value to Abraham Lincoln, Mother Teresa, Albert Schweitzer, the Dalai Lama, Jesus Christ, Gandhi, and Albert Einstein. He is inviolable—and proud of it—in spite of any deficiency of merit. From the egalitarian perspective, in spite of appearances to the contrary, Smith is of equal intrinsic worth as the best citizen in his community. I suggest this is the myth of liberalism, "The Emperor's New Clothes" of our culture. For a further discussion, see my article "On Equal Human Worth: A Critique of Contemporary Egalitarianism" in *Equality: Selected Readings*, ed. Louis P. Pojman and Robert Westmoreland (Oxford University Press, 1996).

could call for a moratorium on executions in California, until reforms were instituted, while retaining it in Arizona. Or we might conclude that a certain district in California applies the death penalty arbitrarily and penalize that district, but not the entire state.

Conclusion

Reiman and I agree that justice demands that some murderers deserve the death penalty, and we agree that we have a prima facie duty to impose the death penalty under certain conditions. We differ somewhat on those conditions. We also differ as to whether the death penalty deters. If I am correct, by abolishing the death penalty we make murder less costly to the criminal and put an increased number of innocent people at risk. We also differ on the relationship of the death penalty to promoting civilization. I have tried to show not only that Reiman lacks a cogent argument for any necessary or strongly contingent connection between the abolition of the death penalty and civilization, but that this institution, properly applied, may actually enhance our quest for a deeply moral society. I have argued that while our criminal justice system and society, as a whole, has injustices, the moral thing to do is to reform both the criminal justice system and society itself. We ought not throw out the baby with the dirty bathwater.

4

Reply to Louis P. Pojman

Jeffrey Reiman

Louis Pojman's essay in favor of the death penalty contains numerous accounts of grisly murders that, no doubt, evoke feelings of anger in the reader and maybe even cause the reader to want to see the murderers killed. The accounts often have this effect on me, too. However, let's be clear: Our job here is not to determine what we *feel* about murderers or what we *want* to do to them. Our job is to figure out what we *should* do, what it is *morally right* to do to murderers. For this, we must consult our reason and come up with arguments rather than feelings. I have presented my arguments against executing murderers; let us look carefully at Pojman's arguments for executing them. Those arguments fall mainly under the rubrics of desert and deterrence. I shall take these up in turn, show that they fail to establish his case, and conclude with a miscellany of other objections to Pojman's defense of the death penalty.

I. Desert, Equivalence, and Duty

Pojman argues that murderers should be executed because they deserve to die and we have a duty to give them what they deserve. These notions are in turn grounded in more general claims, namely, that evildoers deserve evil equivalent in gravity to the evil that they have done (call this *the equivalence thesis*) and that we (or our state) have a duty to give people what they deserve (call this *the duty thesis*). Unless Pojman can establish both the equivalence thesis and the duty thesis, he fails to establish that murderers should be executed because they deserve it.

Pojman begins his argument for the equivalence thesis with a series of

151

appeals to authority (13). Ancient adages, the Eastern idea of karma, words of Cicero, Leibniz, and Kant are marshaled to show the long pedigree of the idea that the good should prosper and the evil should suffer—both in equal measure to their virtue or vice. However, appeals to authority are not very persuasive. They show only that some respectable folks have held an opinion, *not* that that opinion is true. Moreover, Pojman's roster of authorities is marked by the conspicuous absence of Buddha, Socrates, and Jesus, who all taught that we should respond to evil with good.[1] And even among the authorities to whom Pojman does appeal, there is little that actually supports the equivalence thesis as such. For example, Cicero is cited for holding that justice is giving each his due. But this doesn't say what anyone's due is. And Leibniz is cited for holding that it is "morally fitting" that the evil suffer eternal damnation. Pojman thinks that "eternal hell is excessive punishment for human evil," but he asserts that Leibniz's principle of *moral fittingness* is the same principle as what Kant calls the principle of *equality*, that is, the equivalence thesis. However, when Pojman notes that eternal hell is excessive punishment for human evil, he implicitly acknowledges that Leibniz did not understand moral fittingness as equality or equivalence—eternal hell is a lot more evil than any human could have caused.

From here, Pojman turns to our primitive, spontaneous, and involuntary responses of gratitude for favors and resentment for harms. Our primitive desire "to reciprocate and harm" the one who harms us reveals to Pojman "an instinctual duty to harm" the wrongdoer. That this is instinctual to us is supported by Pojman's claim that some animals seem to respond to harm in similar ways. However, the most that an argument like this can show is that resentment and gratitude are natural to us. But our question is what is right, not what is natural. And since much that is natural (aggressiveness, dominance hierarchies, not to mention running around naked in public) needs to be limited or prohibited in light of moral

---

1. Pojman does mention Jesus here, but for commanding that we "Render unto Caesar that which is Caesar's and unto God that which is God's." This statement is about the relationship of political duties to religious duties; it says nothing about punishing or rewarding, nor about requiting good with good and evil with evil. Socrates did, to be sure, believe in punishing the evil. However, he thought that this was justified because he understood punishment as a cure for evil, and thus as benefiting the soul of the punished. See, for example, Plato's *Gorgias*, 478d-e.

considerations, what is natural cannot itself tell us what is right. Indeed, the very notion of "an instinctual duty" strikes me as incoherent. Consider that the sexual instinct is as strong as the instinct for resentment or vindication: Does it make sense to say that we have an instinctual duty to have sex? All that could be instinctive to us is a desire to act some way—be it sexually or vindictively. Perhaps we experience this instinctual desire so strongly as to make it feel like a duty. But feeling one has a duty no more entails that one really has a duty than feeling that one can fly entails that one can fly.

Moreover, while some animals may requite harm with harm, there is no evidence that they aim to requite with harm *equivalent* to what they have suffered. Thus, no support is given to the equivalence thesis even if animal behavior could give such support, which I doubt. In the treatment of our fellows, we aspire (I hope) to do better than animals. Nonetheless, Pojman moves directly from the "primordial reactions" of animals to the "primordial desert-based idea of justice," which, he says,

> has two parts. Every action in the universe has a fitting response in terms of creating a duty to punish or reward, and that response must be *appropriate* in measure to the original action. It follows that evil deeds must be followed by evil outcomes and good deeds by good outcomes, exactly equal or in proportion to the vice or virtue in question. (15)

Note that this passage affirms that evil is to be matched with evil and good with good "exactly equal *or in proportion to* the vice or virtue in question." Recall the discussion of proportional retributivism in my essay. Proportional retributivism calls for punishing criminals who do the worst crime with our worst penalty, punishing those who do the second worst crime with our second worst penalty, and so on—*without insisting on equivalence between crime and punishment.* Since, by his own statement, "appropriateness" can be satisfied with proportionate punishment that is not equivalent to the harm caused, Pojman's formulation *doesn't even assert, much less prove, the equivalence thesis.*

Regarding the duty thesis, Pojman asserts again that the evil deserve evil, that justice entails giving people what they deserve, and thus that, "[s]ince we have a general duty to strive to bring about justice in the world, it follows that we have a duty to try to bring it about . . . [that] wherever possible, the virtuous are rewarded with well-being and the vicious with suffering" (19). Suppose we grant that we have a duty to bring about justice, that justice includes people getting what they deserve, and that the evil deserve punishment and the good deserve reward. What sort of duty do we, then, have? Recall that in my essay I claimed that, while benefactors of humanity deserve rewards, no one necessarily has a duty to give them those rewards. At most, this is a weak and easily overridden duty. Now, since giving the good what they deserve is as much a part of justice as giving the evil what they deserve, our duty to punish the evil can be no stronger than our duty to reward benefactors of humanity. Then, even if we grant Pojman that there is a duty to give people what they deserve, that duty is weak and easily overridden—and thus, in effect, next to no duty at all. In fact, if this is what Pojman's view comes down to, he and I are not far apart. I share with him the belief that it is in general good to give people what they deserve; and my argument needs only the claim that we are not duty-bound to give them everything that they deserve.

Pojman writes that, "by violating the right of another to life, I thereby forfeit my right to life" (30). However, if I forfeit my right to life that means only that if someone kills me, he violates no right, maybe he does no wrong. But this doesn't imply that he has a duty to kill me, as Pojman recognizes. He continues:

> Forfeiture gives the moral and legal authority the right to inflict the criminal with a punishment, but it says nothing about the *duty* of the authority to punish. The principle of just desert completes the theory of retribution. Not only do murderers forfeit their right to life, but they positively deserve their punishment. If they have committed a capital offense, they deserve a capital punishment. If first-degree murder is on the level of the worst types of crimes, as we think it is, then we are justified in imposing the worst type of punishments on the murderer. Death would be the fitting punishment; anything less would indicate that we regarded murder a less serious offense. (30–31)

Note, first, that this passage asserts that the offender's desert implies a duty to punish him, when, as I have shown by inventorying his attempts, the most that Pojman can be said to have proven is that we have a duty here that is no stronger than the duty we have to reward humanity's benefactors. Then the passage asserts that capital criminals deserve capital punishments, when, as I have shown by inventorying his attempts, Pojman has not proven the equivalence thesis upon which this assertion is based. And the passage concludes with two sentences that imply that equivalence is not even necessary after all. Consider that the last sentence only follows from the one before it if death is our worst type of punishment. If rape or castration were our worst punishments, then it would follow that these were the fitting punishments for the murderer. And if life in prison without parole were our worst type of punishment, it would be the fitting punishment for murder. Rather than showing that death is the only fitting punishment for murder, Pojman's argument here leads to the conclusion that our worst punishment is the fitting punishment for murder—and nothing has been said to show that that must be death.

I conclude, then, that Pojman has not proven either the equivalence thesis or the duty thesis. He has not proven that justice or desert requires that we execute murderers. Nor has he proven that justice or desert cannot be satisfied with, say, life in prison without parole—legally, a "civil death"—or even with a long prison term, such as twenty years.

II. Deterrence: Common Sense and the Best Bet Argument

Pojman says of the criticism of Isaac Ehrlich's deterrence research: "One criticism . . . is that if he had omitted the years 1962 to 1969, he would have had significantly different results" (38). The criticism is far more serious than this sounds. Ehrlich studied the deterrent effect of the death penalty for the period 1933 to 1969 and found that each execution may have deterred as many as eight murders. When the period from 1963 to 1969 is eliminated, there aren't merely "different results"; rather, *no significant deterrent effect shows up at all!* But if the death penalty deters, how come this didn't show up between 1933 and 1963—particularly in view of the fact that executions were carried out very frequently in the 1930s?[2] One is almost tempted to say that Ehrlich has effectively proven that the death penalty is *not* a superior deterrent to imprisonment. But I will not argue that here.

Pojman recognizes that the empirical studies do not support a greater deterrent effect of capital punishment, but he claims that the studies are inconclusive for two reasons: first, because of the low likelihood of death

---

2. See, for example, U.S. National Criminal Justice Information and Statistics Service, *Capital Punishment 1978* (Washington, DC: Law Enforcement Assistance Administration, December 1979), 18.

penalties and, second, because of the so-called lighthouse effect (according to which, we see the cases where deterrence fails, but not those where it succeeds). Neither of these reasons is very persuasive. As to the first, death sentences were carried out quite regularly in the Depression Era, as already mentioned, and studies covering this period (even Ehrlich's!) show no increased deterrence due to capital punishment. And as to the lighthouse effect, note that the studies that show no difference in murder rates due to the death penalty compare murder rates in two jurisdictions that are similar except that one has and the other does not have the death penalty. Consequently, if the death penalty prevented murders that life imprisonment failed to prevent, this would show up in higher murder rates in the states without the death penalty. Thus this research is not subject to the lighthouse effect. My view is that the studies show no increased deterrent impact from capital punishment because there is none, for reasons that I shall suggest below.

Pojman, contending that the research has not proven that the death penalty does not deter more than life imprisonment, seeks to bolster his case by putting forth the so-called best bet argument, which he takes to be agnostic (39) on the issue of whether the death penalty is a superior deterrent to imprisonment, and he follows this argument with the commonsense argument, which purports to prove that, whatever the research shows, the death penalty is a greater deterrent after all. Since I think that the best bet argument is not really agnostic, but in fact gets some of its force from the commonsense argument, I take up the commonsense argument first.

We have already seen the commonsense argument formulated by Ernest van den Haag and Michael Davis. Pojman follows suit. The argument starts from the premise that "what people (including potential criminals) fear more will have a greater deterrent effect on them," and it goes on to say that, since people fear death more than life in prison, they "will be deterred more by the death penalty" than by other available punishments, such as life in prison (45). I have already contended, in my essay that the first premise here is a nonstarter. As David Conway pointed out, the fact that one penalty is feared more than another does not imply that the more feared penalty deters more than the less feared, since the less feared penalty may already deter me as much as I can be deterred. Says Conway,

> given the choice, I would strongly prefer one thousand years in hell to eternity there. Nonetheless, if one thousand years in hell were the penalty for

some action, it would be quite sufficient to deter me from performing that action. The additional years would do nothing to discourage me further. Similarly, the prospect of the death penalty, while worse, may not have any greater deterrent effect than does that of life imprisonment.[3]

Since this argument was made more than twenty years ago and still has not deterred van den Haag and Davis and now Pojman from using the commonsense argument, I am convinced that more must be said to show just how devastating the implications of this point are for any version of the commonsense argument. Conway's argument shows that the commonsense argument contains a questionable premise, namely, the idea that *people's disinclination to act in some way rises continuously and without limit as the fearsomeness of the penalty for that act rises.* Without this premise, the commonsense argument fails. If people's disinclination doesn't keep rising but instead tops out at some point, it is no longer possible to infer from the greater fearfulness of the death penalty its greater deterrent impact since people's disinclination may have topped out at life imprisonment. What is really devastating about Conway's point is that the continuously rising disinclination premise is part of a technical theory, and no part of common sense. Those who put forth the commonsense argument are really putting forth a theory that isn't commonsensical at all, and they're calling it common sense!

What theory is this that underlies the idea that disinclination continuously correlates with fearfulness? It is some version of psychological hedonism of the sort that one finds in textbooks of neoclassical economic theory, in which people are thought to seek continuously to maximize their net satisfaction. What we have here, then, is not the behavior of commonsense folks. It's the behavior of idealized rational consumers![4] The giveaway is Pojman's claim that criminals do cost-benefit analyses before deciding to break the law (46). Beware of equivocation here. I don't doubt that would-be criminals consider costs and benefits of potential crimes in a rough manner. I will shortly suggest a "model" of how they do so. What

---

3. See note 50 and accompanying text in my essay.

4. Michael Davis, to his credit, effectively admits this in acknowledging that his version of the commonsense argument is about *rational agents* rather than real people, and later, when he asserts that the commonsense method yields conceptual truths. But, then, it is misleading to call this common sense. Only a formalized theory of rational judgment could yield conceptual truths. See note 49 in my essay.

is highly implausible, however, is that criminals do cost-benefit analyses in the technical sense of that term, such that every increment of cost and every increment of benefit are taken into account. This is what we have to think at least a significant number of criminals are doing in order to ignore the social science findings and insist, as Pojman (and van den Haag and Davis) do, that an increase in penalty from life in prison to execution will figure in the motivation of potential murderers enough to deter additional murders. And that is simply implausible.

When John Stuart Mill tried to introduce qualitative differences in pleasures into utilitarianism, he was already responding to the implausibility of psychological hedonism understood on the model of Jeremy Bentham's calculus of pleasures and pains. (How often do you reach a decision between alternative courses of action by summing the pleasures and pains of each and following the option with the highest net sum of satisfaction? How often do you even think of pleasures as measurable and summable? Do you suppose that the pleasure of falling in love or discovering a cure for cancer is equal to the pleasure from some—even a very large—number of cheeseburgers?) If there are qualitative differences of pleasures, then it is not possible to sum up pains and pleasures and pursue maximum net satisfaction because qualitatively different pleasures are strictly incommensurable.

In any event, if there are qualitative differences in pleasures, there are surely also qualitative differences in pains and thus in fearfulness—and no longer any reason to expect that disinclination will rise continuously with fearfulness. It seems to me that this is confirmed when we observe the actual judgments and behavior of commonsensically rational people, instead of reading a theory into them. Rather than finely calibrating their reactions to increasingly negative outcomes, commonsense people seem to batch negative outcomes into qualitative groupings, such as "worth a great effort to avoid," "worth a substantial effort to avoid," and "worth only a minor effort to avoid." So being killed painfully or painlessly, being locked in prison for your whole life or for much of your life, being paralyzed, being blinded, and losing both arms or both legs are all, irrespective of their relative differences in awfulness, worth a great effort to avoid. Breaking a bone, losing a finger, getting a serious (but not permanently damaging) beating, and being injured seriously (but not gravely and permanently) in a car accident are worth a substantial effort to avoid. And getting a splinter, stubbing a toe, and falling in the street, as well as worse but very unlikely things, such as getting hit by lightening, killed in a train derailment, or contracting a rare and terrible disease, are worth only a minor effort to avoid.

I do not insist on the details of this description. I say only that it is something like what commonsensically rational people do in the face of statistically possible negative outcomes, and there's nothing irrational about it, unless one is already assuming a theory of rationality, such as that used in economics.[5] Then, when you think of potential criminals, it's only commonsensical to suppose that they do the same, treating any serious criminal penalty as "worth a great effort to avoid." I contend that the so-called cost-benefit analyses that Pojman thinks some criminals engage in amount to no finer calculation than this. And this is not only closer to the actual way in which commonsense folks treat risks, it also fits perfectly with the majority of social science studies on the death penalty, which show that the difference between life in prison and death does not alter people's inclination or disinclination to commit murder—just as if would-be murderers had batched these two penalties under one rubric and acted accordingly. I conclude that the commonsense argument for the death penalty is an impostor. It is a theory of rational behavior and not even a very plausible one. The commonsense argument fails for lack of common sense.

Pojman tries to bolster the commonsense argument with anecdotal evidence of the greater deterrent effect of capital punishment, but anecdotes are no basis upon which to justify a policy, particularly one that includes killing people. Anecdotes are afflicted with the arbitrariness of how they (rather than other stories with contrary morals) come to our attention. Moreover, anecdotes yield uncertain lessons because they rely on the judgments made by the people who figure in the anecdotes, judgments that may be false or one-sided or merely mirroring conventional and potentially

---

5. To give the economists their due, it is worth noting that the description of people's ways of dealing with statistically negative outcomes sketched here is fully compatible with the theory of rational consumer behavior when that theory is thought of as applying to very large numbers of individuals rather than as describing any particular individual's actual psychology. If people classify outcomes in the rough way I have here suggested they do, and if they choose in light of these classifications, their choices will tend to increase their satisfaction. If you plot a very large enough number of such choices, the lumpiness of each person's classification system will be averaged out by that of the others, and their choices will appear simply to follow increased net satisfaction in a smoothly incremental way.

groundless beliefs. For example, that an anecdote tells of a crook who says he stopped using a gun because the death penalty was instituted does not prove that that is the real reason why he stopped. He might, for example, have been influenced by news reports of a crackdown on crime, or by a television show about criminals getting caught, or by a dozen other influences that may work on his mind without his full awareness of their impact. It is precisely because of these limitations on the truth content of anecdotes that we have recourse to the more controlled methods of social science. To use anecdotes to improve on social science is like going to a shaman because you don't like what your doctor has told you.

I turn now to the best bet argument. The best bet argument holds that, because execution *might* deter murderers, it is better to execute murderers than not to. Executing murderers may deter someone from killing an innocent person, and if not, all we have lost is one dead murderer. Not executing may have no impact on future criminals, but if there are any who would have been deterred by execution, then we have failed to stop the killing of an innocent person. Since it seems worse to fail to stop the killing of the innocent than to kill a murderer without a deterrent gain, our best bet is to execute murderers.

I put off dealing with the best bet argument until now because that argument looks very weak without the commonsense argument accompanying it. For unless there is some reason to expect the death penalty to be a superior deterrent to life in prison, the best bet argument calls for the merest toying with human beings, which seems offensive even when the human beings are murderers. It is one thing to kill murderers when there is reason to think it will protect innocents, but to kill them because of the bare possibility that this might happen seems like exactly the kind of disrespectful treatment of the murderer that Kant condemned. So, without either a showing from social science or from common sense that the death penalty is likely to save lives, I think the best bet argument fails.

Some people may resist this conclusion, holding that, since murderers are of less worth than innocent people (Pojman puts their comparative value at 1 to 1,000 [41]), the bare possibility that executing a murderer might save an innocent is enough to justify the death penalty as our best bet. There is, I think, a further argument against this approach that I think refutes it finally. Recall that in my essay, I argued that, by refraining from executing murderers, the state will contribute to the general repugnance of murder, and I speculated that *this will lead to fewer murders over time.*

Moreover, there is a line of social science research defending the so-called brutalization hypothesis, which purports to show that murders increase in the period following executions and that these are real increases (not just changes in timing).[6] If either or both of these claims are plausible, then the outcomes facing us in the best bet argument are dramatically changed. Now, in addition to no evidence that the death penalty deters more murders, there is the additional possibility that the death penalty increases the number of murders. Then, there is no reason to bet on executions over life imprisonment in the name of future innocent victims. Executions may protect them or jeopardize them. With that, the best bet argument evaporates.

III. Concluding Miscellany

Pojman repeats van den Haag's argument against the claim that the biased way in which the death penalty is administered disqualifies it as a legitimate punishment policy. Pojman argues that that is a problem with the application of the penalty, not with the death penalty itself (56). And he repeats van den Haag's argument against the claim that poverty is a cause of crime. Pojman points out that crime rates in absolutely poorer countries are often lower than ours (3). In my essay, I showed that the first of these van den Haagian arguments saves the justice of the death penalty *in principle* at the price of leaving standing the argument against instituting it *in practice* and that the second of these van den Haagian arguments rests on an oversimplified reading of the claim about poverty and crime (119, 127–28).

More important, Pojman thinks he has gotten rid of the bias argument in pointing out that a slightly higher percentage of whites arrested for murder are executed than the percentage of blacks arrested for murder who get executed (58n72). He ignores the presence of racist bias in arrest practices[7] and the well-documented bias in the imposition of the death

---

6. See note 54 and accompanying text in my essay.

7. For example, in 1993, respondents to the Department of Justice's National Criminal Victimization Survey reported that 32 percent of their assailants in violent victimizations (rape, robbery, and aggravated assault) were perceived to be black, whereas 45 percent of those arrested for rape, robbery, and aggravated assault that year were black (U.S. Department of Justice, Bureau of Justice Statistics, *Sourcebook of Criminal Justice Statistics, 1994*, ed. Kathleen Maguire and Ann L. Pastore [Washington, DC: U.S. Government Printing Office, 1995], Table 3.28, p. 243; Table 4.11, p. 388).

penalty by race of the victim and the way in which this bias undermines the state's moral authority to impose the death penalty.[8] Moreover, this evidence of racist bias comes after the Supreme Court threw out death penalty statutes in 1972 (because of arbitrariness and discrimination) and then allowed new death penalty statutes in 1976 (held to have removed the main sources of arbitrariness and discrimination).[9] In short, the bias occurred *after* the system was reformed, suggesting that the problem runs too deep to be corrected by reform. Finally, Pojman does accept that there is economic bias against the poor in the imposition of capital punishment (58n72), and that is equally undermining of the state's moral authority to impose the penalty.

Pojman puts forth something that he calls "the Golden Rule argument for the death penalty" (51). Instead of an argument, however, one finds a series of rhetorical questions, such as "if you had kidnapped a young girl, placed her in your trunk, and then killed her, what punishment do you think would be fitting for *you?*," which Pojman assumes his readers will answer in ways that show their agreement on the rightness of capital punishment. Note, first of all, that this has little to do with the Golden Rule, which asks you to treat people as you would want to be treated by them, and thus at most asks, "If you did some awful crime, how would you *want* to be treated?"—a question to which most folks would probably answer, "with mercy." Kant regarded the Golden Rule as of limited worth, in part because "the criminal would on this ground be able to dispute with the judges who punish him."[10] Further, Pojman ought to pose his questions to a thoughtful objector to the death penalty. I suspect that Pojman would not get the answers he expects. And that should be enough to show that he has put forth as an argument what is no more than a set of intuitions, his own, coupled with the unverified assumption that others will share them and that they are probative—neither of which seems to be the case.

Finally, Pojman contends that those opponents of capital punishment who support a woman's right to abortion—such as Supreme Court Justice William Brennan—are inconsistent in allowing the killing of fetuses who

8. See notes 77 and 78 and accompanying text in my essay.
9. *Furman v Georgia*, 408 US 238 (1972); and *Gregg v Georgia*, 428 US 153 (1976).
10. Immanuel Kant, *Grounding for the Metaphysics of Morals*, trans. J. W. Ellington (Indianapolis, IN: Hackett Publishing, 1981; originally published 1785), 37n.

are "innocent of any wrongdoing" but opposing the killing of murderers who "deserve death" (63). As applied to Brennan, the charge is way off-base, inasmuch as he was not rendering moral decisions, but determining what the U.S. Constitution requires. However, even as moral decisions, there is no inconsistency here whatsoever. Pojman acknowledges that those in the pro-choice camp hold that "fetuses are not *persons*."[11] Having recognized this, Pojman goes on, without argument, to affirm in effect that a fetus is morally comparable to an adult human being because the "fetus progressively nears personhood." One might just as well argue that a long fly ball that goes foul only by inches ought to get some of the credit given to a home run because it's so close. However near to personhood it may be, a fetus is not yet a person. What Pojman fails to see is that, here, as in baseball, a miss is as good as a mile. Not being a person, a fetus does not yet have a person's right to life, and thus a fetus is morally incomparable to a murderer, who (whatever else he is) is a person. There is no more inconsistency in saying that it is wrong to kill (guilty) persons but okay to kill (innocent) nonpersons than it would be to say that it is wrong to kill (guilty) murderers but okay to kill (innocent) animals.

---

11. See, for example, Michael Tooley, *Abortion and Infanticide* (Oxford: Clarendon Press, 1983); Mary Anne Warren, "On the Moral and Legal Status of Abortion," in *The Problem of Abortion*, 2nd ed., ed. Joel Feinberg (Belmont, CA: Wadsworth Publishing, 1984), 110–14; S. I. Benn, "Abortion, Infanticide, and Respect for Persons," in *Problem of Abortion*, ed. Feinberg, 135–144; Jeffrey Reiman, "Abortion, Infanticide, and the Asymmetric Value of Human Life," in *Journal of Social Philosophy* 27, no. 3 (Winter 1996): 181–200; and Jeffrey Reiman, *Critical Moral Liberalism: Theory and Practice* (Lanham, MD: Rowman & Littlefield, 1997), 189–210.

Index

moral dignity. *See* dignity

moral education, 69–70n3

moral reform. *See* repentance

Morningside Heights (New York), 3

Morris, Herbert, 7, 33; Davis and, 75; on unfair advantage, 10–11, 74, 78

Moses (prophet), 19, 53

motivation, 45, 56–57, 158. *See also* intention; *mens rea*

murder: abortion and, 63–64; advancing civilization and, 116, 118; aggravating factors in, 51; Best Bet Argument on, 39; discriminatory definition of, 123–25; in imaginary town, 143; inclination to, 159; interracial, 122; judicial error as, 54; just response to, 119, 120; laws on, 32n34, 57; lighthouse effect and, 156; in natural state, 84n24; in prisons, 62, 126; proportional punishment of, 20, 93; public complicity in, 9, 29; retributive punishment of, 30–31; unfair advantage from, 85; in Western Europe, 141n4; worst punishment for, 155; wrongfulness of, 105–6. *See also* homicide

murder deterrence, 149, 158, 160–61; in Cicero, 47; Ehrlich on, 37, 101, 155; Gernstein on, 46, 50; Hogan on, 49; Layson on, 38; Mill on, 48; state duty in, 53, 116

murderers: desert of, 30, 67, 134, 143, 149, 151; executed, 49, 58n72; forfeiture by, 33, 40–41, 43, 44, 65, 154; Golden Rule and, 51–52; Kant on, 9, 29, 92n32; life imprisonment of, 62, 98, 99, 118; milder punishment of, 68; multiple, 31, 64, 94–95, 96, 99; pain for, 141–42; personhood of, 163; race of, 58, 122; relative value of, 36, 40, 41, 42, 43, 50, 160; repentance by, 34; responsibility of, 25–26, 35, 61–62, 65, 120–21; socioeconomic status of,

128; van den Haag- Conway debate on, 106–7n55

murder victims: Best Bet Argument on, 40, 41; families of, 99; female, 27–28, 51; interstate transfer of, 48, 140; potential injustice to, 67, 68, 117; relative value of, 50; respect for, 61; theoretical resuscitation of, 44, 51

Murphy, Jeffrie, 130–31, 137n2

Murrah Federal Building, 4, 51

mutilation. *See* physical mutilation

Nathanson, Stephen, 38, 44, 53n64, 56–57

National Academy of Sciences, 101

National Center for Injury Prevention and Control, 2n3

National Center of Health Statistics, 2

National Criminal Victimization Survey, 161n7

national defense, 6

Native Americans, 58n72, 126–27, 144

natural state. *See* state of nature

Nazism, 117, 137–38

Netherlands, 32

neurological manipulation, 26, 33–34

neuroses, 25

New Delhi, 3

New York City, 2, 3, 4

Nietzsche, Friedrich, 108, 144, 145–46

nonnegligent manslaughter, 49

Northern Ireland, 52

Nozick, Robert, 126

occupational diseases, 123–24

offenses against the person. *See* crimes against the person

Ohio, 122

Oklahoma City bombing (1995), 4, 51

organ transplants, 138–39

Orwell, George, 115

pain. *See* physical pain; psychological pain

painkillers, 108n57, 145

About the Authors

Louis Paul Pojman grew up in Cicero, Illinois. He attended New Brunswick Theological Seminary before becoming a minister of a black church in Bedford-Stuyvesant, Brooklyn in the 1960s. He was a civil rights activist, leading integration projects and participating in demonstrations. In 1969 he was a Fulbright Fellow at the University of Copenhagen, and in 1970 he was a Rockefeller Fellow at Hamburg University. He received his Ph.D. in philosophy from Oxford University in 1977. He has taught at the University of Notre Dame, the University of Texas at Dallas and the University of Mississippi before coming to the United States Military Academy at West Point.

Louis Pojman is the author or editor of over twenty books and seventy-five articles. He has won several research and teaching awards, including the Burlington Northern Award for Outstanding Teaching and Scholarship (1988) and the Outstanding Scholar/Teacher in the Humanities at the University of Mississippi (1994). He and his wife are avid hikers and environmentalists. He is a vegetarian, a bicyclist and a member of Amnesty International.

Jeffrey Reiman is William Fraser McDowell Professor of Philosophy at American University in Washington, D.C. Born in Brooklyn, New York, in 1942, Reiman received his B.A. in philosophy from Queens College in 1963 and his Ph.D. in philosophy from Pennsylvania State University in 1968. He was a Fulbright Scholar in India during 1966–67.

Reiman joined the American University faculty in 1970 in the Center for the Administration of Justice (now called the Department of Justice, Law and Society of the School of Public Affairs). After several years of holding a joint appointment in the Justice program and the Department of Philosophy and Religion, he joined the Department of Philosophy and Religion full-time in 1988, becoming director of the Master's Program in

Philosophy and Social Policy. He was named William Fraser McDowell Professor of Philosophy in 1990.

Reiman is a member of the Phi Beta Kappa and Phi Kappa Phi honor societies and president of the American University Phi Beta Kappa chapter. He is the author of *In Defense of Political Philosophy* (Harper & Row, 1972), *Justice and Modern Moral Philosophy* (Yale University Press, 1990), *Critical Moral Liberalism: Theory and Practice* (Rowman & Littlefield, 1997), and *The Rich Get Richer and the Poor Get Prison: Ideology, Class, and Criminal Justice* (5th edition, Allyn & Bacon, 1998), and more than fifty articles in philosophy and criminal justice journals and anthologies.